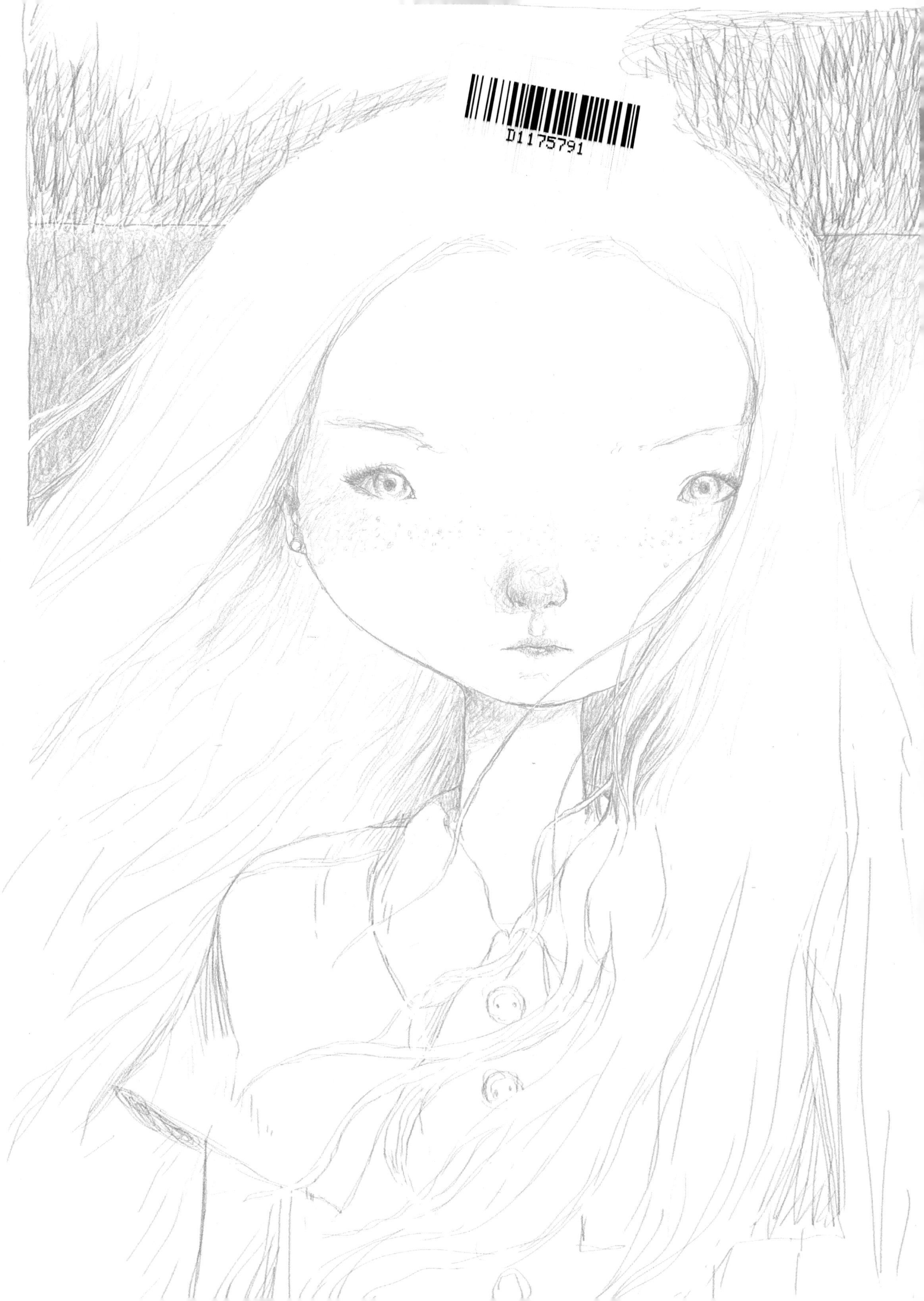

1000 Storms

Tony Sandoval

Written and illustrated
by
Tony Sandoval

Translation by Jeremy Melloul
Localization, Editing, and Layout by Mike Kennedy
Production Assistance by Chris Northrop

MAGNETIC™

ISBN: 978-1-951719-13-5
Library of Congress Control Number: 2021904937

1000 Storms, published 2021 by Magnetic Press, LLC.
Originally published in French under the title Mille Tempetes, by Tony Sandoval © BELG Prod SARL, 2018.
www.groupepaquet.net. All rights reserved.

Printed in China.

10 9 8 7 6 5 4 3 2 1

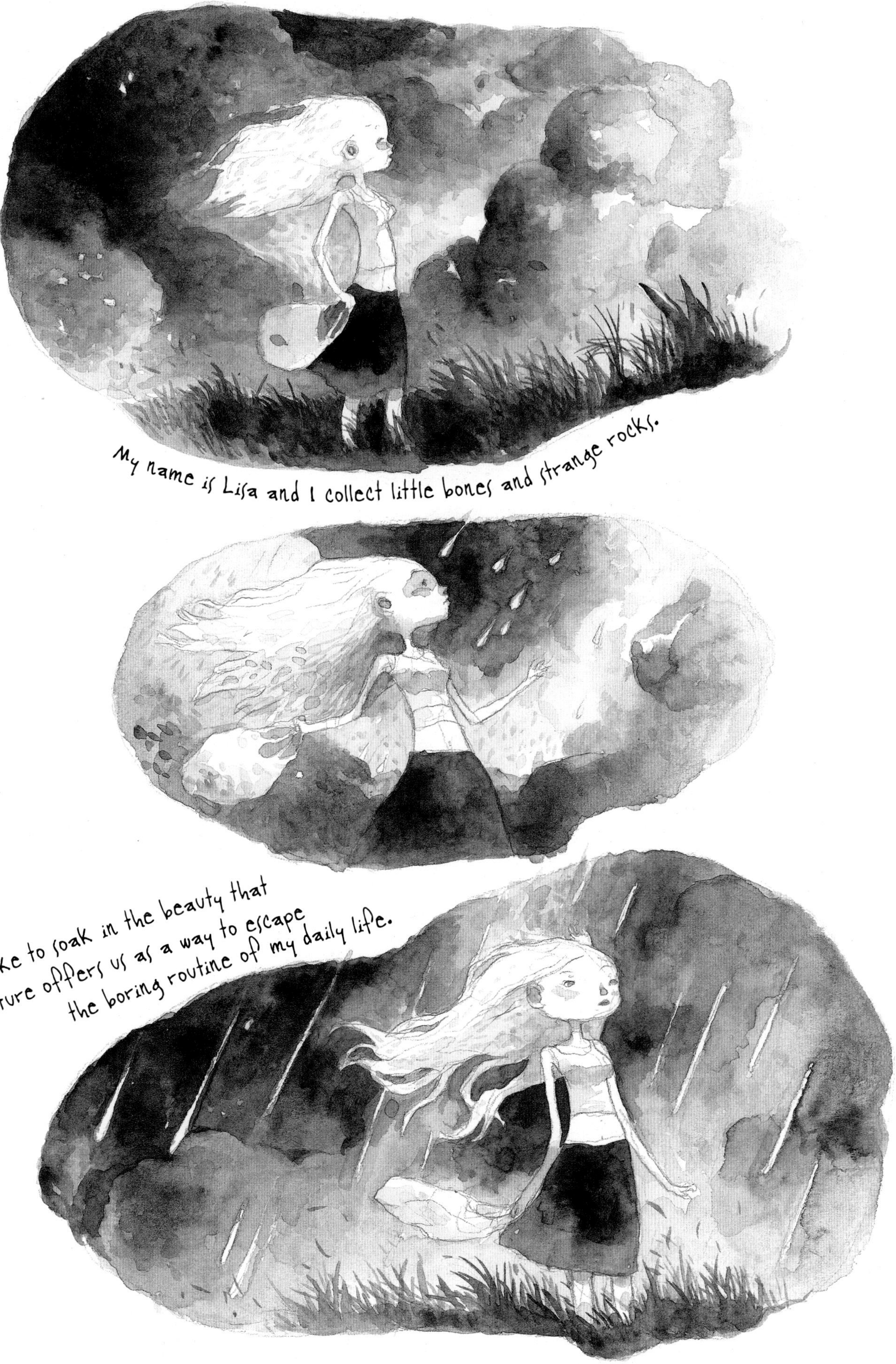
My name is Lisa and I collect little bones and strange rocks.
I like to soak in the beauty that nature offers us as a way to escape the boring routine of my daily life.

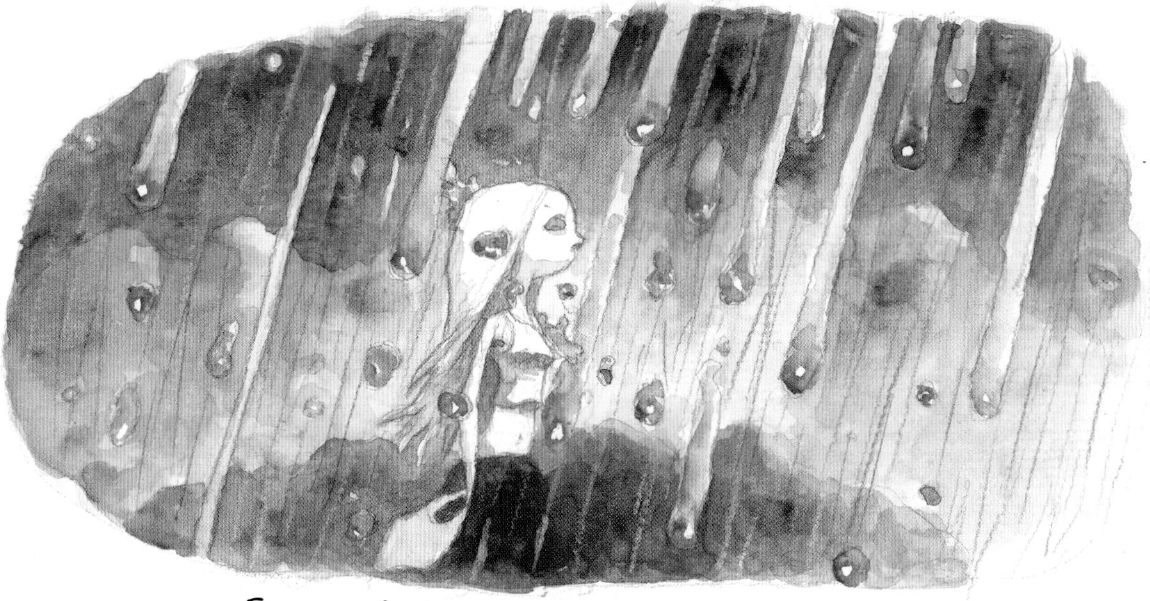

Far away from my godmother's strict rules...

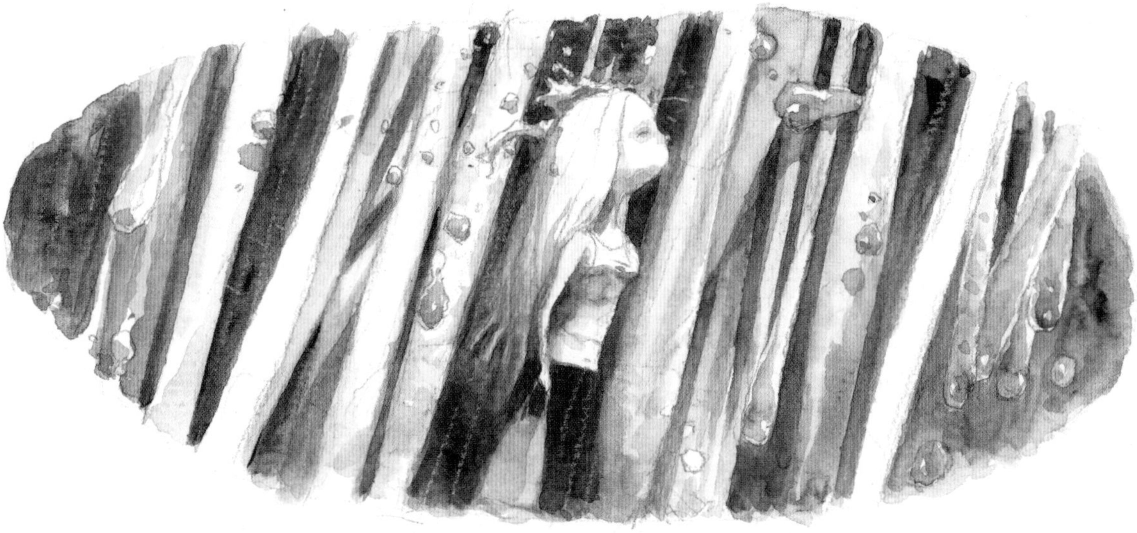

...and her son's childish pranks.

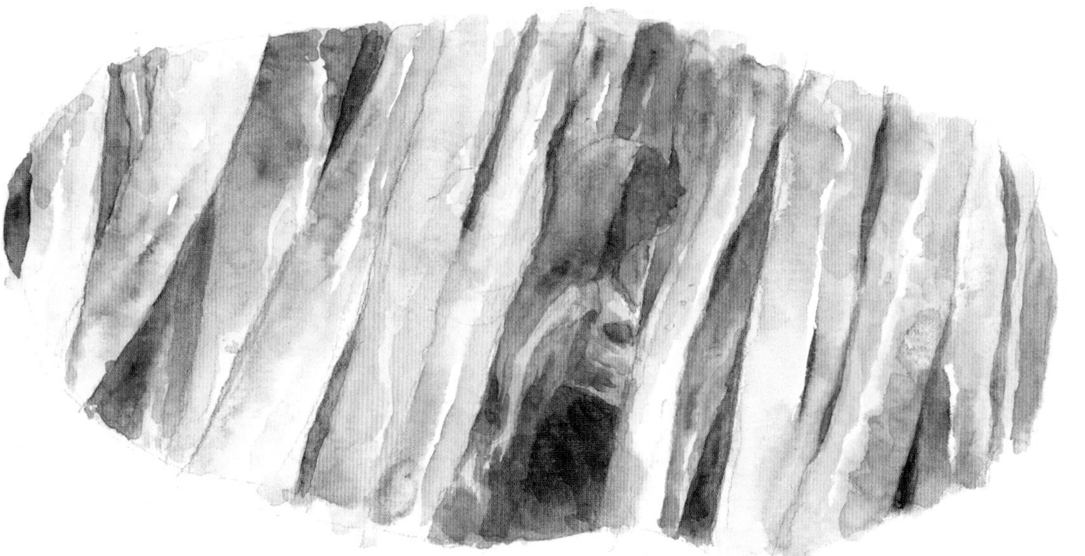

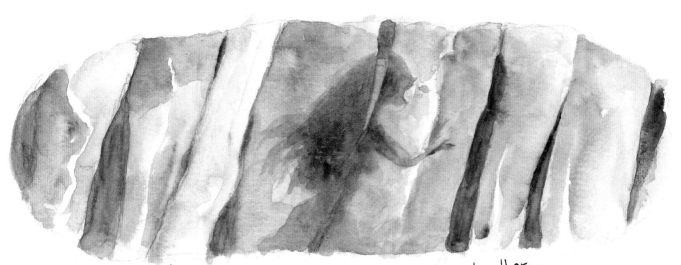

Far from the laughter of the other kids playing together.

Far from the gulf that separates me from my father.

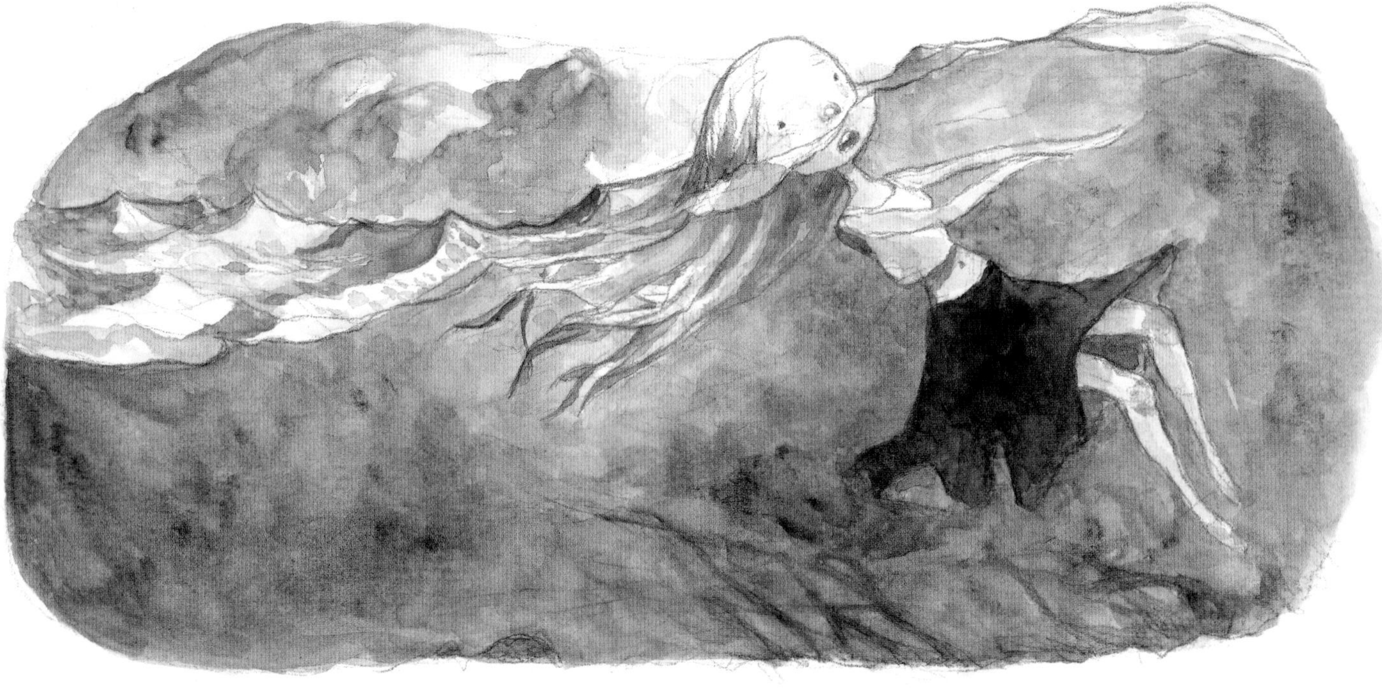

But most of all, far from the void left by the death of my mother...

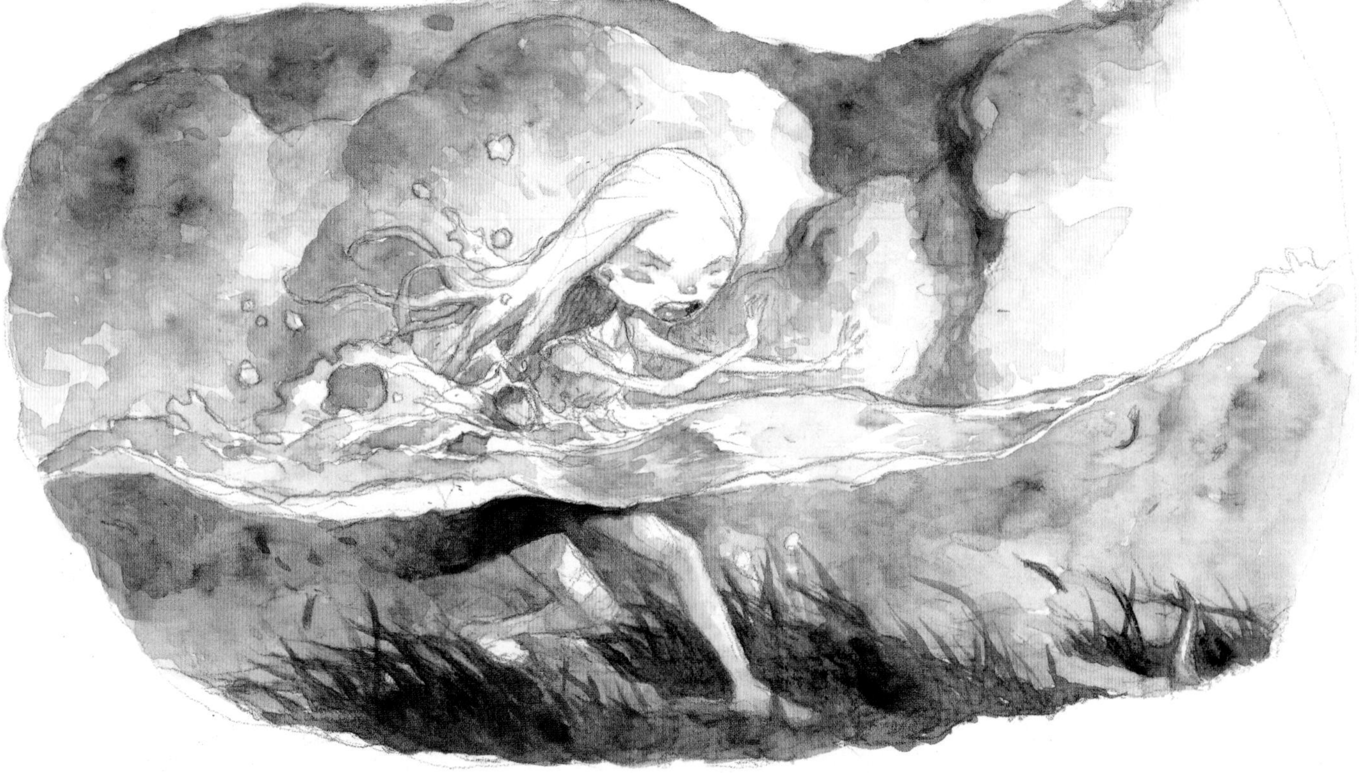

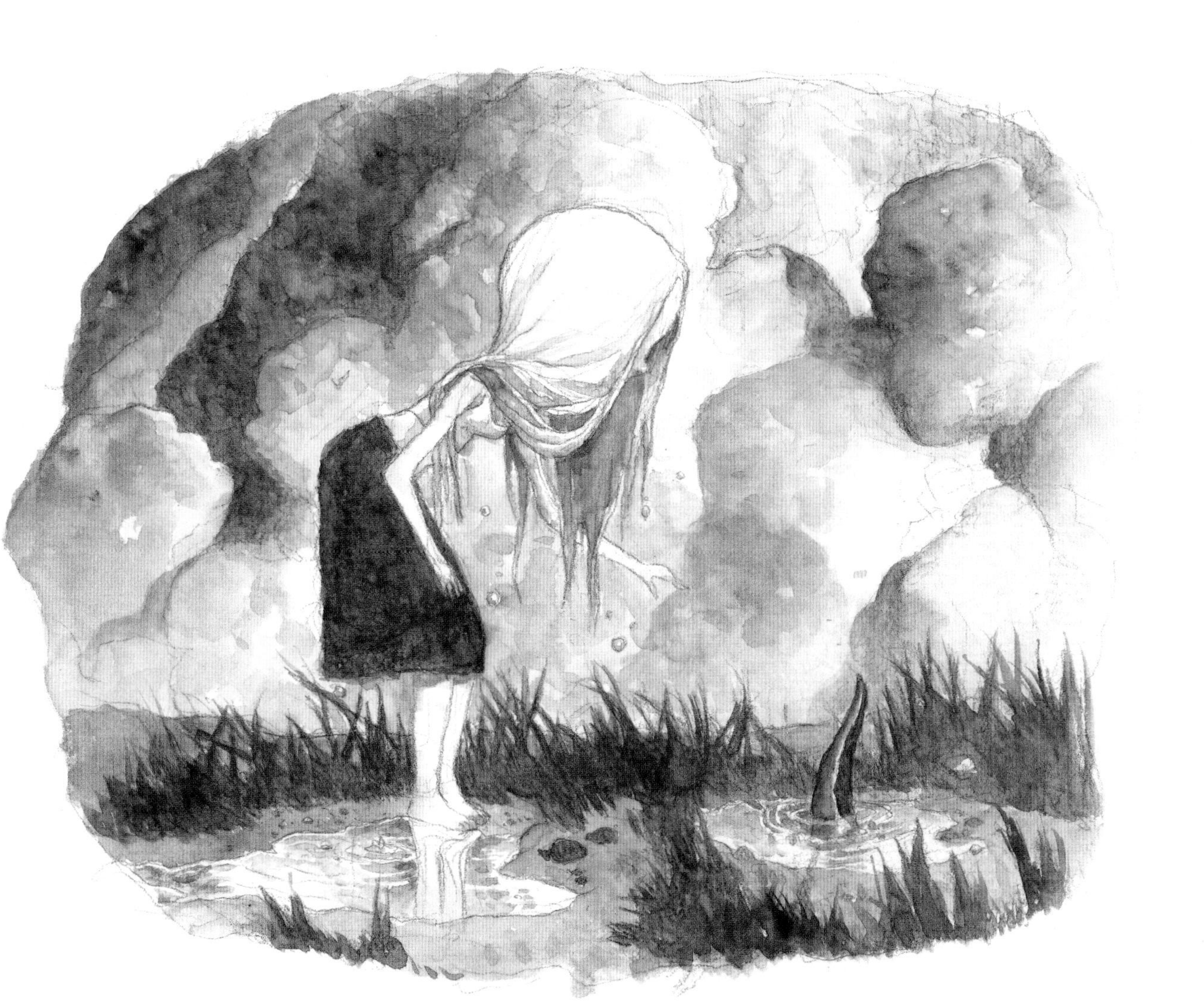

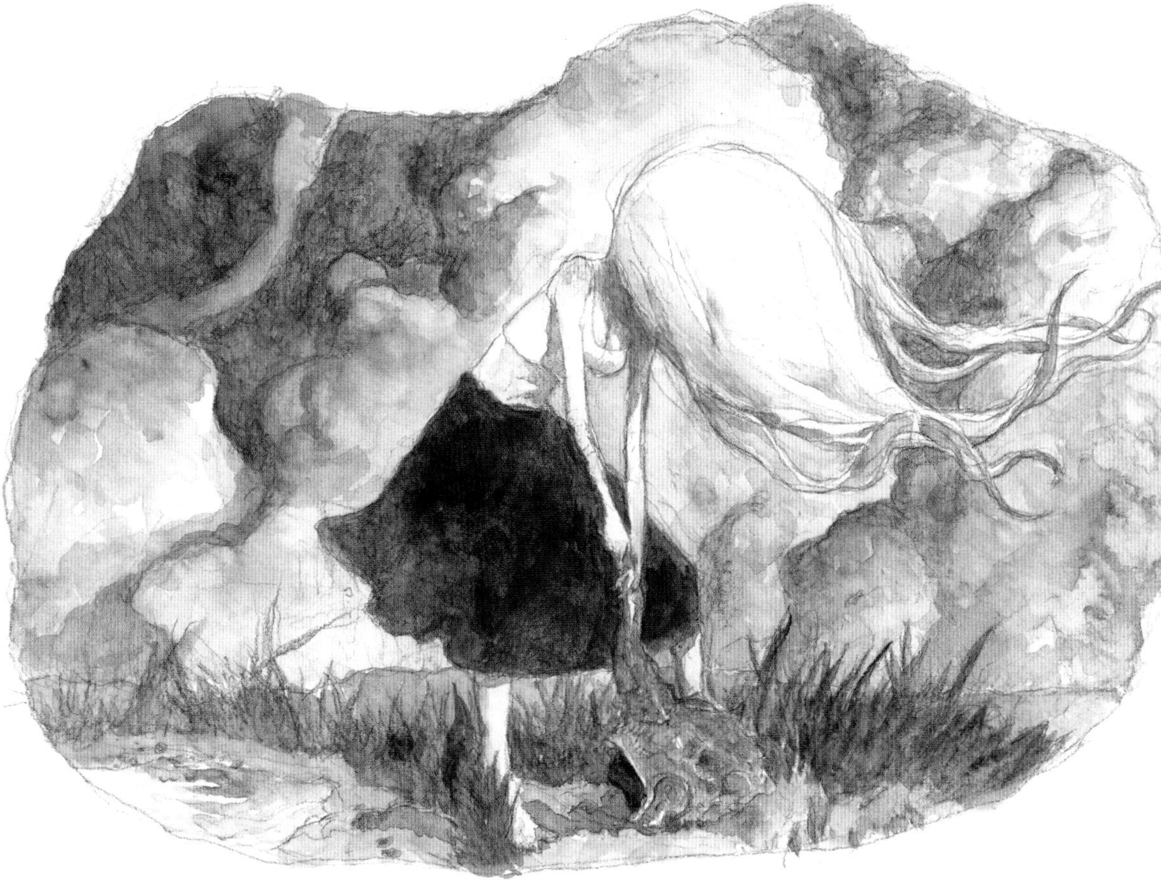

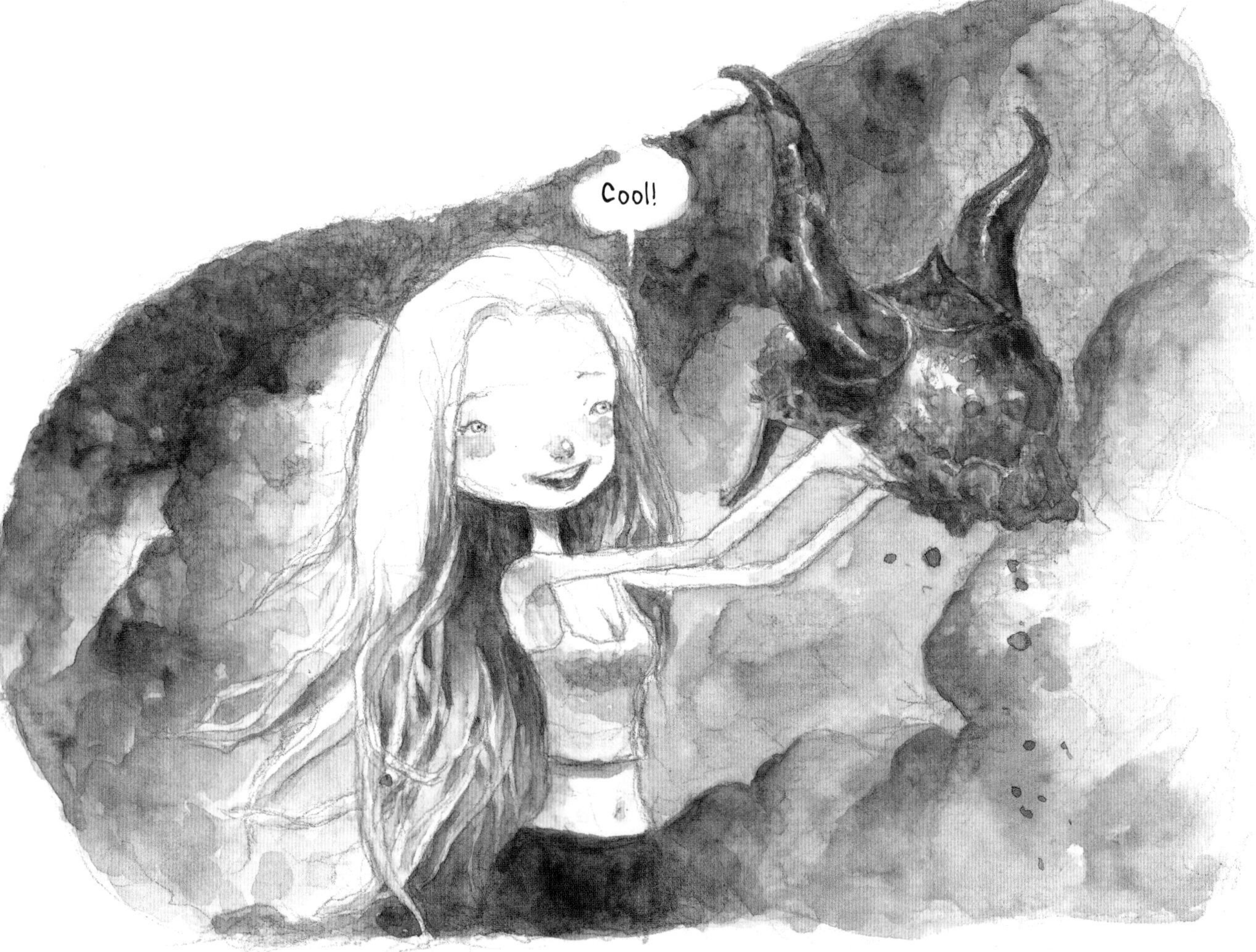
Cool!

My name is Lisa and I collect pretty things.

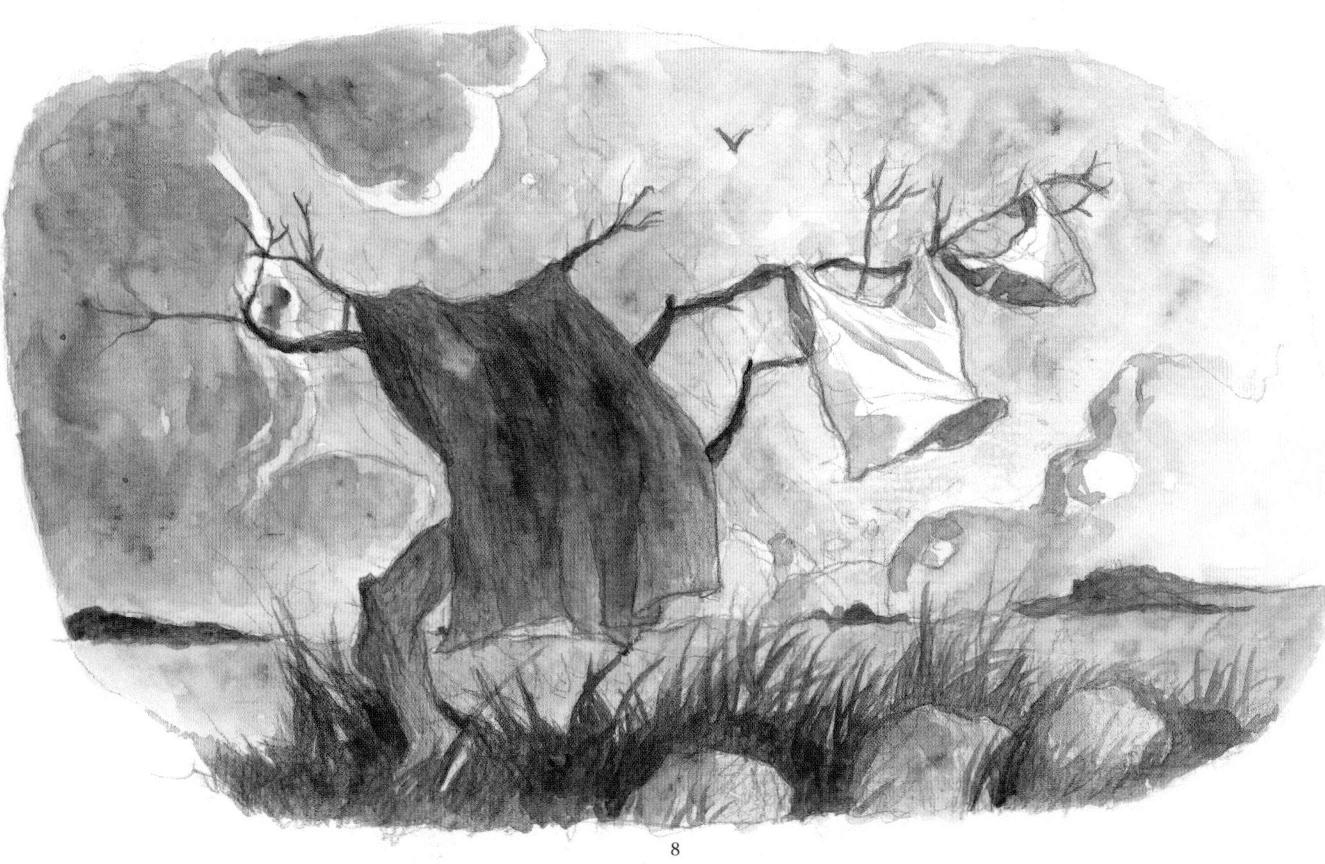

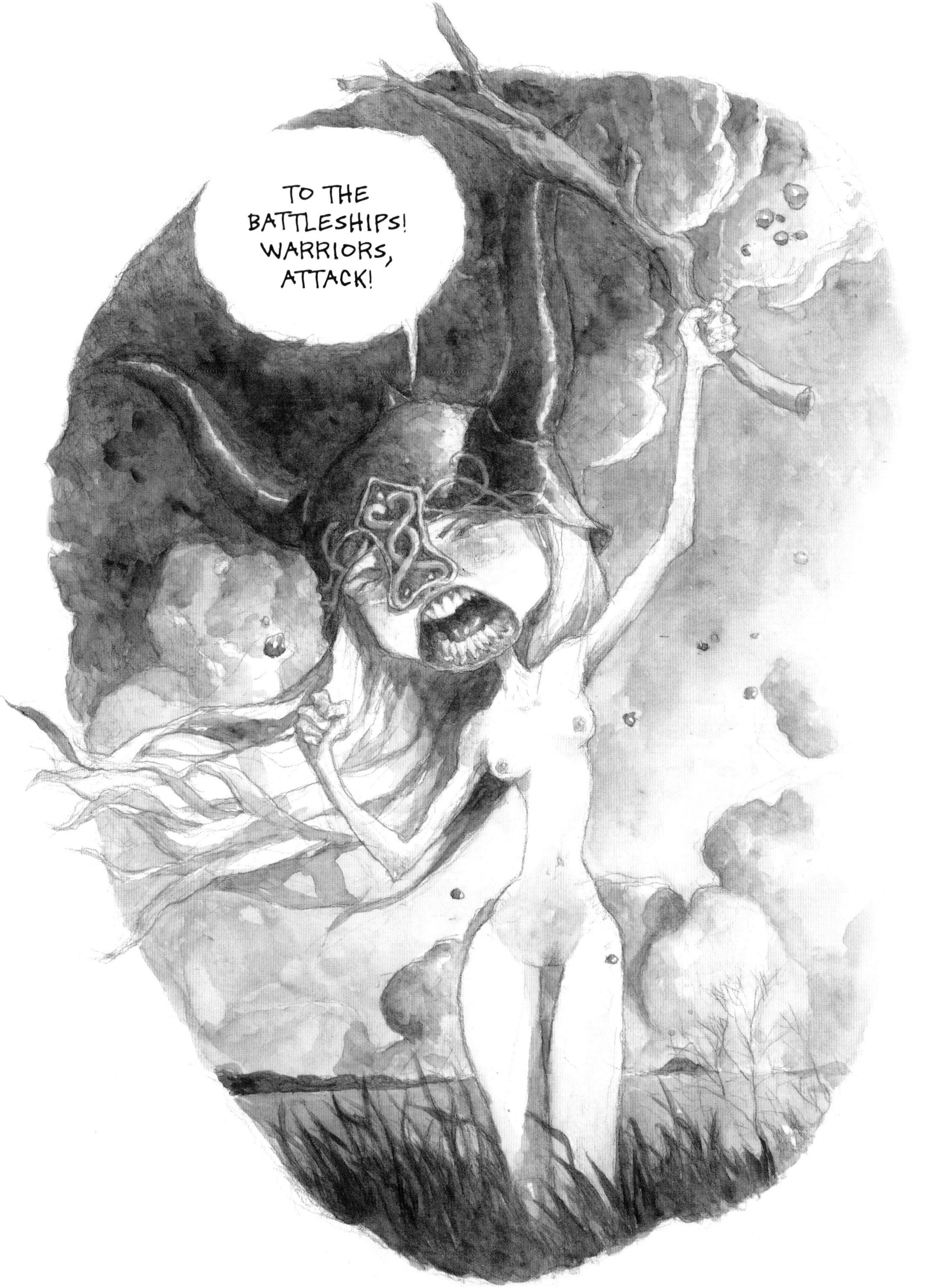
TO THE BATTLESHIPS! WARRIORS, ATTACK!

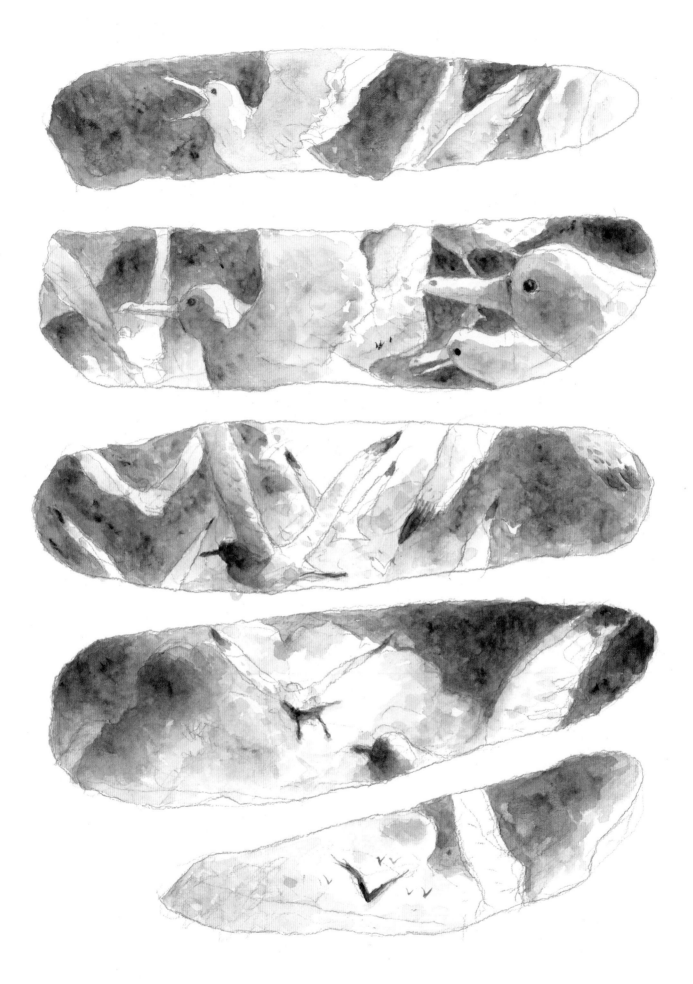

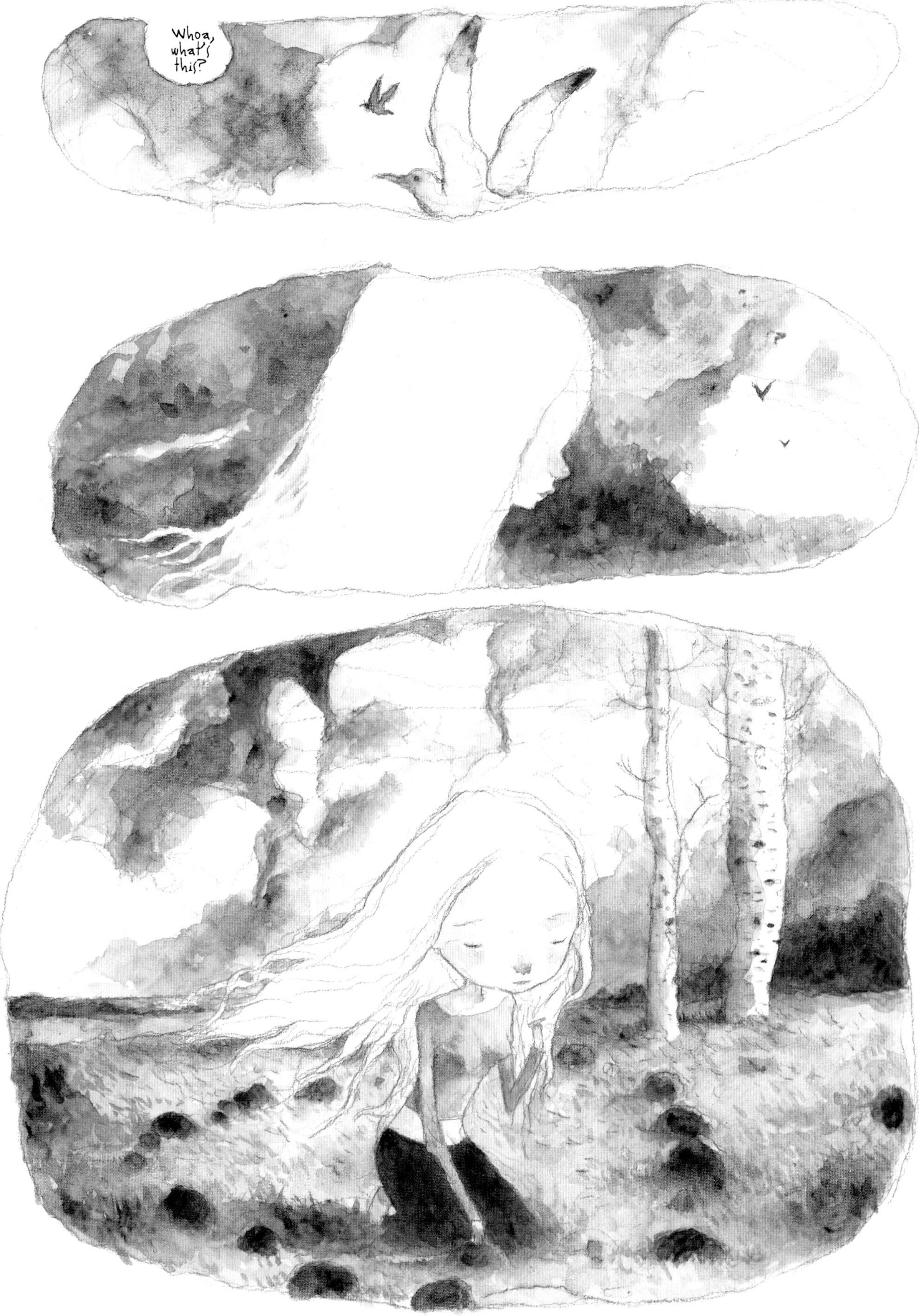
Whoa, what's this?

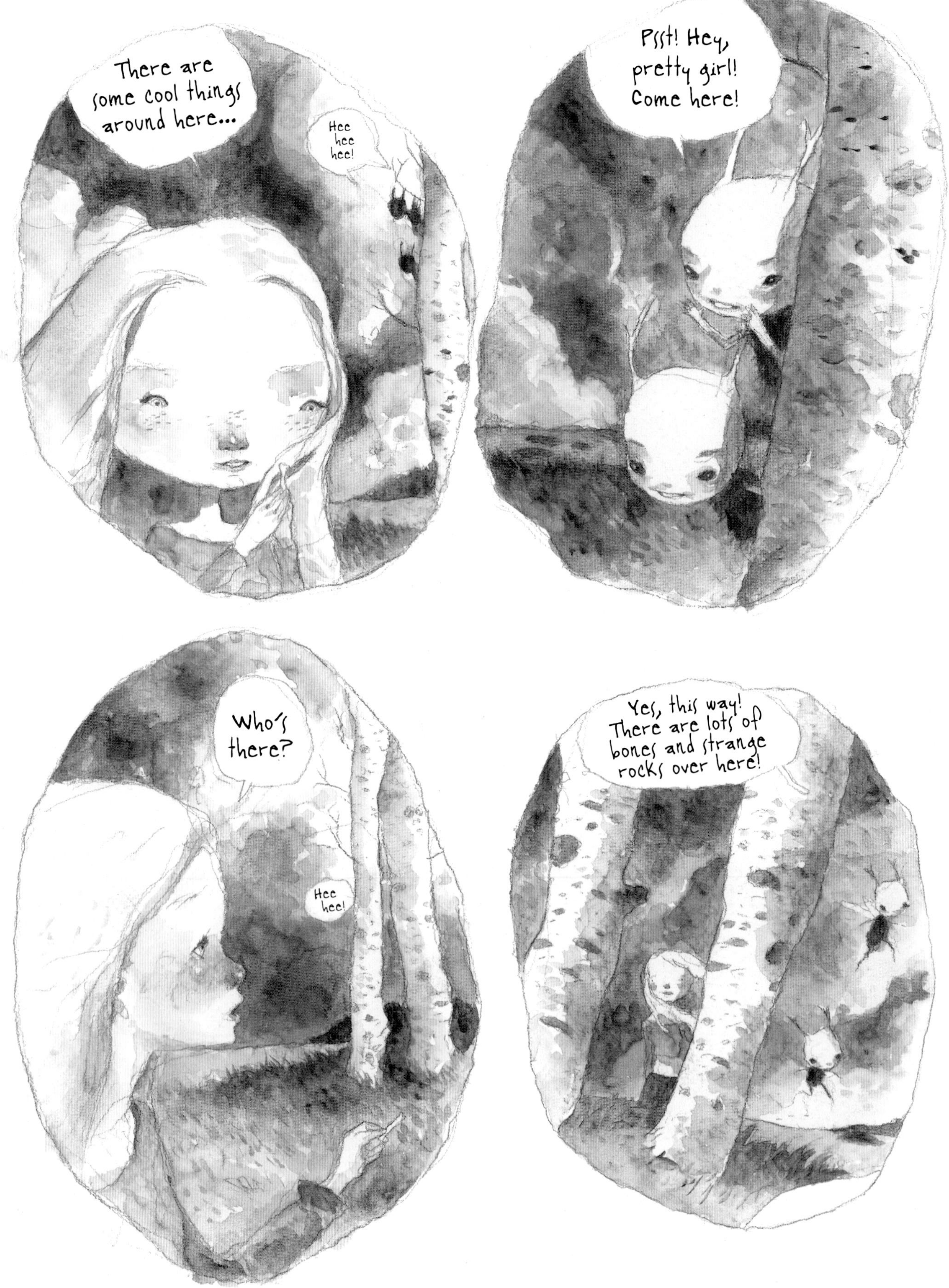
There are some cool things around here...
Hee hee hee!
Psst! Hey, pretty girl! Come here!
Who's there?
Hee hee!
Yes, this way! There are lots of bones and strange rocks over here!

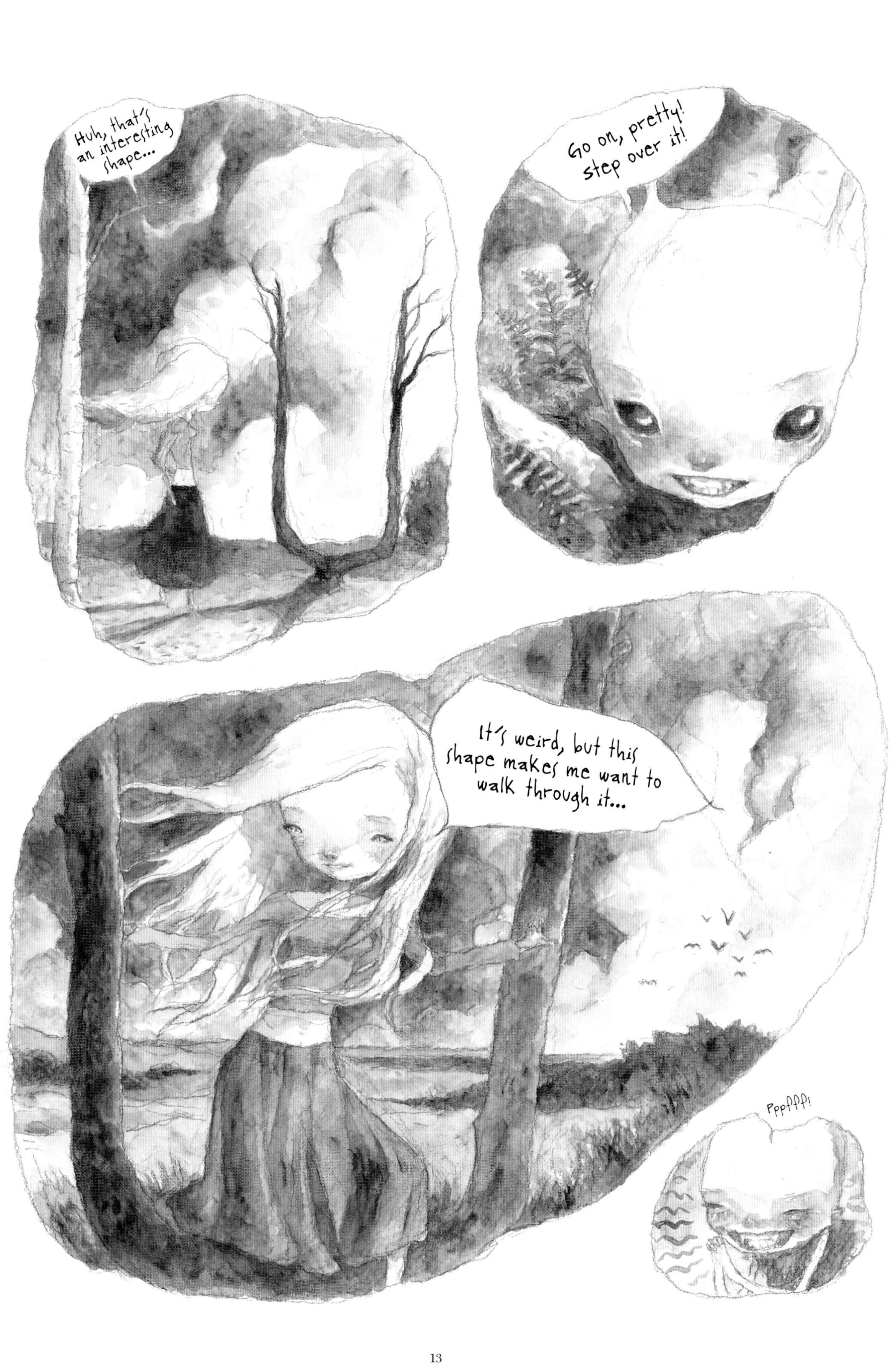
Huh, that's an interesting shape...
Go on, pretty! Step over it!
It's weird, but this shape makes me want to walk through it...
Pppfff!

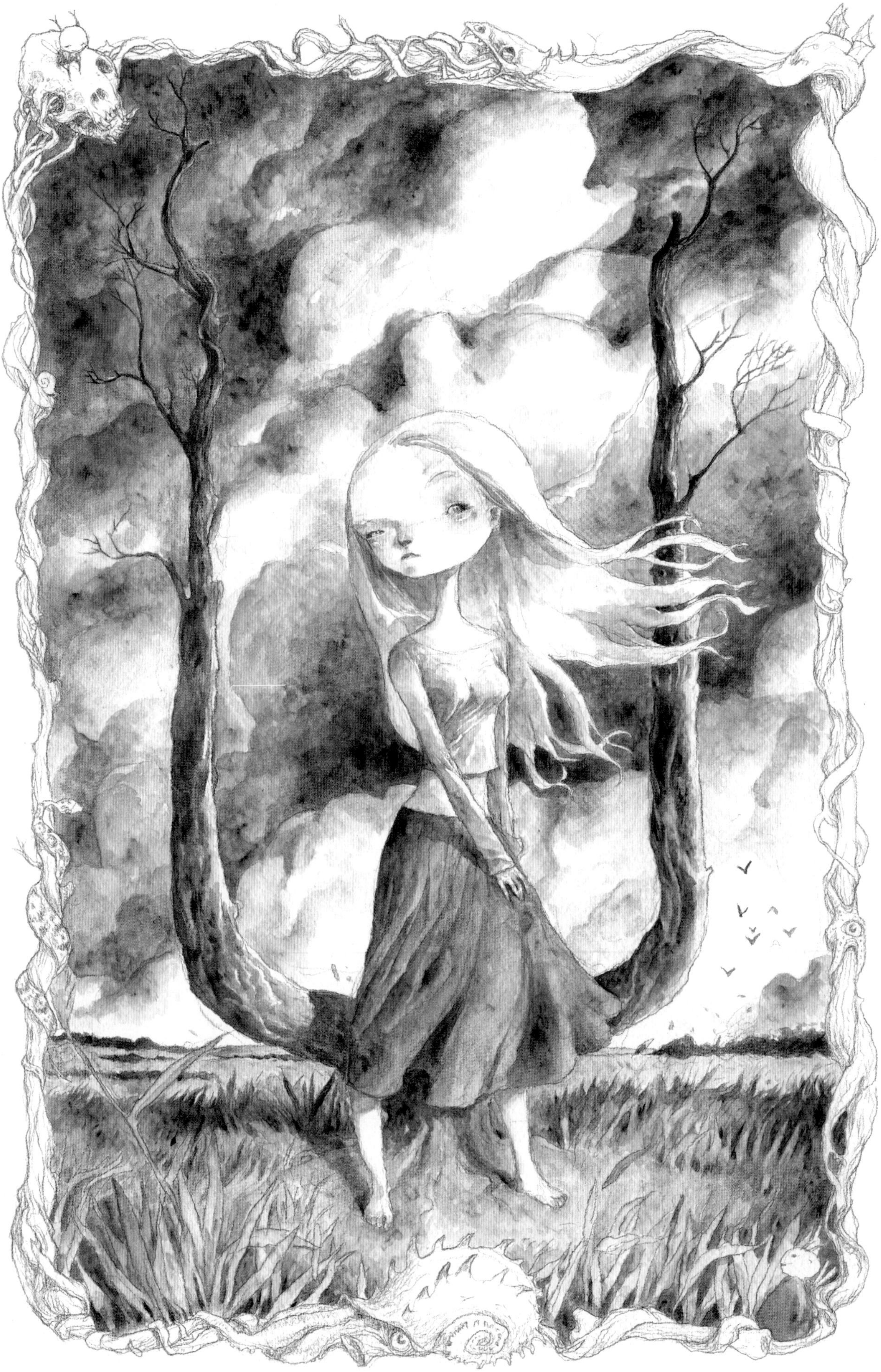

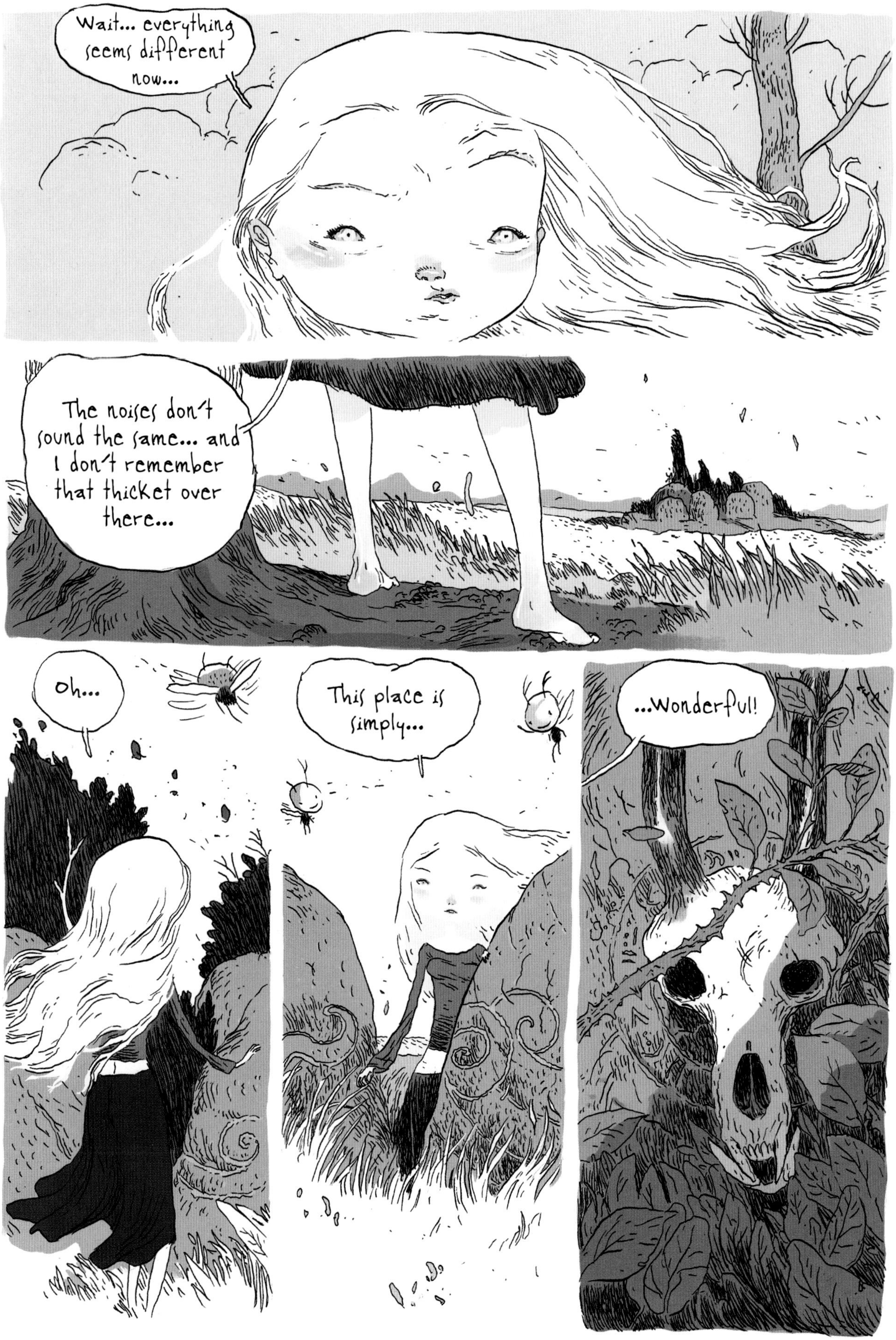
Wait... everything seems different now...
The noises don't sound the same... and I don't remember that thicket over there...
Oh...
This place is simply...
...Wonderful!

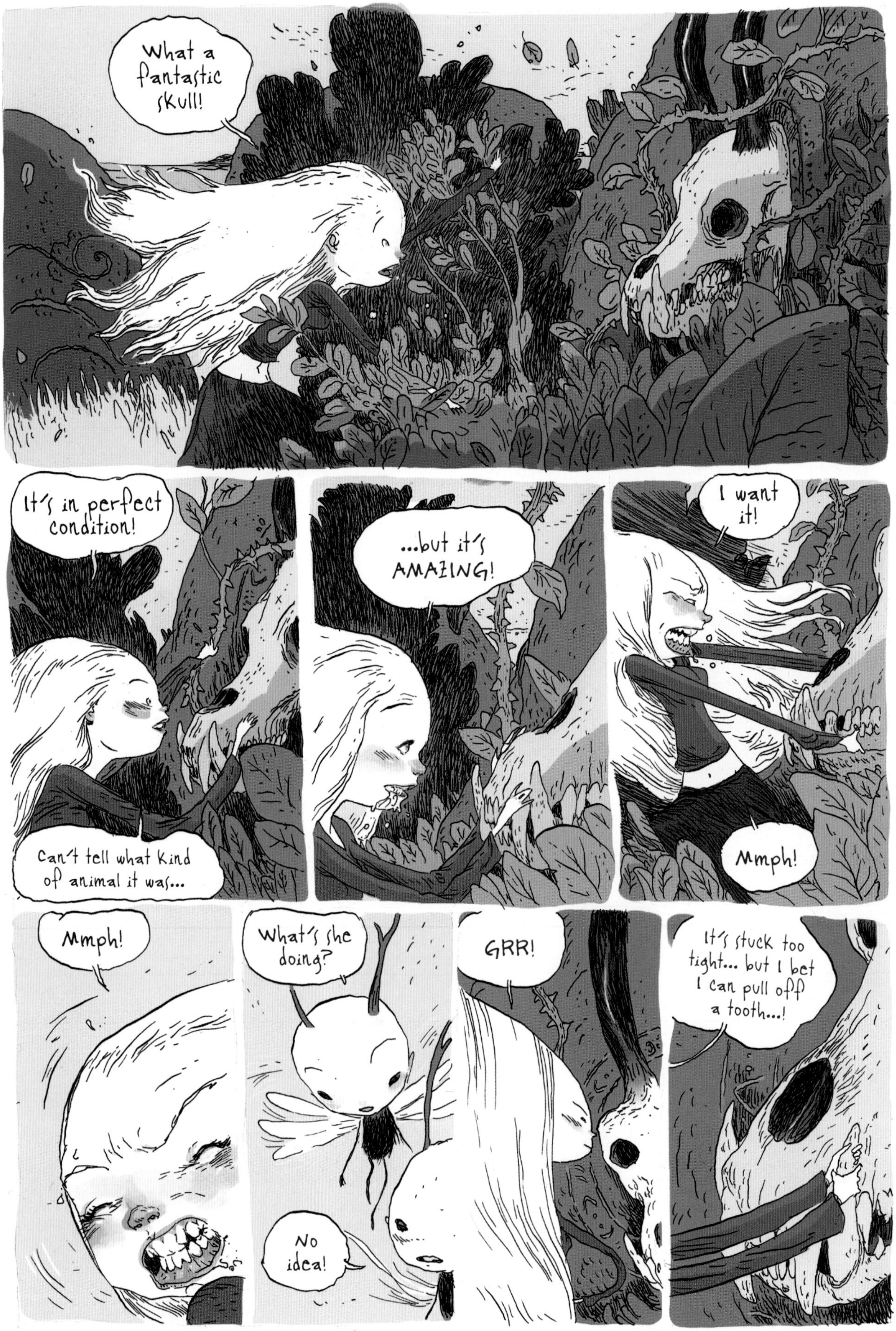
What a fantastic skull!
It's in perfect condition!
Can't tell what kind of animal it was...
...but it's AMAZING!
I want it!
Mmph!
Mmph!
What's she doing?
No idea!
GRR!
It's stuck too tight... but I bet I can pull off a tooth...!

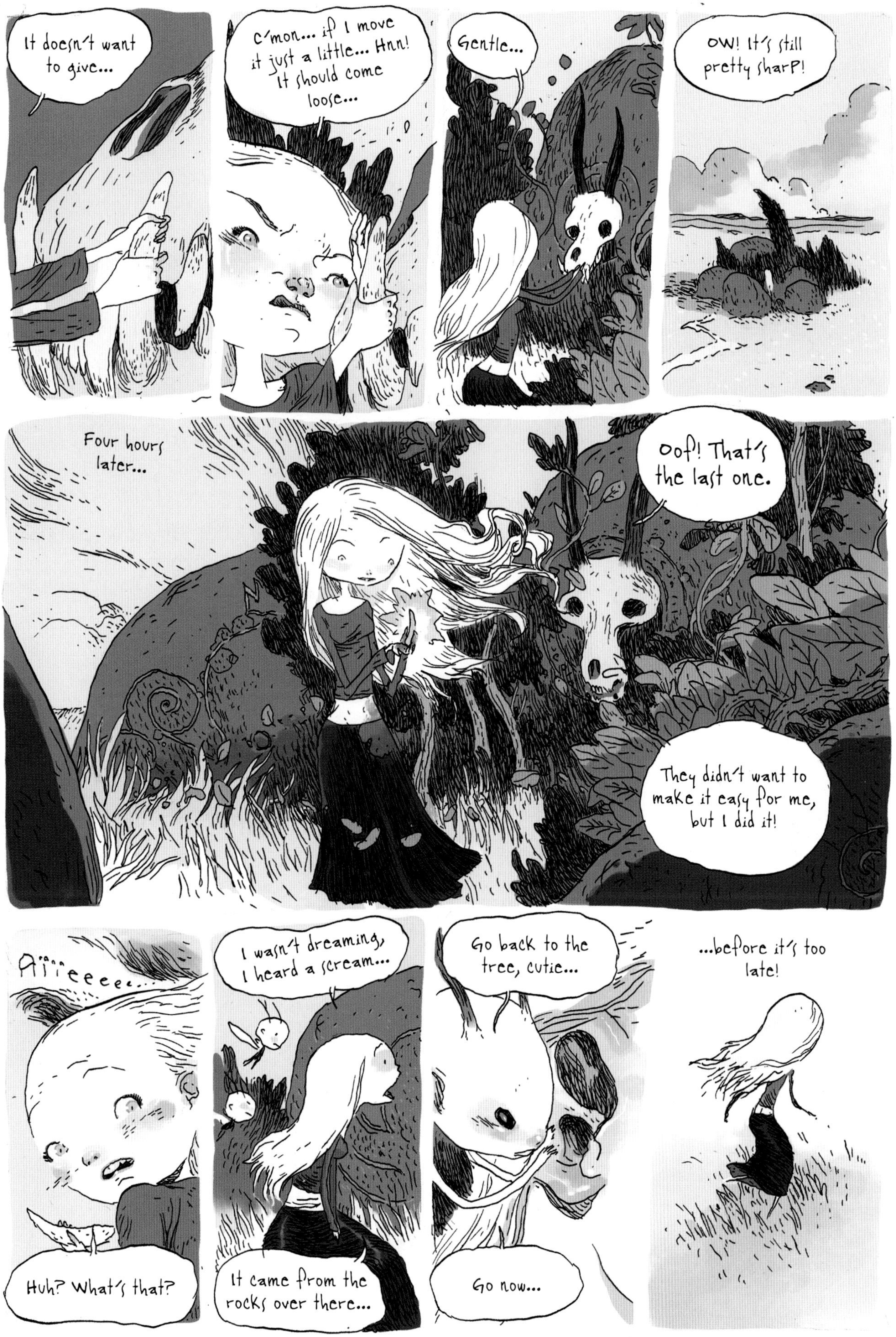
It doesn't want to give...
C'mon... if I move it just a little... Hnn! It should come loose...
Gentle...
OW! It's still pretty sharp!
Four hours later...
Oof! That's the last one.
They didn't want to make it easy for me, but I did it!
Aiiieeee...
Huh? What's that?
I wasn't dreaming, I heard a scream...
It came from the rocks over there...
Go back to the tree, cutie...
Go now...
...before it's too late!

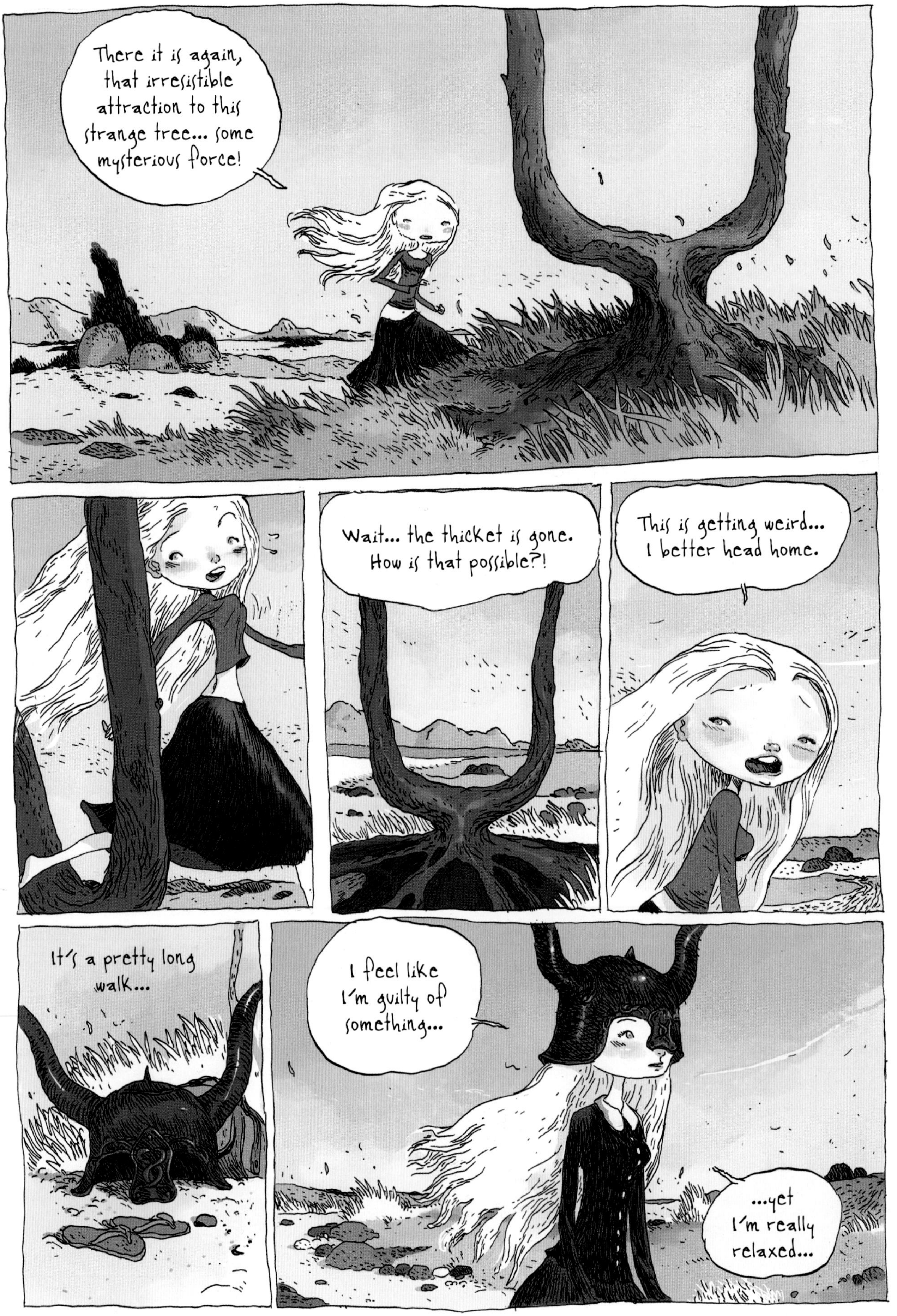
There it is again, that irresistible attraction to this strange tree... some mysterious force!
Wait... the thicket is gone. How is that possible?!
This is getting weird... I better head home.
It's a pretty long walk...
I feel like I'm guilty of something...
...yet I'm really relaxed...

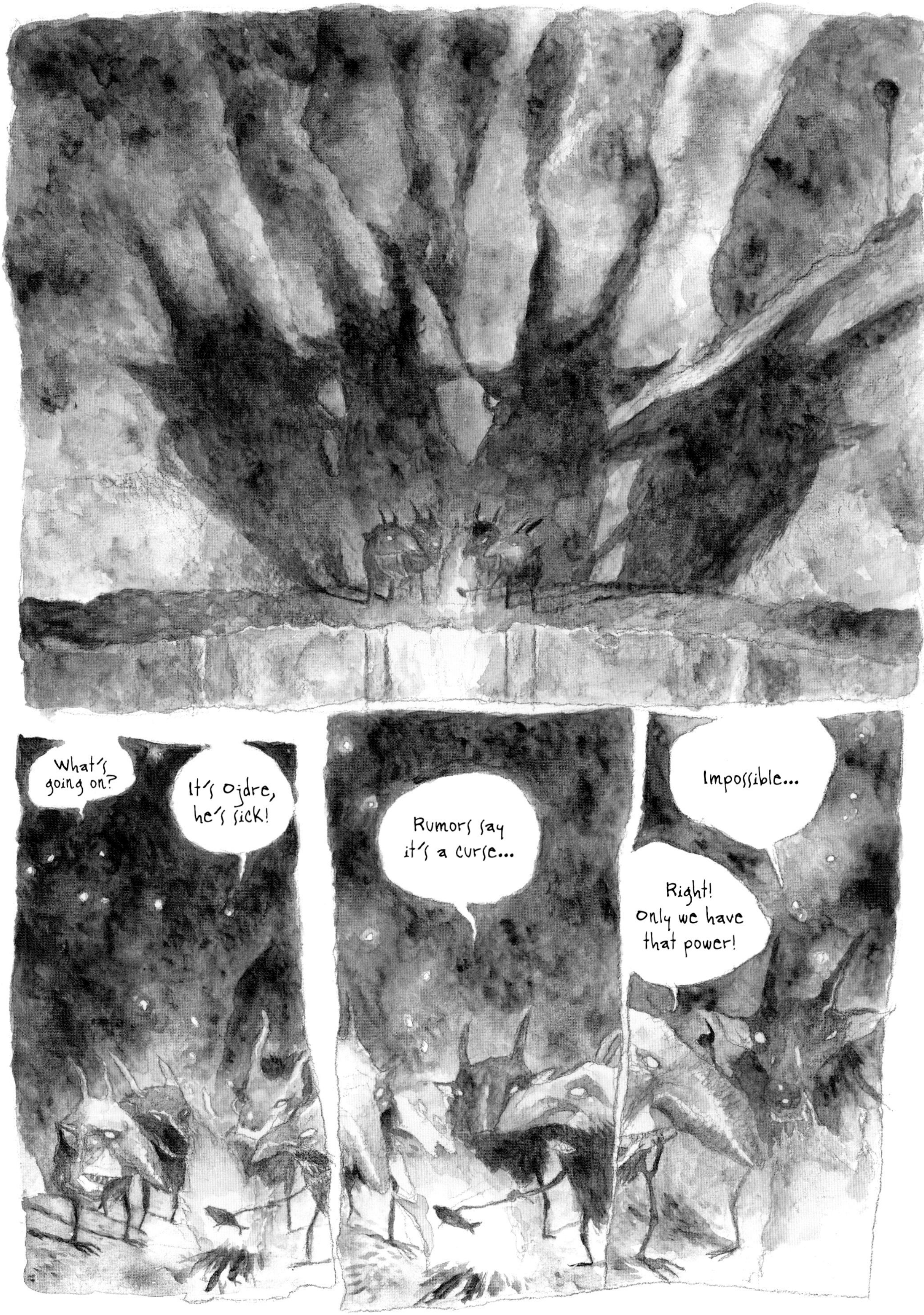
What's going on?
It's Ojdre, he's sick!
Rumors say it's a curse...
Impossible...
Right! Only we have that power!

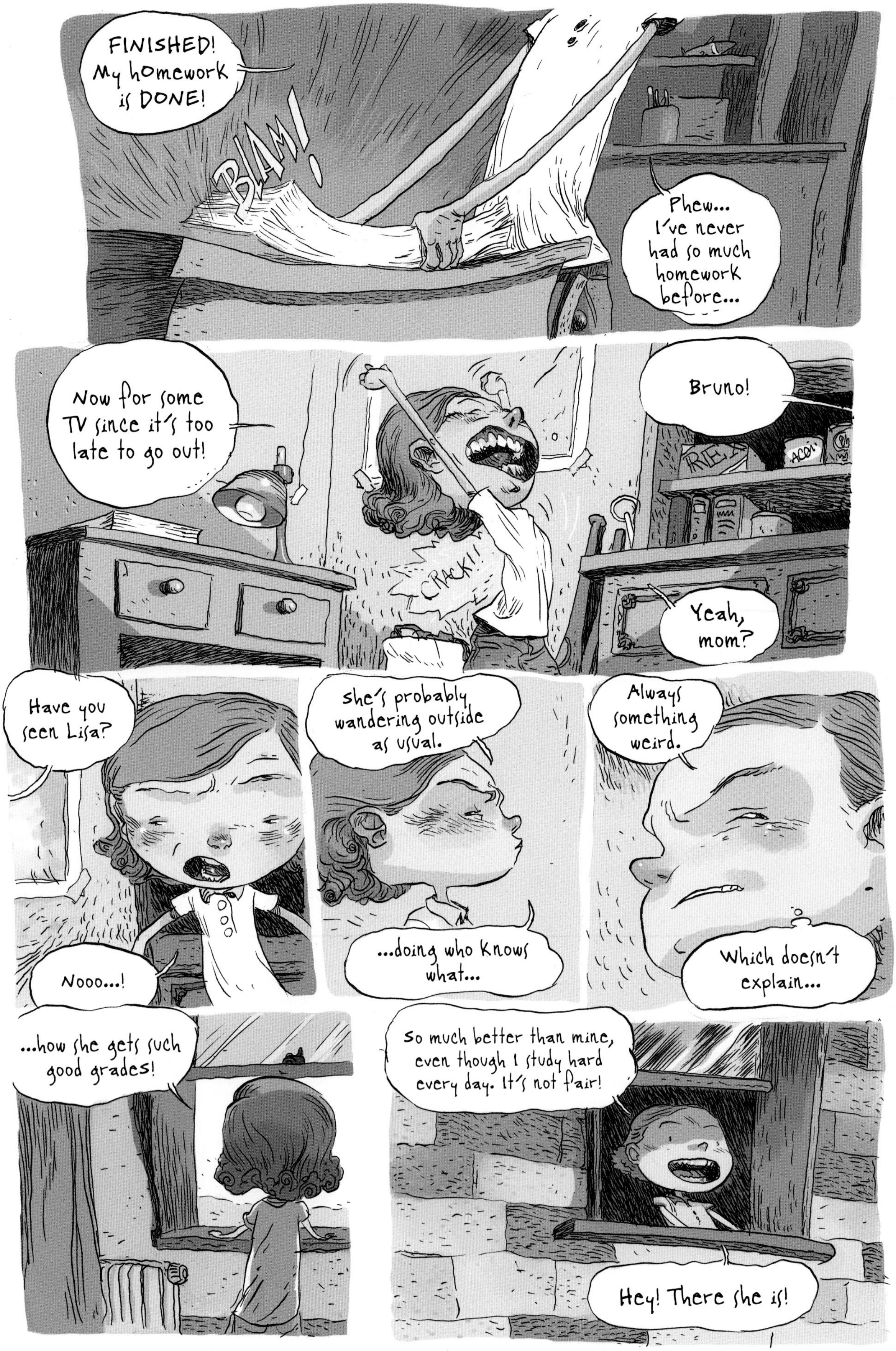
FINISHED! My homework is DONE!
BLAM!
Phew... I've never had so much homework before...
Now for some TV since it's too late to go out!
Bruno!
CRACK!
Yeah, mom?
Have you seen Lisa?
Nooo...!
She's probably wandering outside as usual.
...doing who knows what...
Always something weird.
Which doesn't explain...
...how she gets such good grades!
So much better than mine, even though I study hard every day. It's not fair!
Hey! There she is!

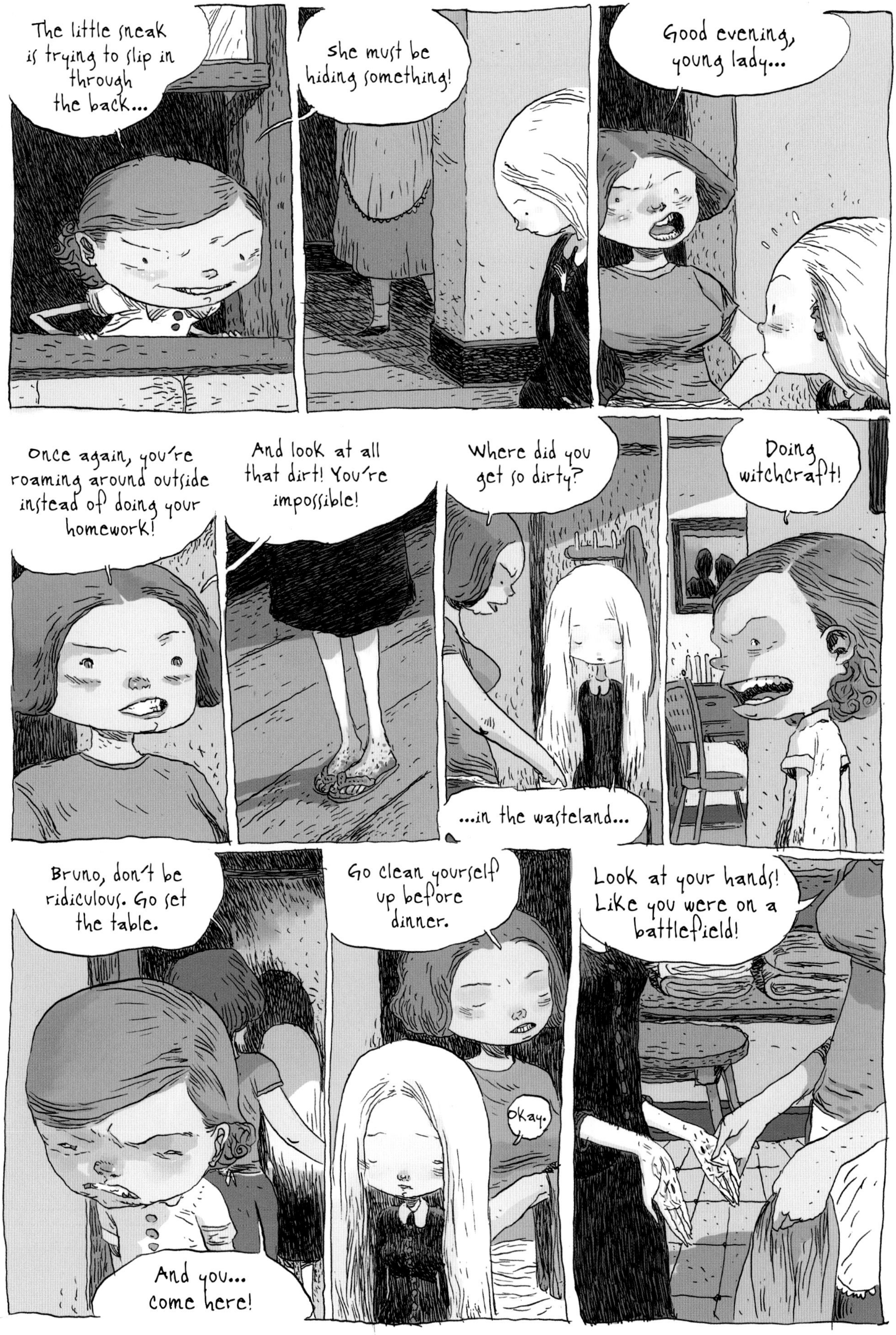
The little sneak is trying to slip in through the back...
she must be hiding something!
Good evening, young lady...
Once again, you're roaming around outside instead of doing your homework!
And look at all that dirt! You're impossible!
Where did you get so dirty?
...in the wasteland...
Doing witchcraft!
Bruno, don't be ridiculous. Go set the table.
And you... come here!
Go clean yourself up before dinner.
Okay.
Look at your hands! Like you were on a battlefield!

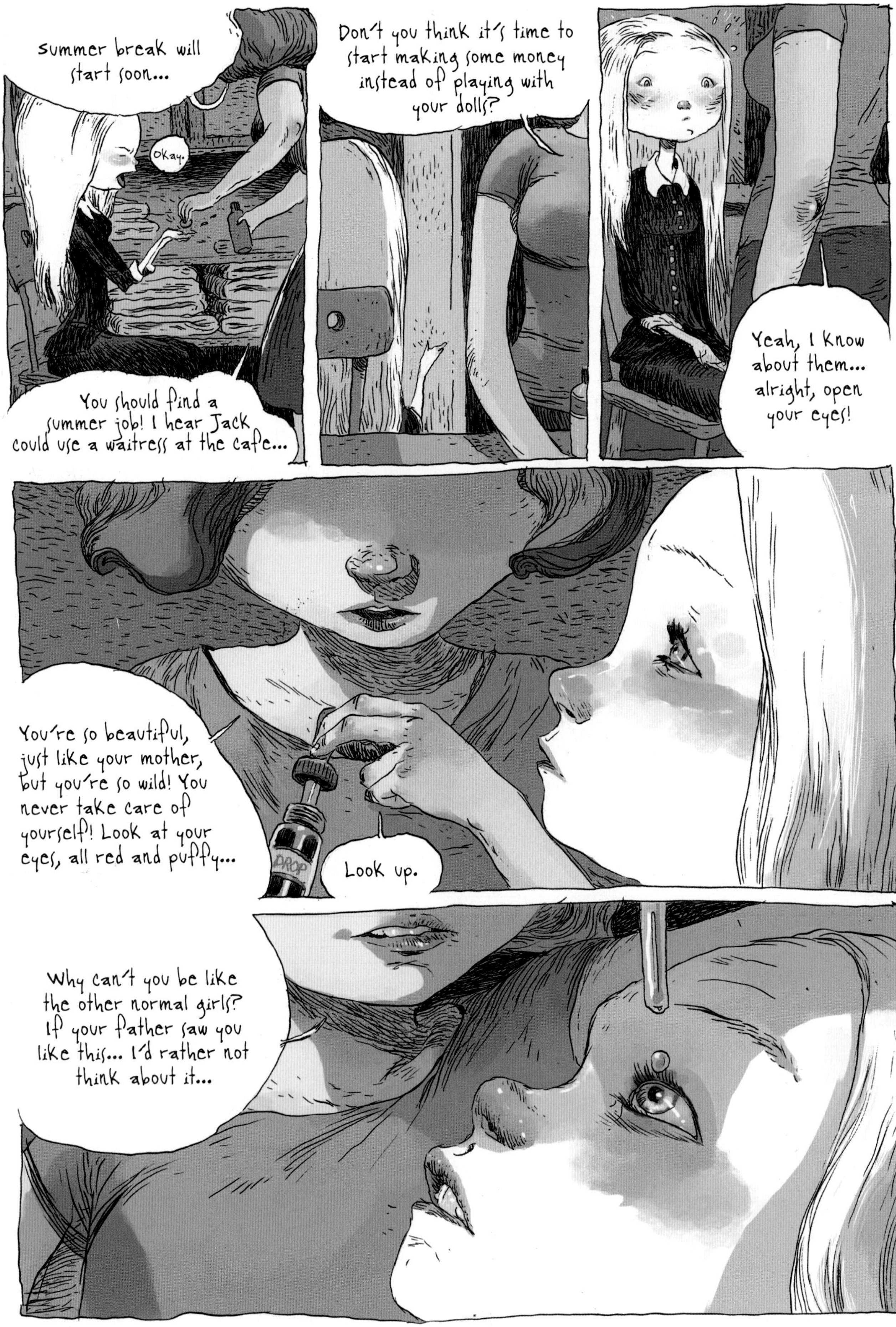
Summer break will start soon...
Okay.
You should find a summer job! I hear Jack could use a waitress at the cafe...
Don't you think it's time to start making some money instead of playing with your dolls?
Yeah, I know about them... alright, open your eyes!
You're so beautiful, just like your mother, but you're so wild! You never take care of yourself! Look at your eyes, all red and puffy...
DROP
Look up.
Why can't you be like the other normal girls? If your father saw you like this... I'd rather not think about it...

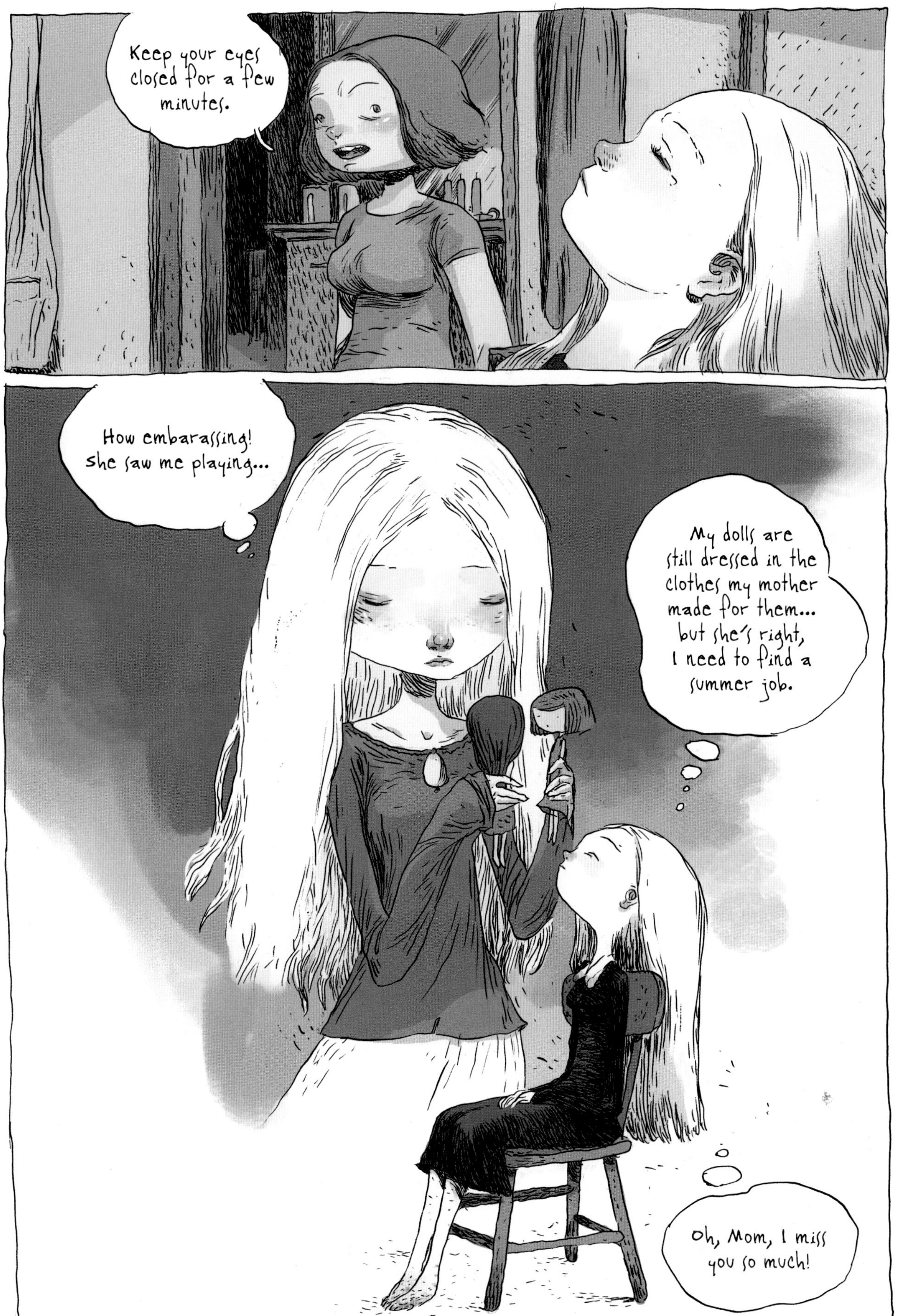
Keep your eyes closed for a few minutes.
How embarassing! she saw me playing...
My dolls are still dressed in the clothes my mother made for them... but she's right, I need to find a summer job.
Oh, Mom, I miss you so much!

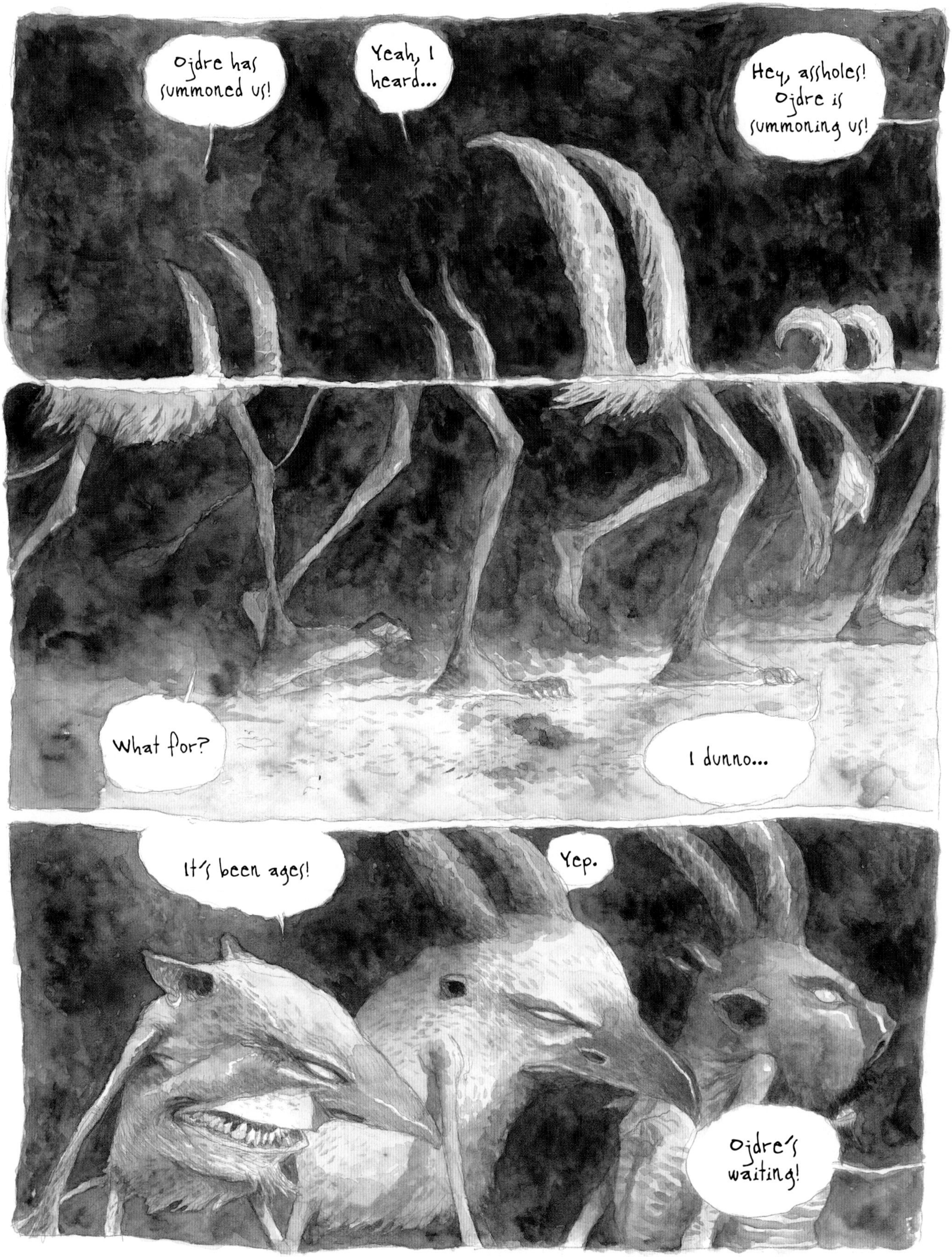
Ojdre has summoned us!
Yeah, I heard...
Hey, assholes! Ojdre is summoning us!
What for?
I dunno...
It's been ages!
Yep.
Ojdre's waiting!

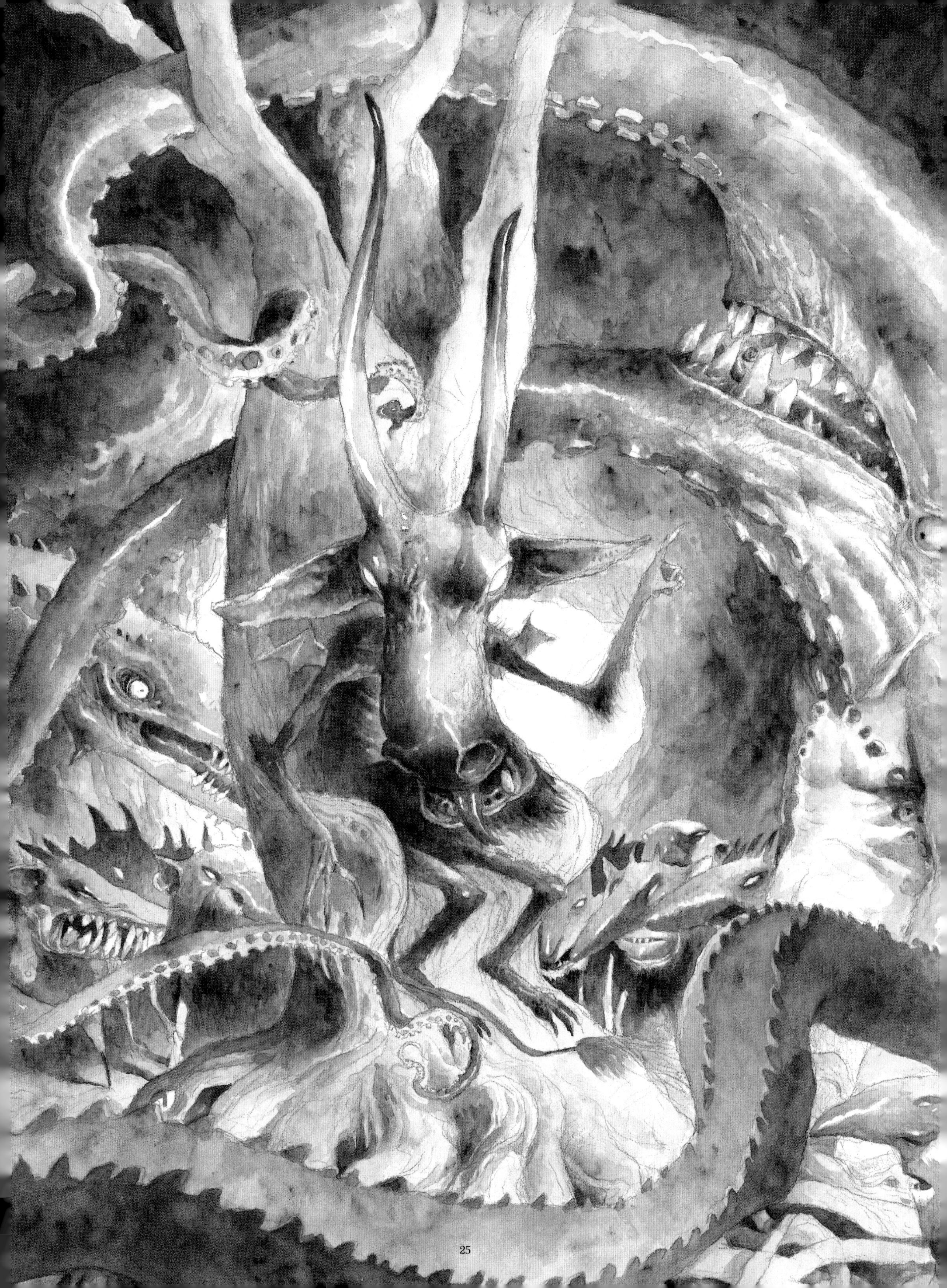

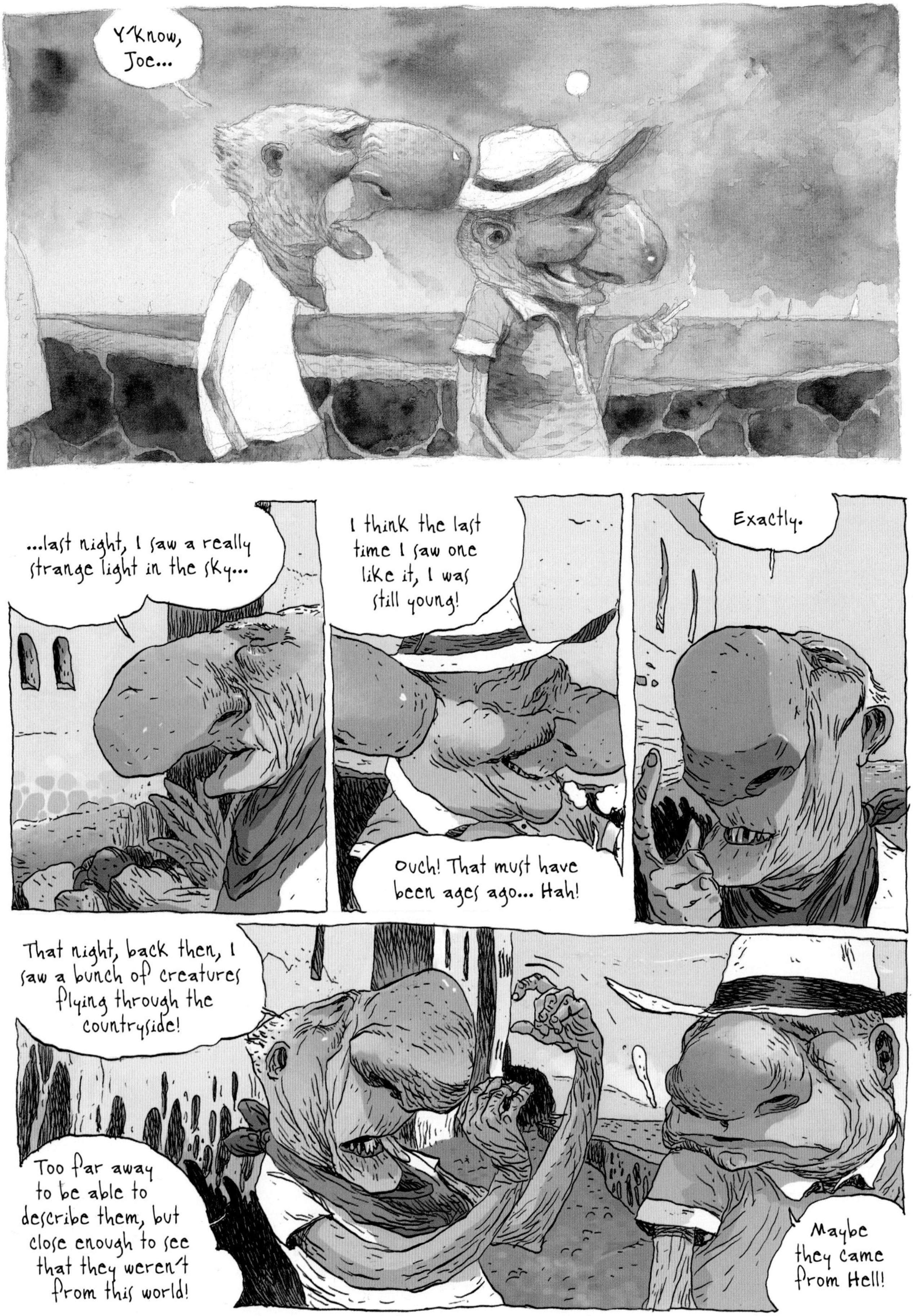
Y'Know, Joe...
...last night, I saw a really strange light in the sky...
I think the last time I saw one like it, I was still young!
Ouch! That must have been ages ago... Hah!
Exactly.
That night, back then, I saw a bunch of creatures flying through the countryside!
Too far away to be able to describe them, but close enough to see that they weren't from this world!
Maybe they came from Hell!

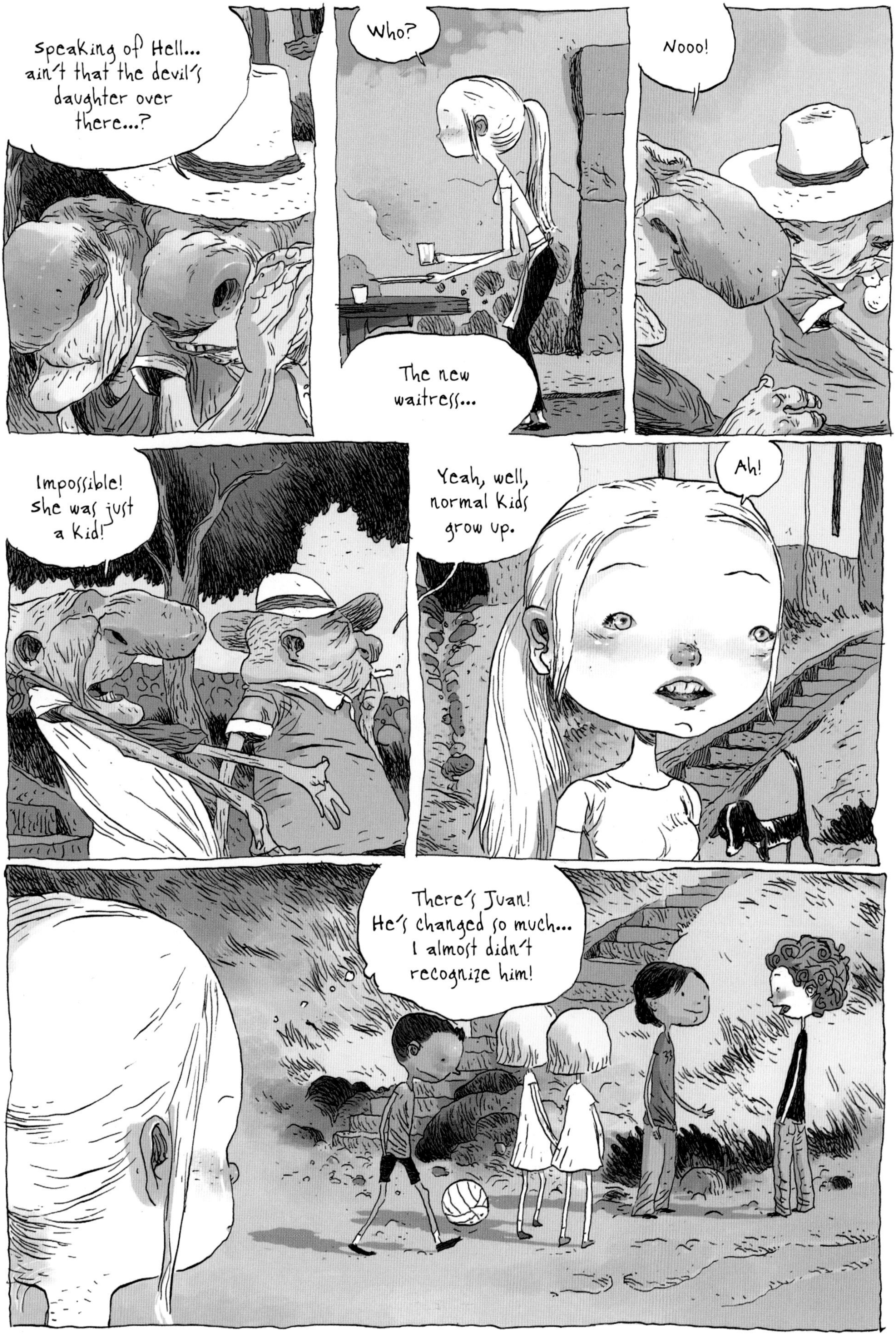
Speaking of Hell... ain't that the devil's daughter over there...?
Who?
The new waitress...
Nooo!
Impossible! She was just a kid!
Yeah, well, normal kids grow up.
Ah!
There's Juan! He's changed so much... I almost didn't recognize him!

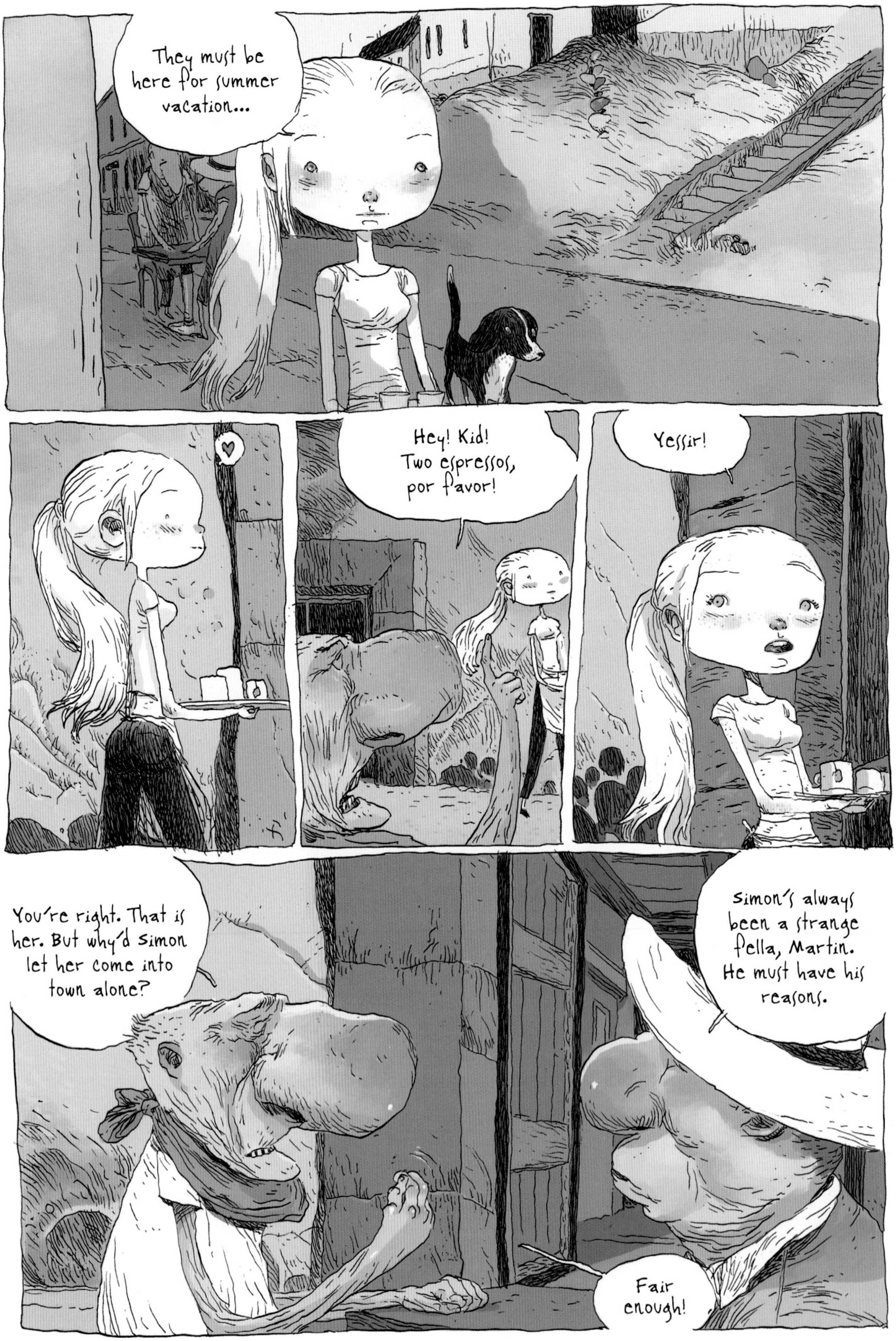

They must be here for summer vacation...
Hey! Kid! Two espressos, por favor!
Yessir!
You're right. That is her. But why'd Simon let her come into town alone?
Simon's always been a strange fella, Martin. He must have his reasons.
Fair enough!

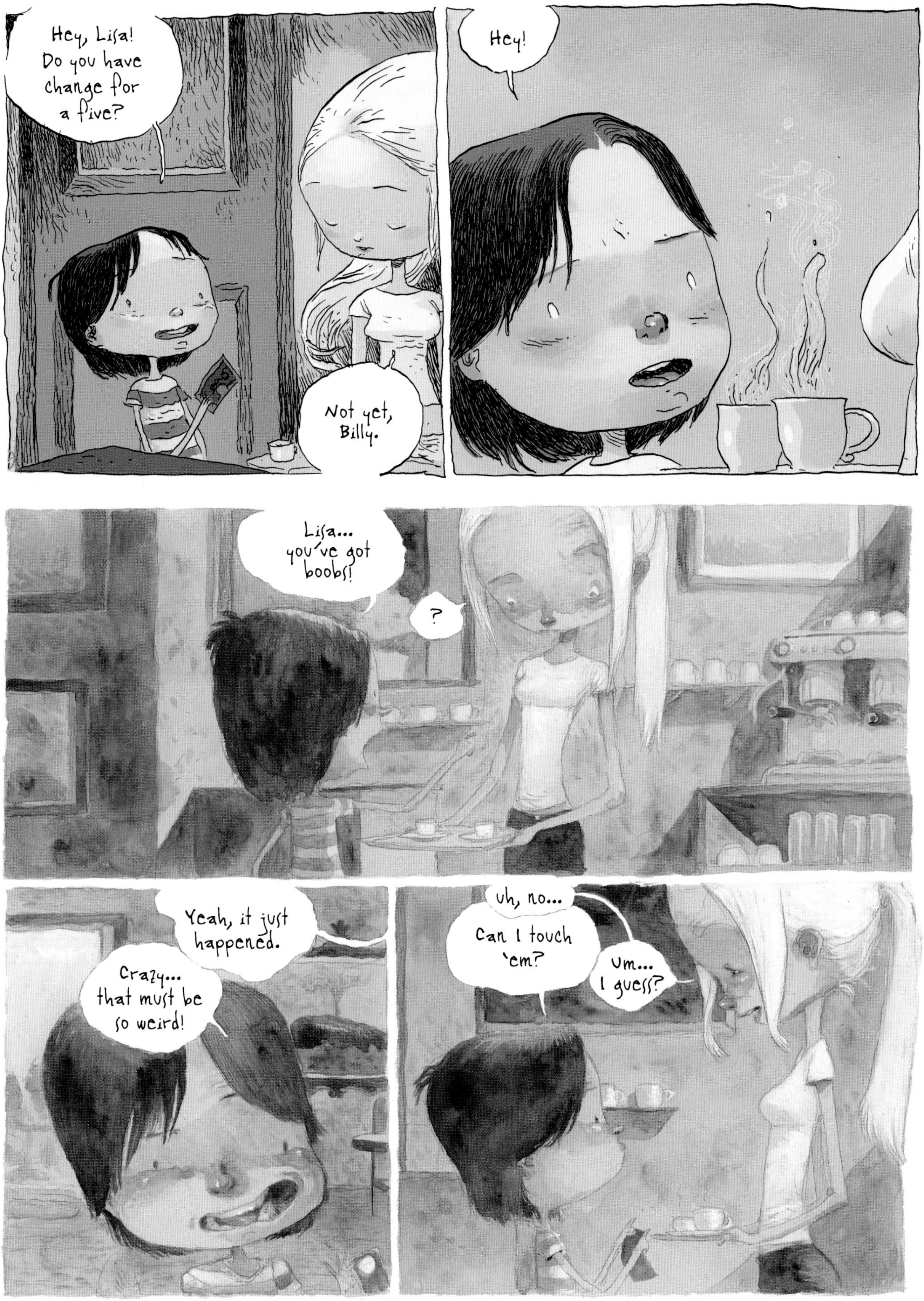

Hey, Lisa! Do you have change for a five?
Not yet, Billy.
Hey!
Lisa... you've got boobs!
?
Yeah, it just happened.
Crazy... that must be so weird!
Uh, no...
Can I touch 'em?
Um... I guess?

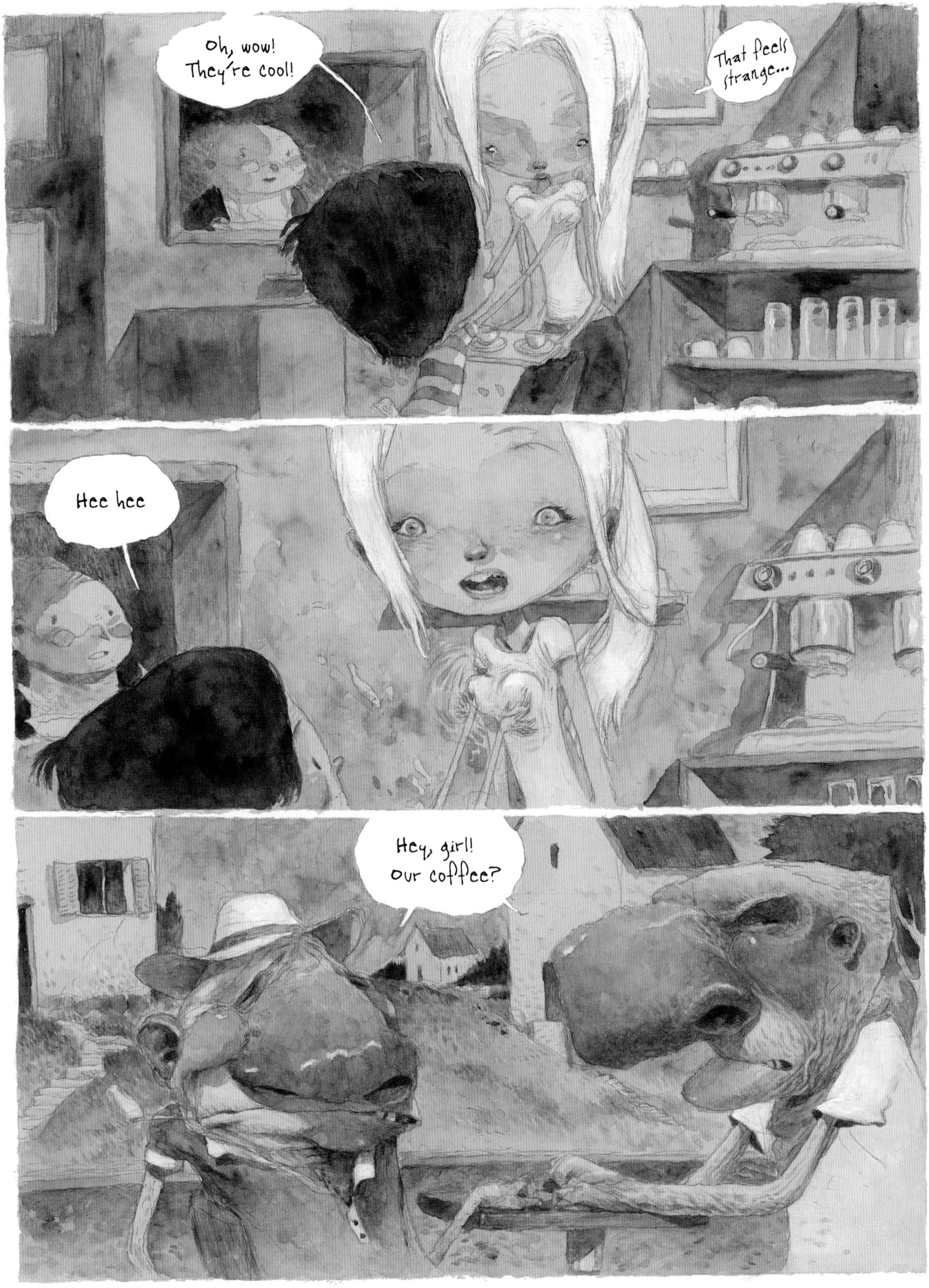
Oh, wow! They're cool!
That feels strange...
Hee hee
Hey, girl! Our coffee?

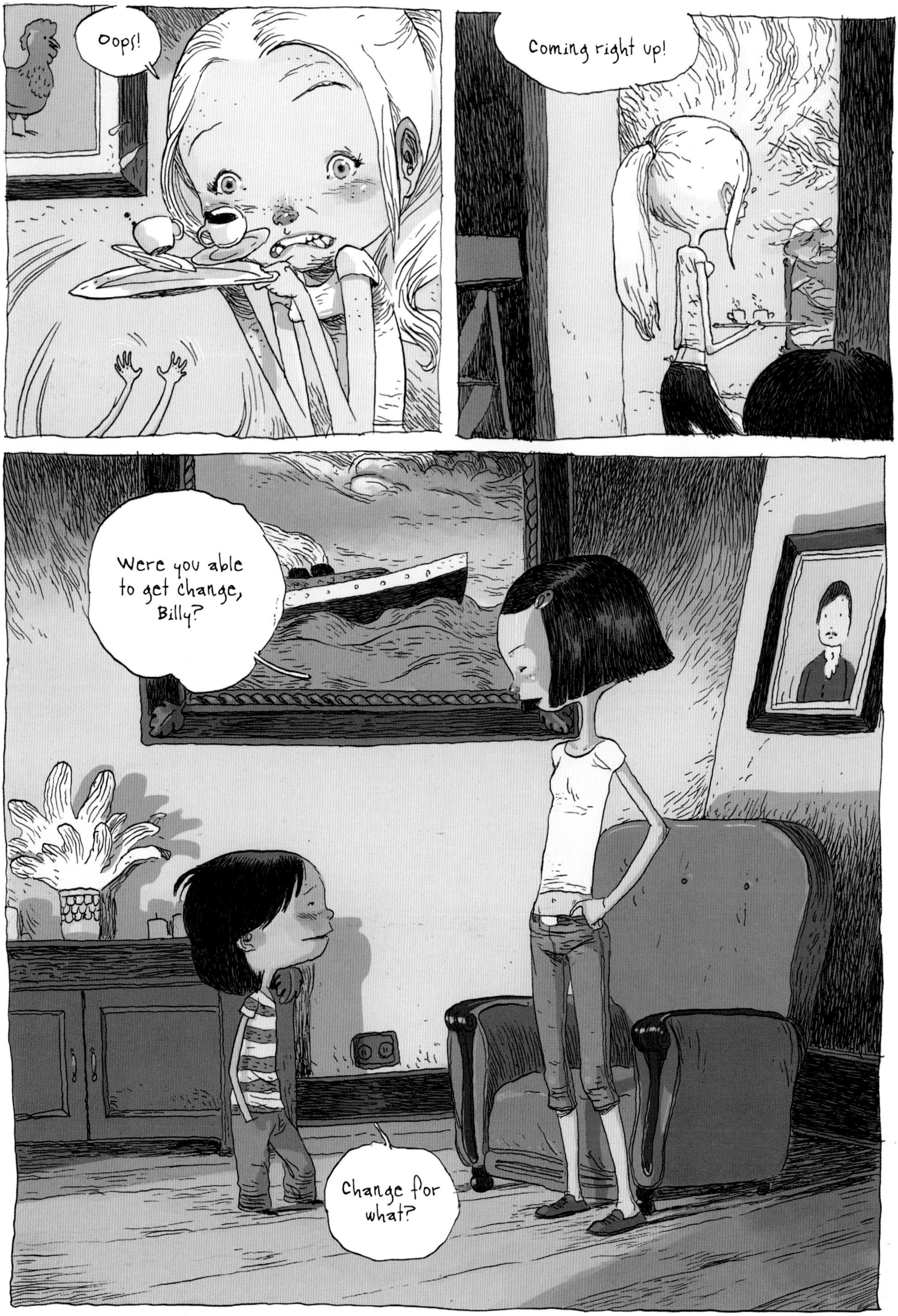
Oops!
Coming right up!
Were you able to get change, Billy?
Change for what?

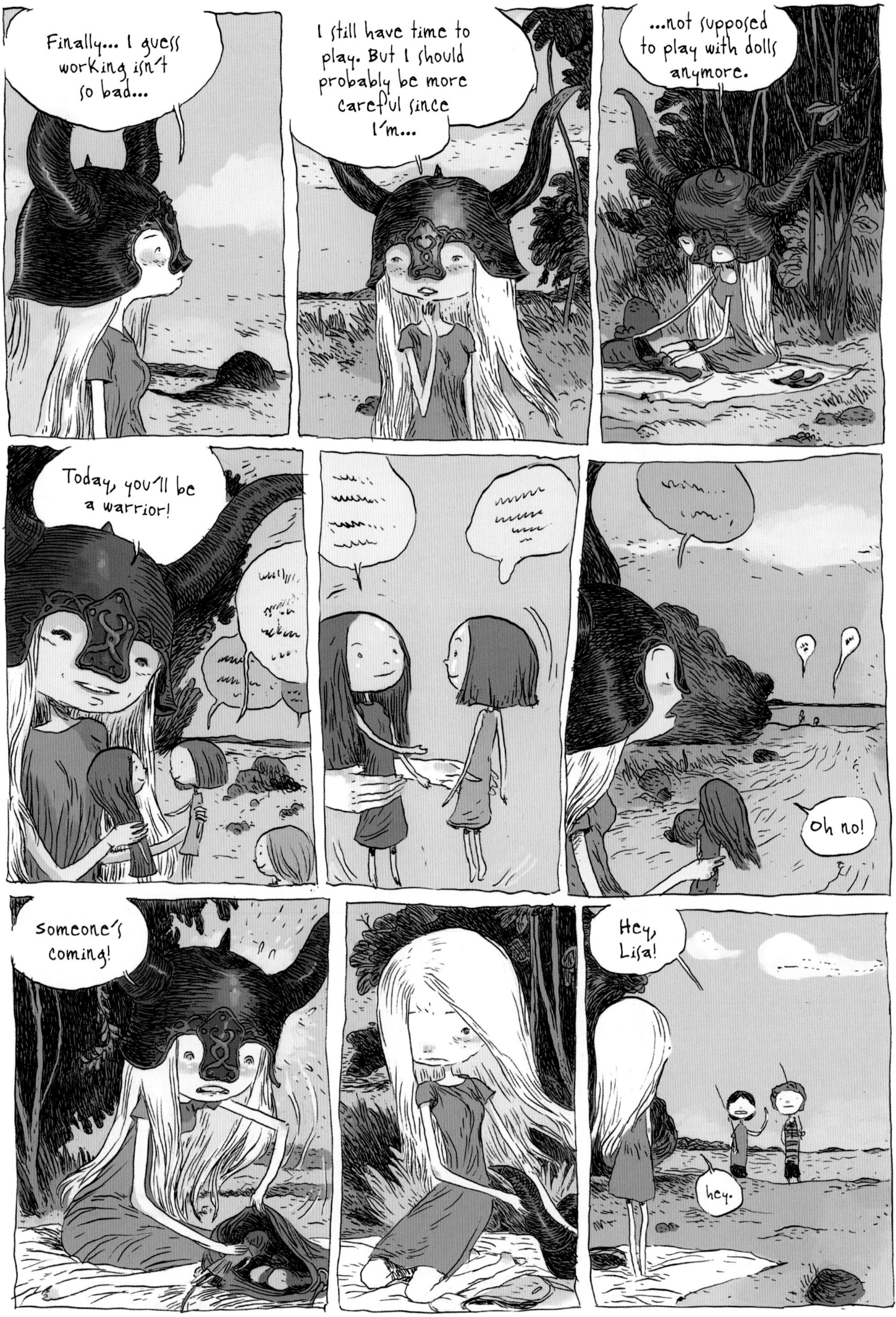
Finally... I guess working isn't so bad...
I still have time to play. But I should probably be more careful since I'm...
...not supposed to play with dolls anymore.
Today, you'll be a warrior!
Oh no!
Someone's coming!
Hey, Lisa!
hey.

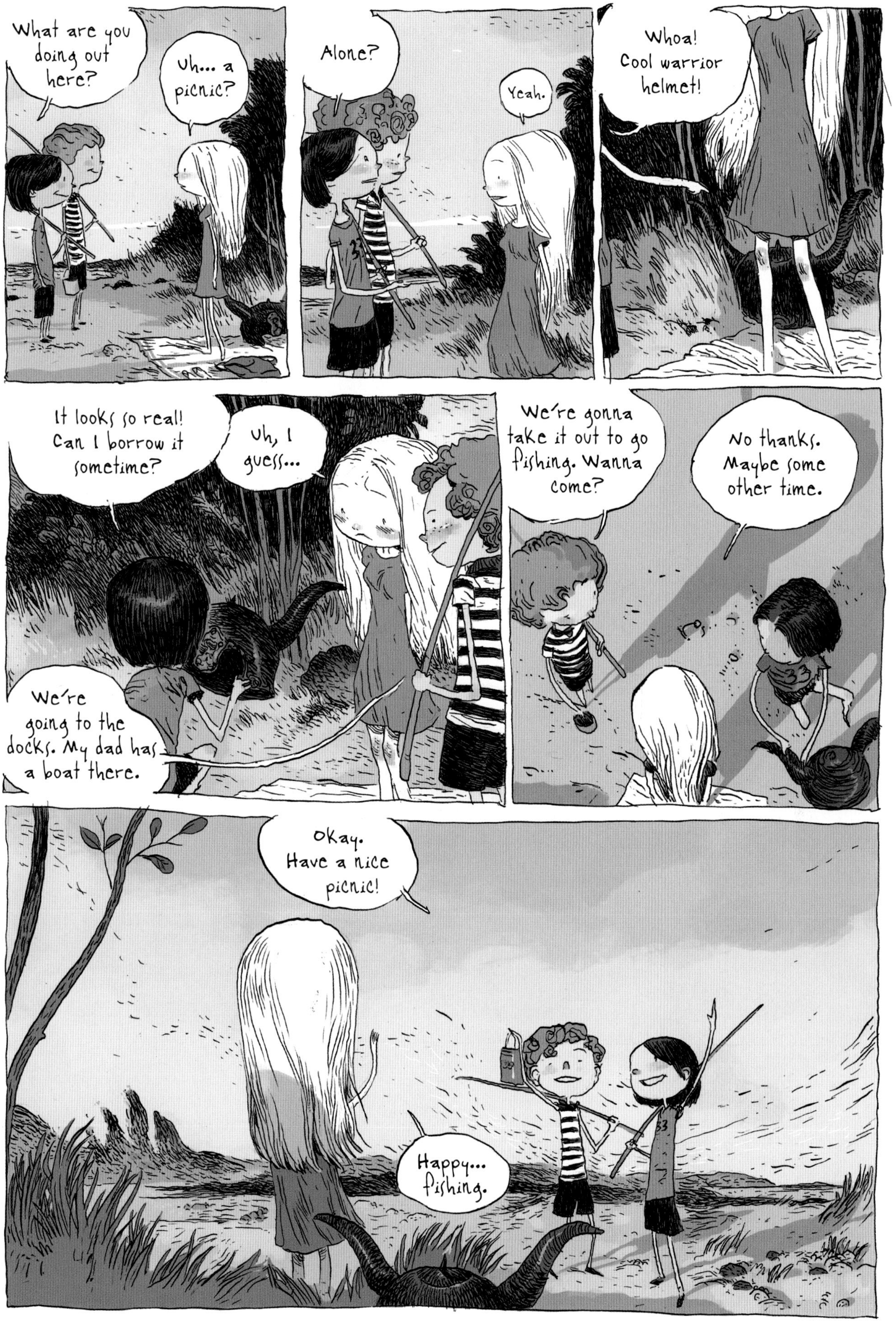
What are you doing out here?
Uh... a picnic?
Alone?
Yeah.
Whoa! Cool warrior helmet!
It looks so real! Can I borrow it sometime?
Uh, I guess...
We're going to the docks. My dad has a boat there.
We're gonna take it out to go fishing. Wanna come?
No thanks. Maybe some other time.
Okay. Have a nice picnic!
Happy... fishing.

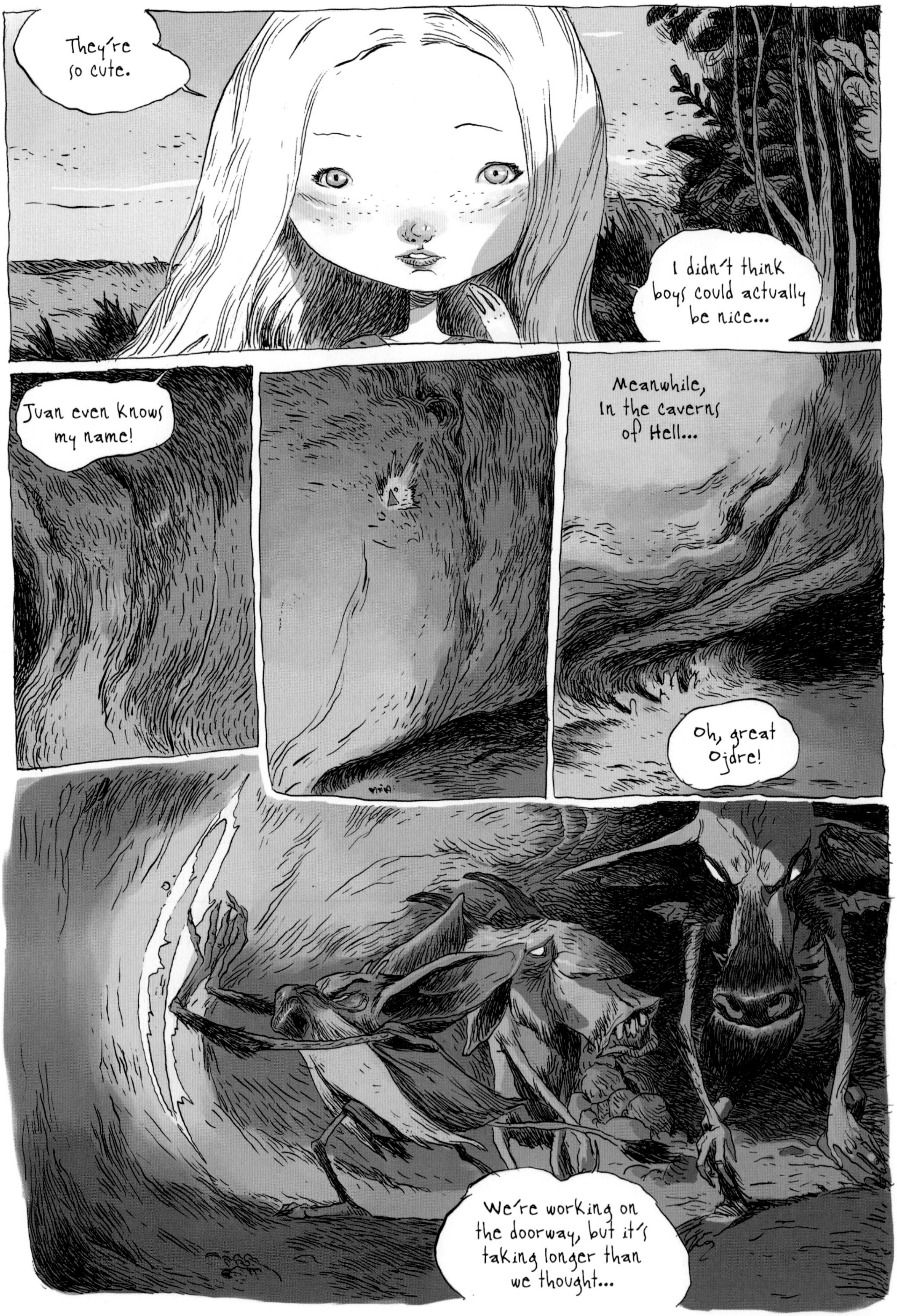
They're so cute.
I didn't think boys could actually be nice...
Juan even knows my name!
Meanwhile, In the caverns of Hell...
Oh, great Ojdre!
We're working on the doorway, but it's taking longer than we thought...

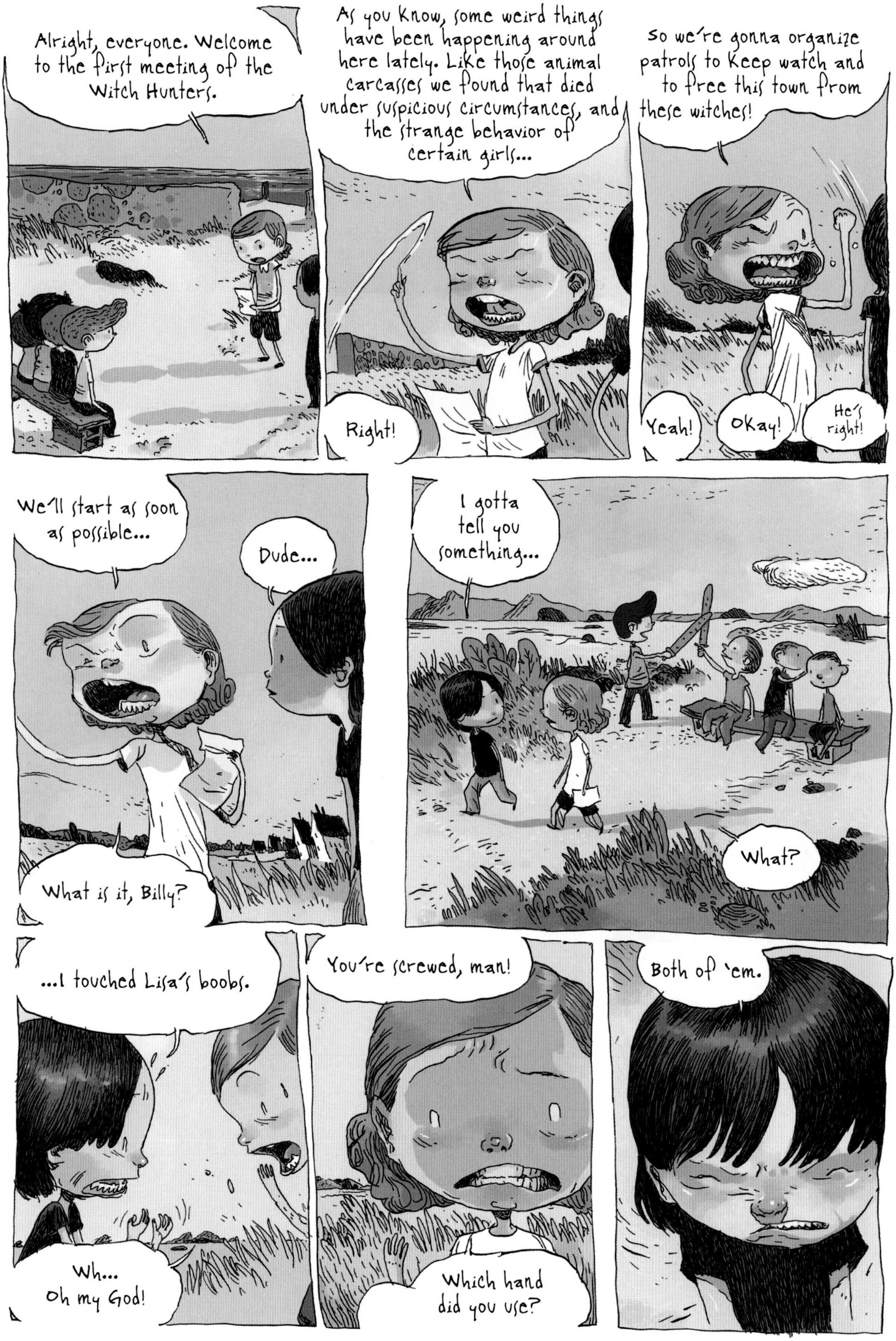
Alright, everyone. Welcome to the first meeting of the Witch Hunters.
As you know, some weird things have been happening around here lately. Like those animal carcasses we found that died under suspicious circumstances, and the strange behavior of certain girls...
Right!
So we're gonna organize patrols to keep watch and to free this town from these witches!
Yeah!
Okay!
He's right!
We'll start as soon as possible...
Dude...
What is it, Billy?
I gotta tell you something...
What?
...I touched Lisa's boobs.
Wh... Oh my God!
You're screwed, man!
Which hand did you use?
Both of 'em.

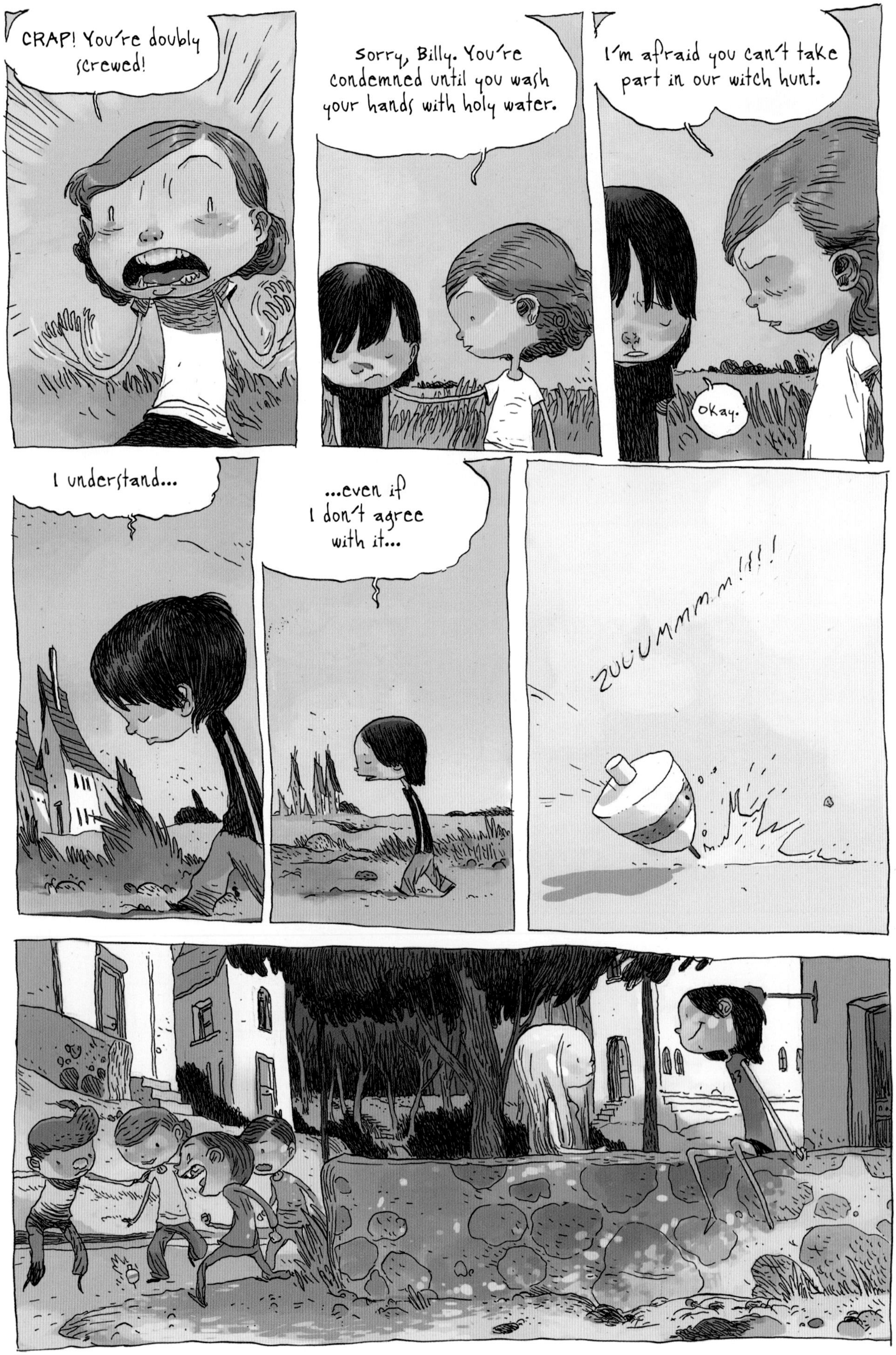
CRAP! You're doubly screwed!
Sorry, Billy. You're condemned until you wash your hands with holy water.
I'm afraid you can't take part in our witch hunt.
Okay.
I understand...
...even if I don't agree with it...
ZUUUMMMMm!!!!

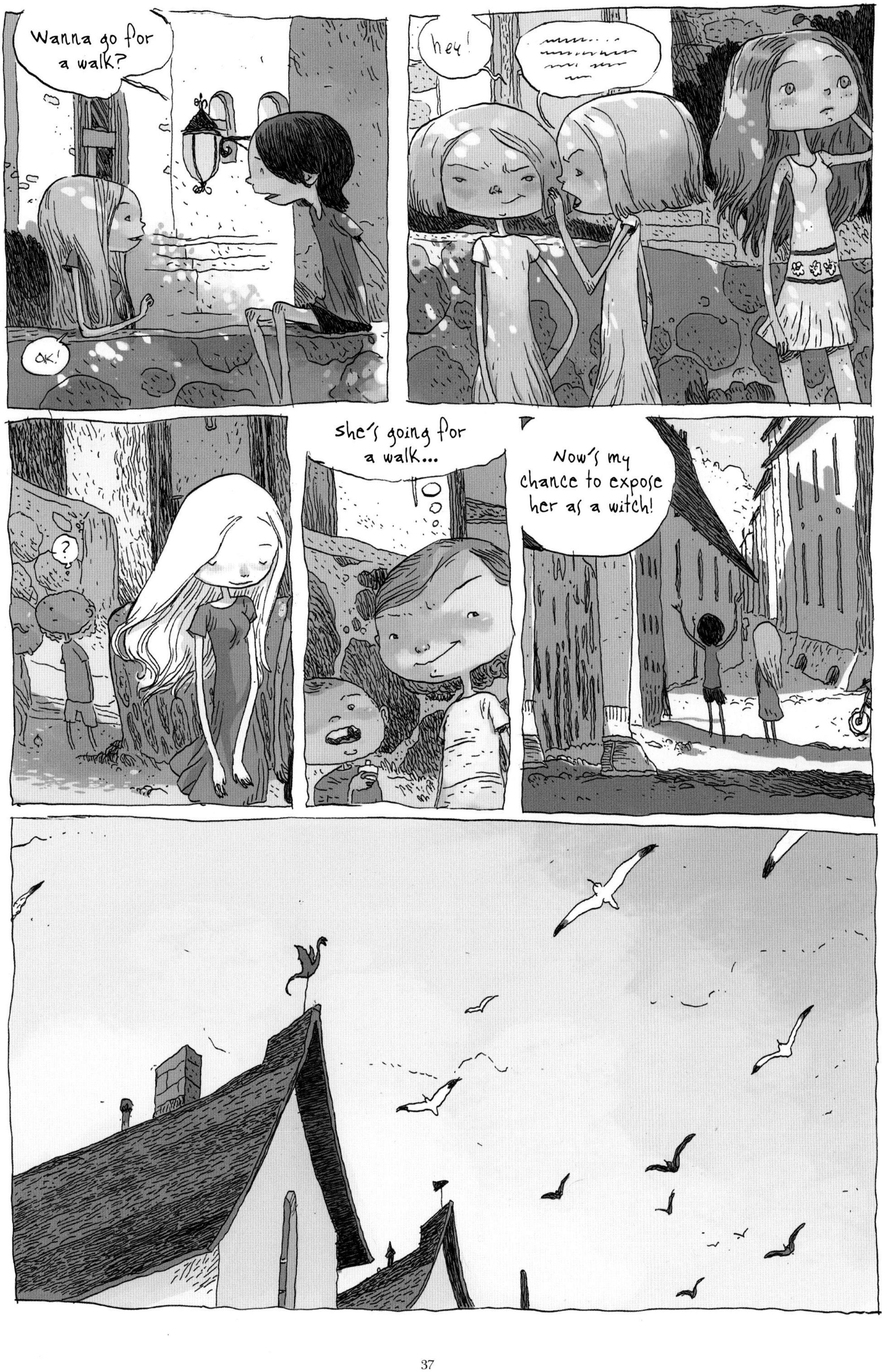
Wanna go for a walk?
OK!
hey!
she's going for a walk...
Now's my chance to expose her as a witch!

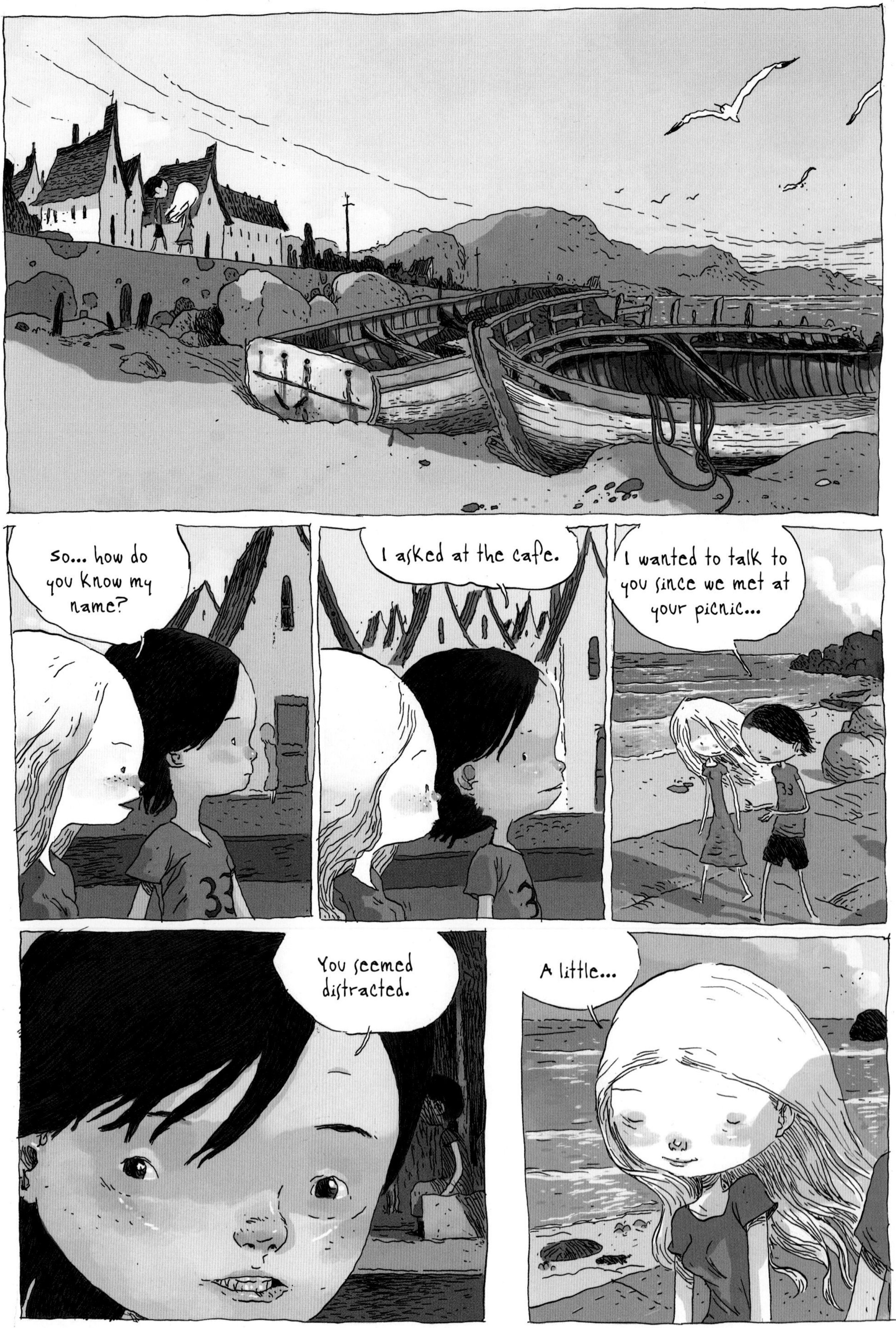
So... how do you know my name?
I asked at the cafe.
I wanted to talk to you since we met at your picnic...
You seemed distracted.
A little...

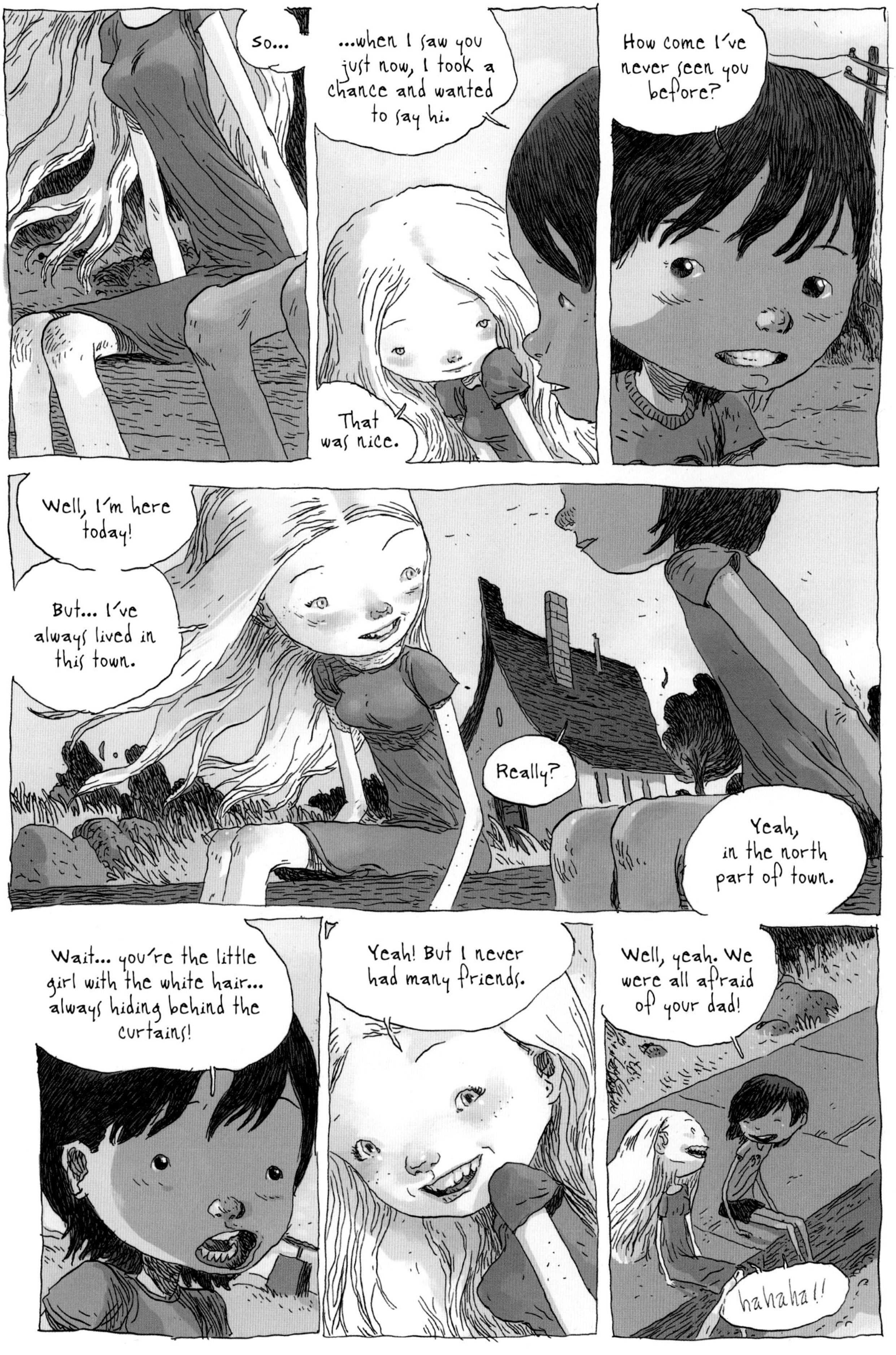
So...
...when I saw you just now, I took a chance and wanted to say hi.
That was nice.
How come I've never seen you before?
Well, I'm here today!
But... I've always lived in this town.
Really?
Yeah, in the north part of town.
Wait... you're the little girl with the white hair... always hiding behind the curtains!
Yeah! But I never had many friends.
Well, yeah. We were all afraid of your dad!
hahaha!!

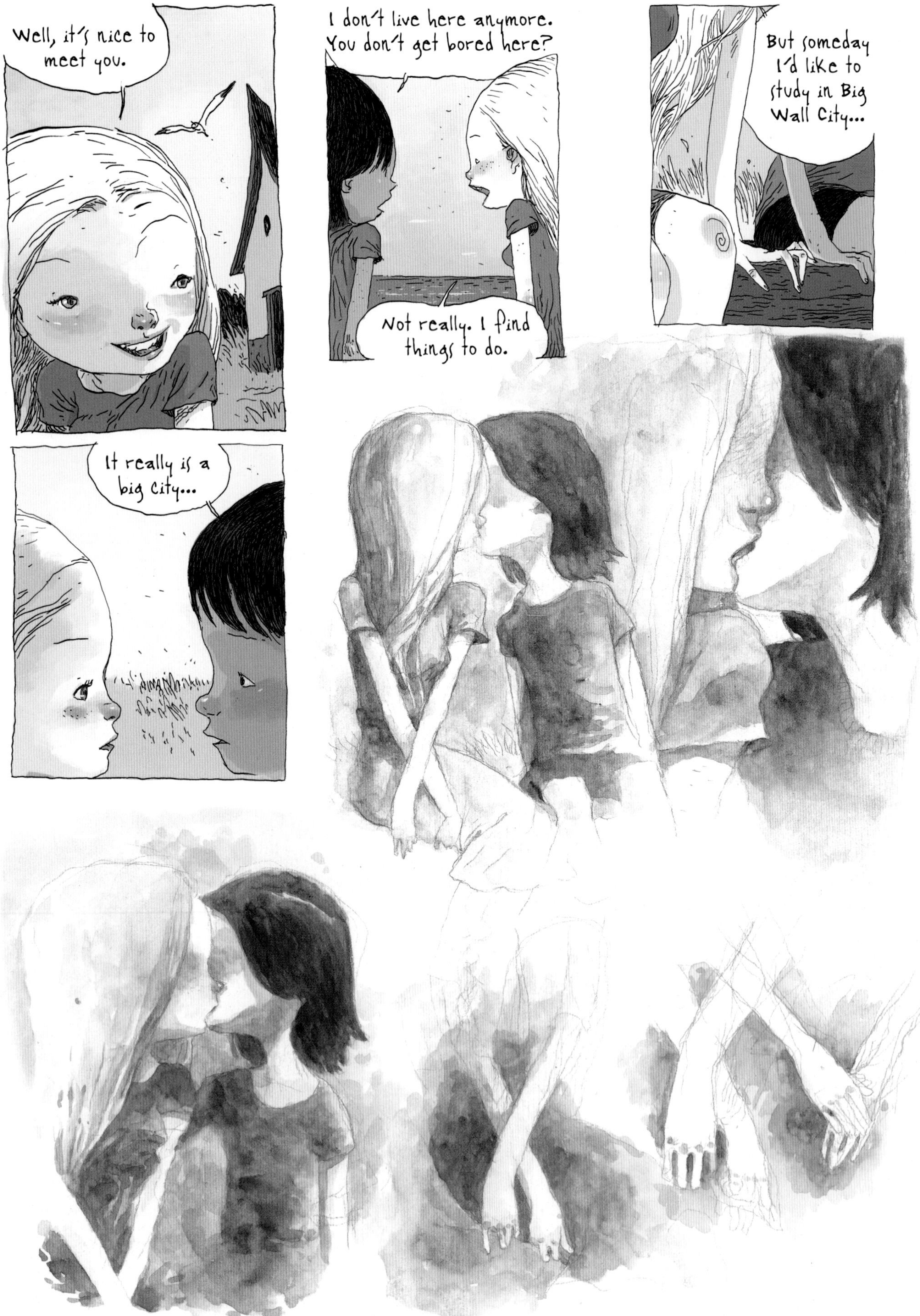
Well, it's nice to meet you.
I don't live here anymore. You don't get bored here?
Not really. I find things to do.
But someday I'd like to study in Big Wall City...
It really is a big city...

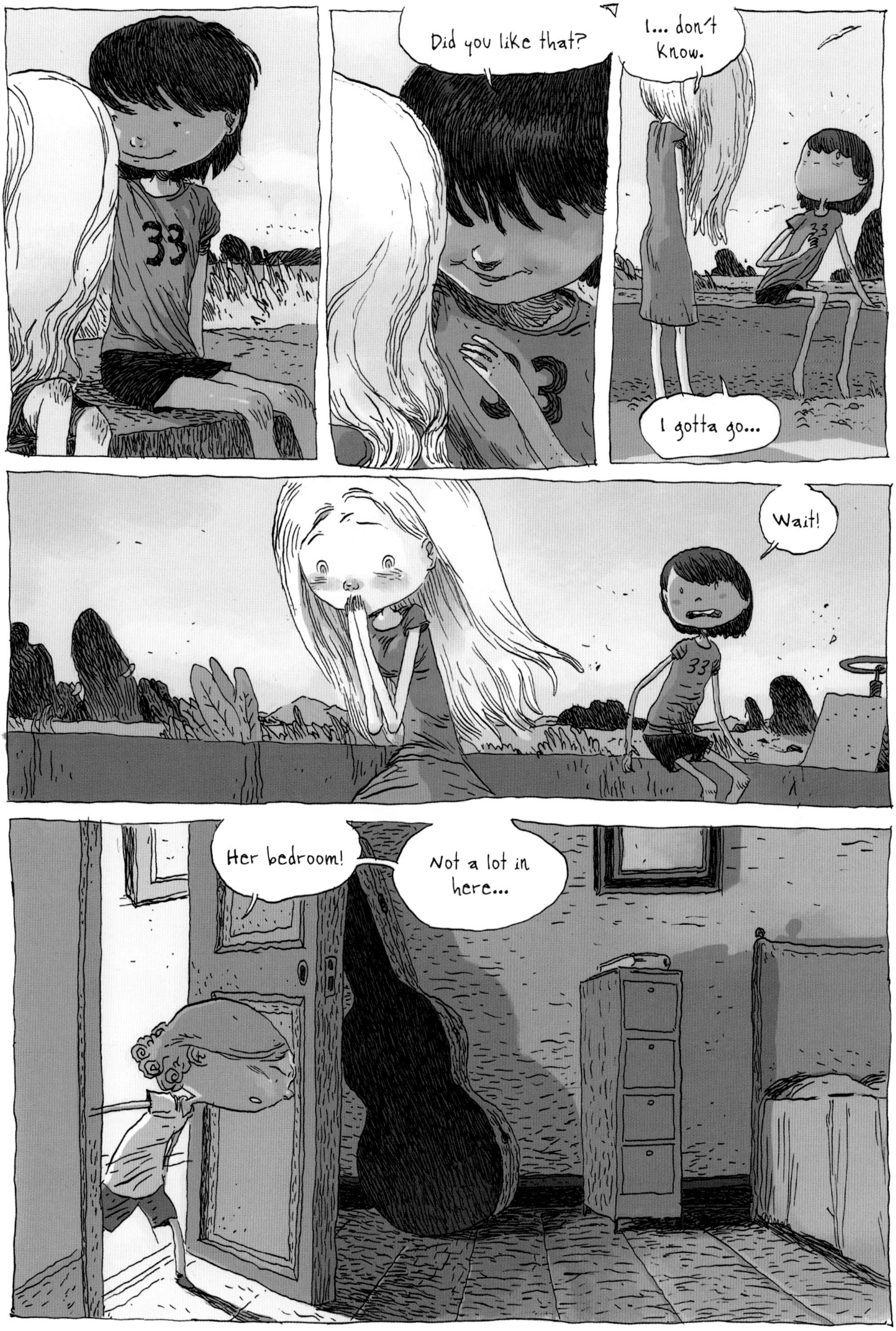
Did you like that?
I... don't know.
I gotta go...
Wait!
Her bedroom!
Not a lot in here...

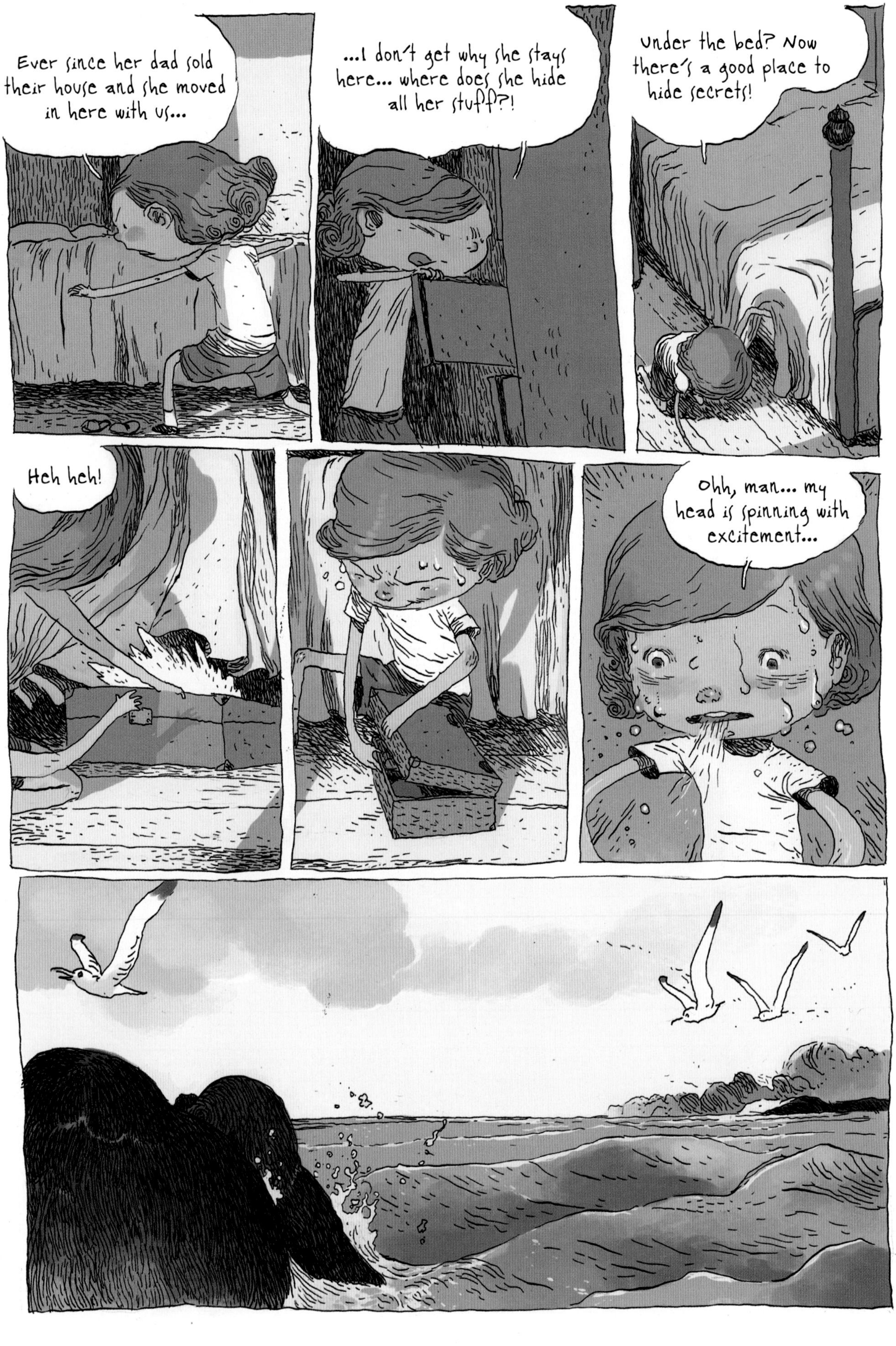
Ever since her dad sold their house and she moved in here with us...
...I don't get why she stays here... where does she hide all her stuff?!
Under the bed? Now there's a good place to hide secrets!
Heh heh!
Ohh, man... my head is spinning with excitement...

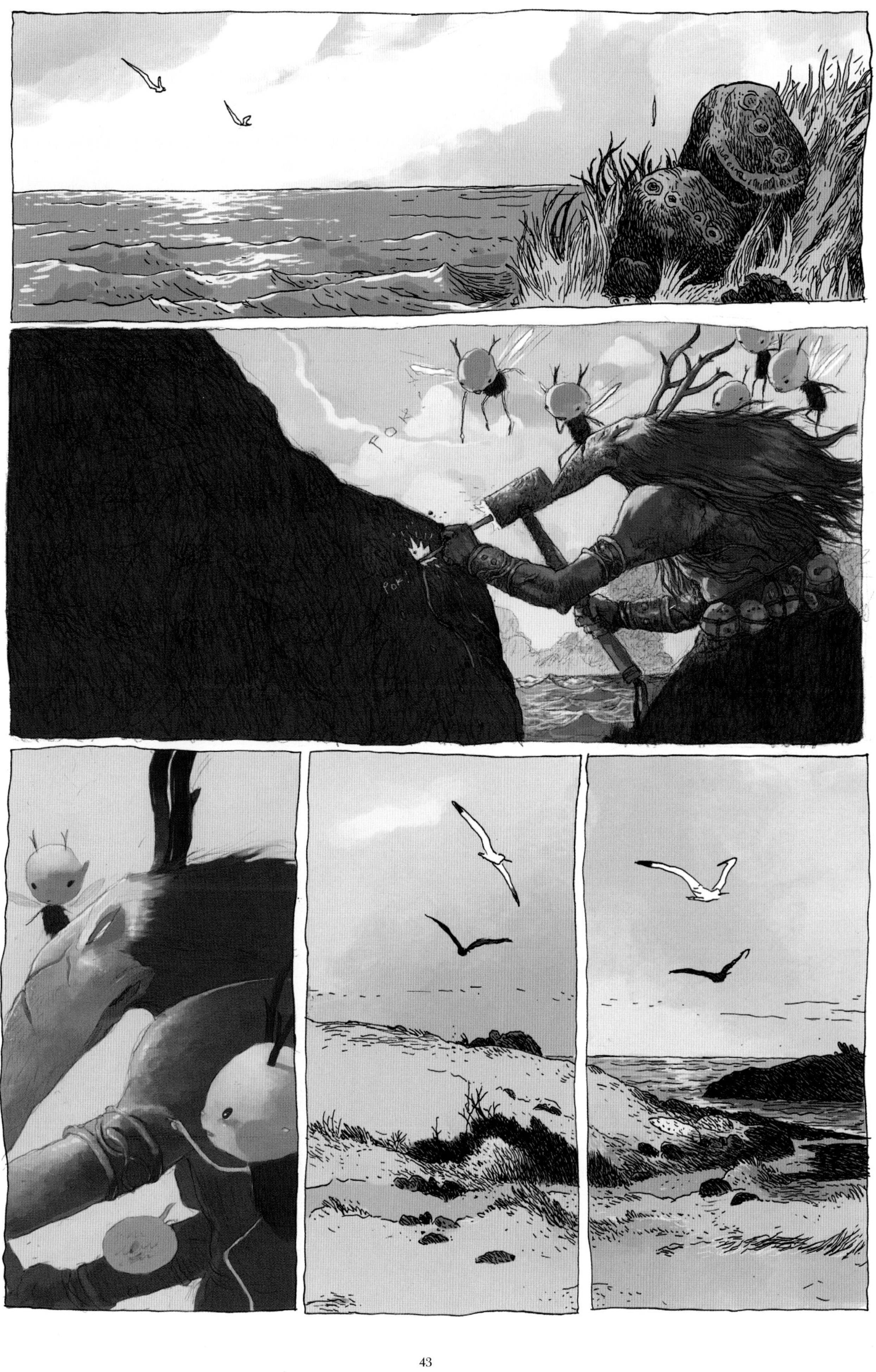
POK!
POK!

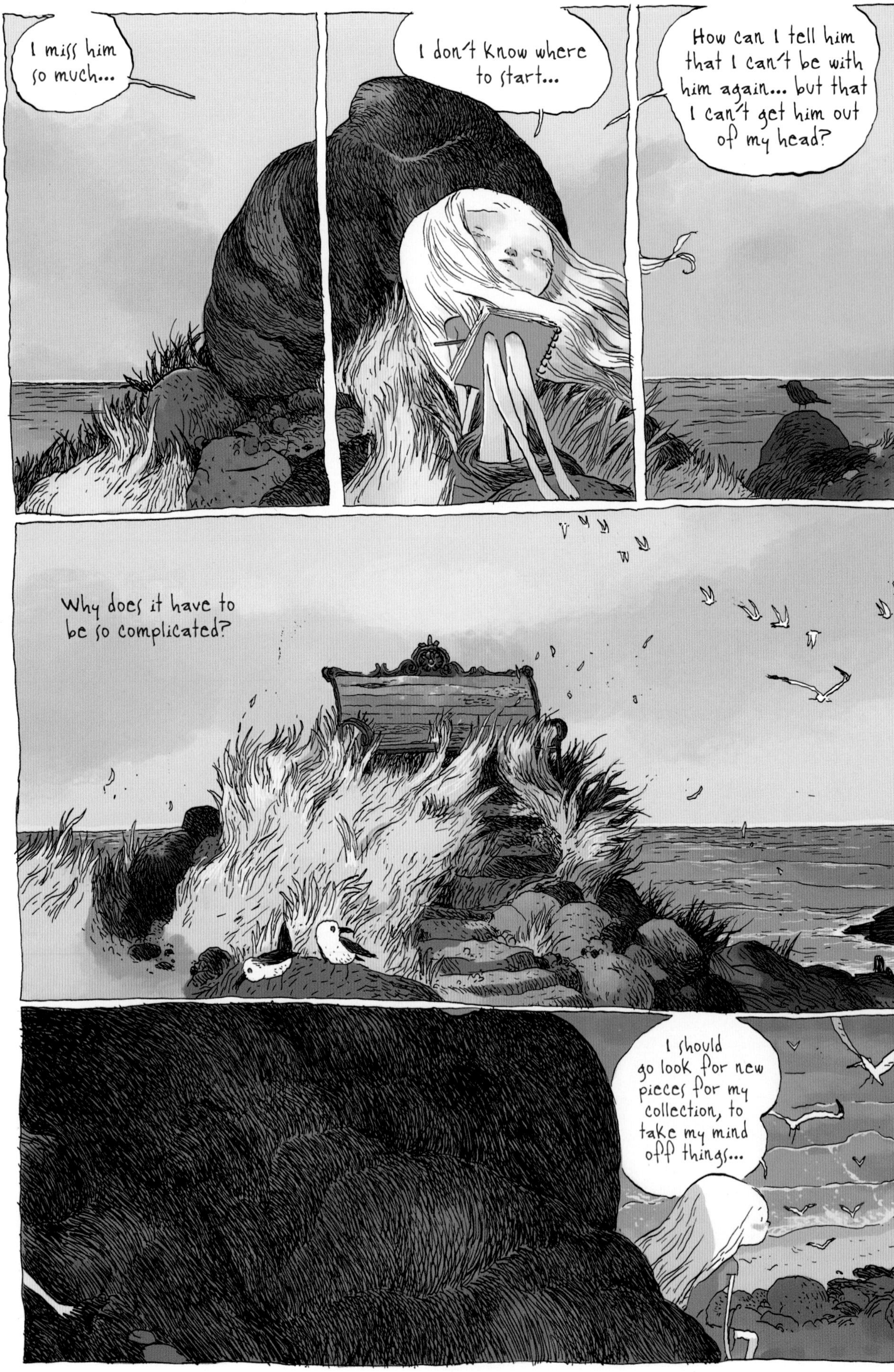

I miss him so much...
I don't know where to start...
How can I tell him that I can't be with him again... but that I can't get him out of my head?
Why does it have to be so complicated?
I should go look for new pieces for my collection, to take my mind off things...

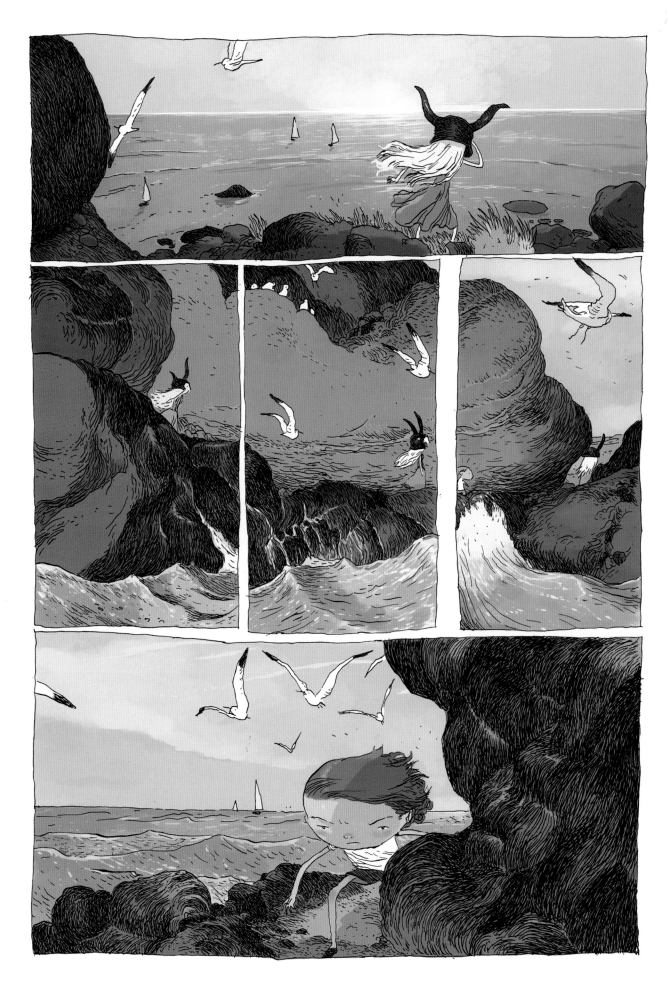

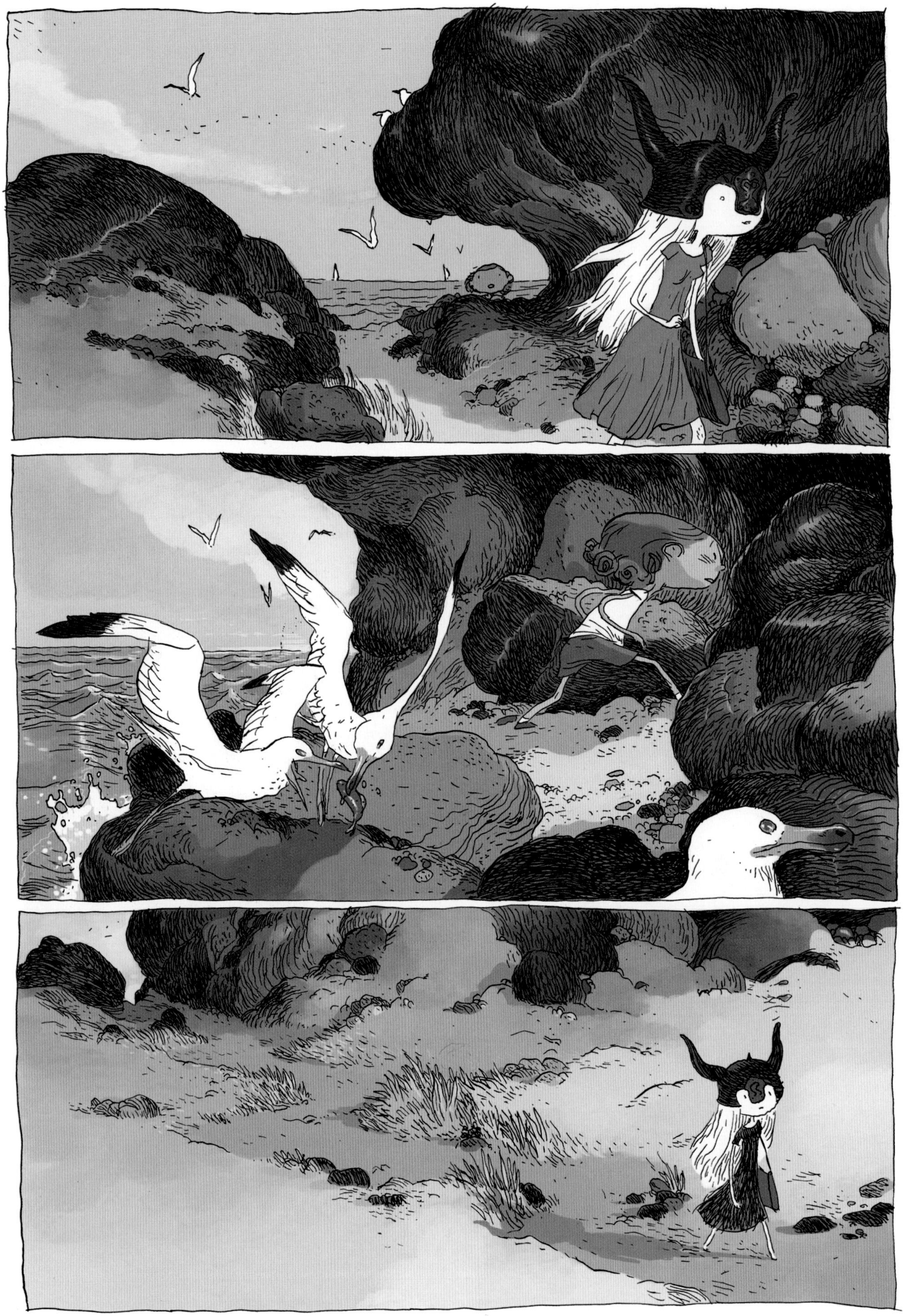

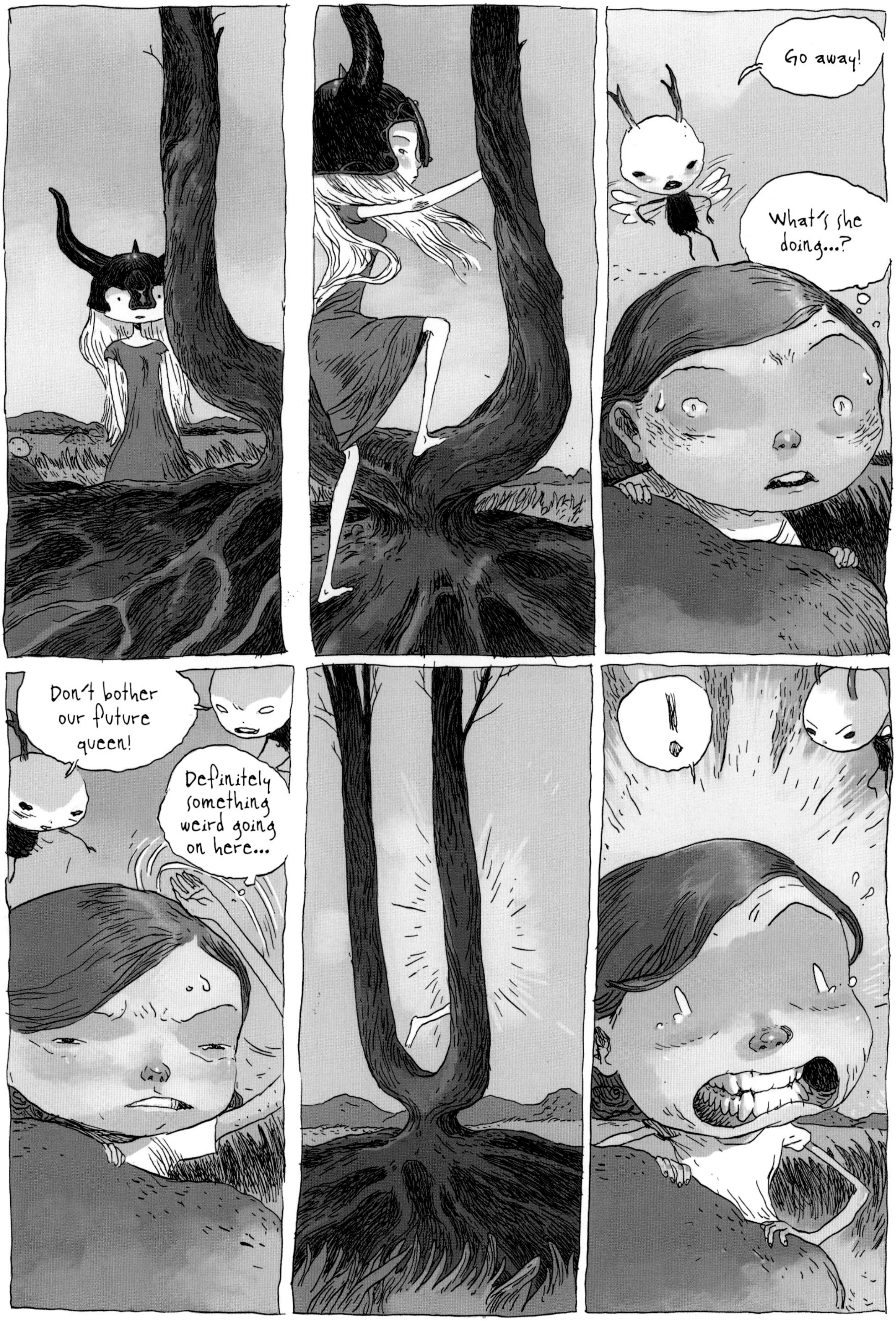
Go away!
What's she doing...?
Don't bother our future queen!
Definitely something weird going on here...
!

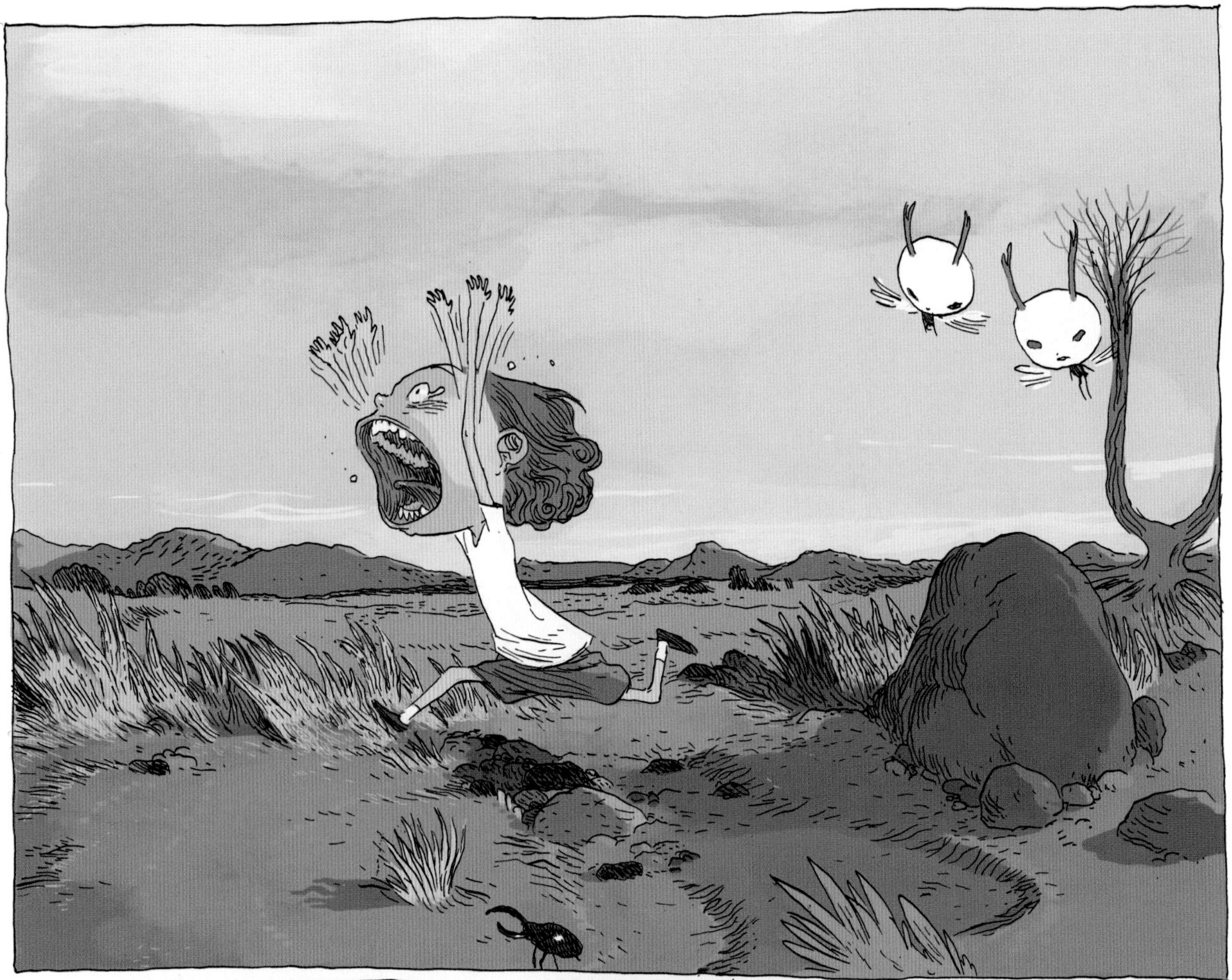

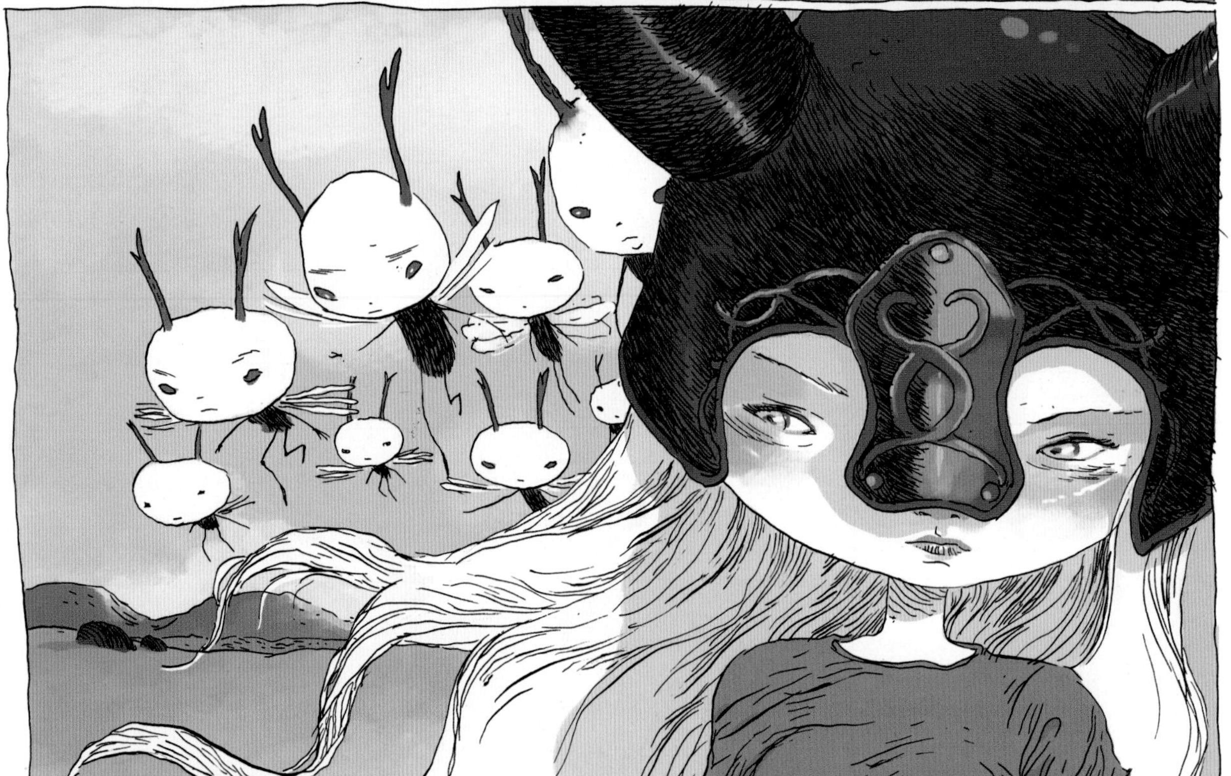

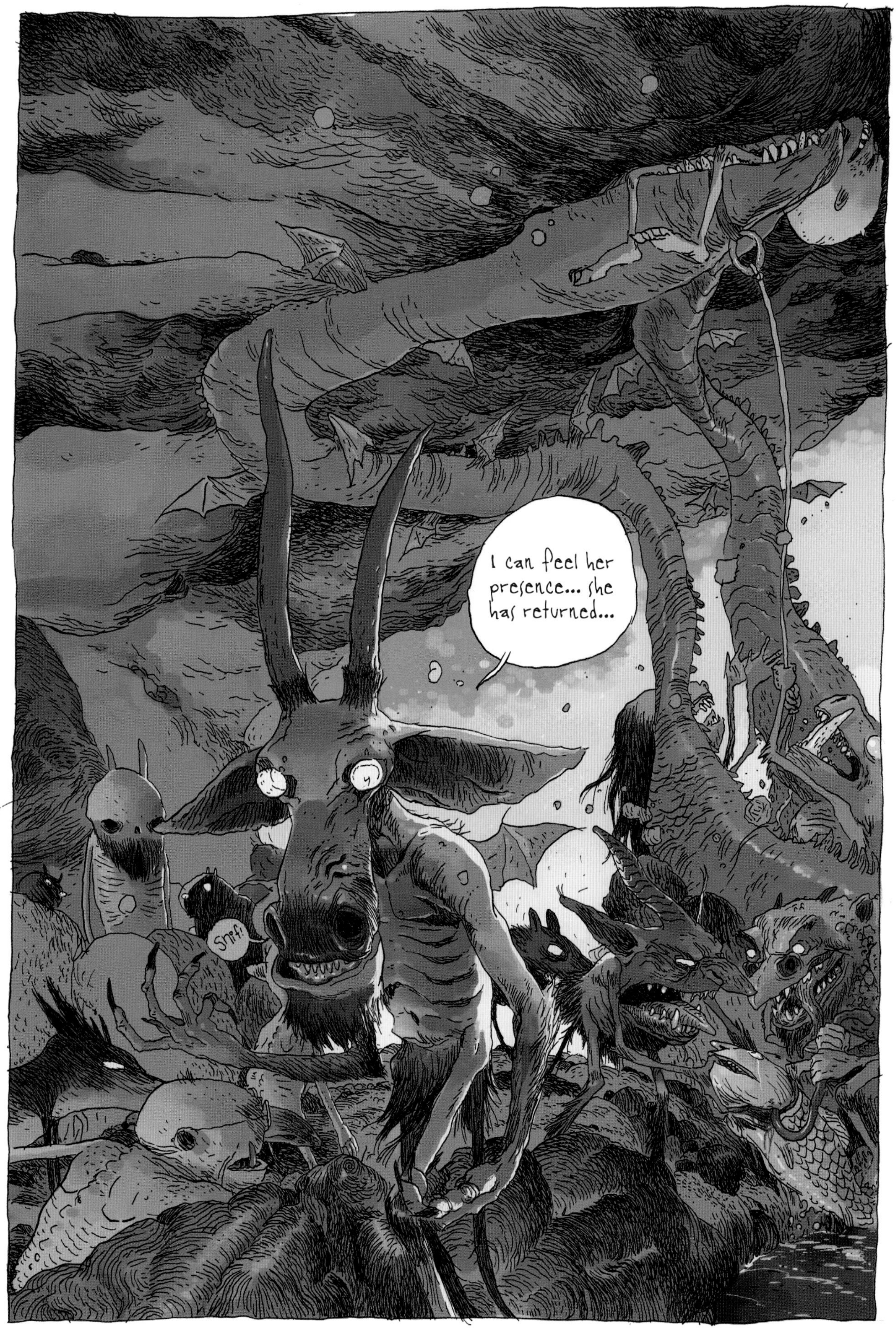
I can feel her presence... she has returned...
Snif!

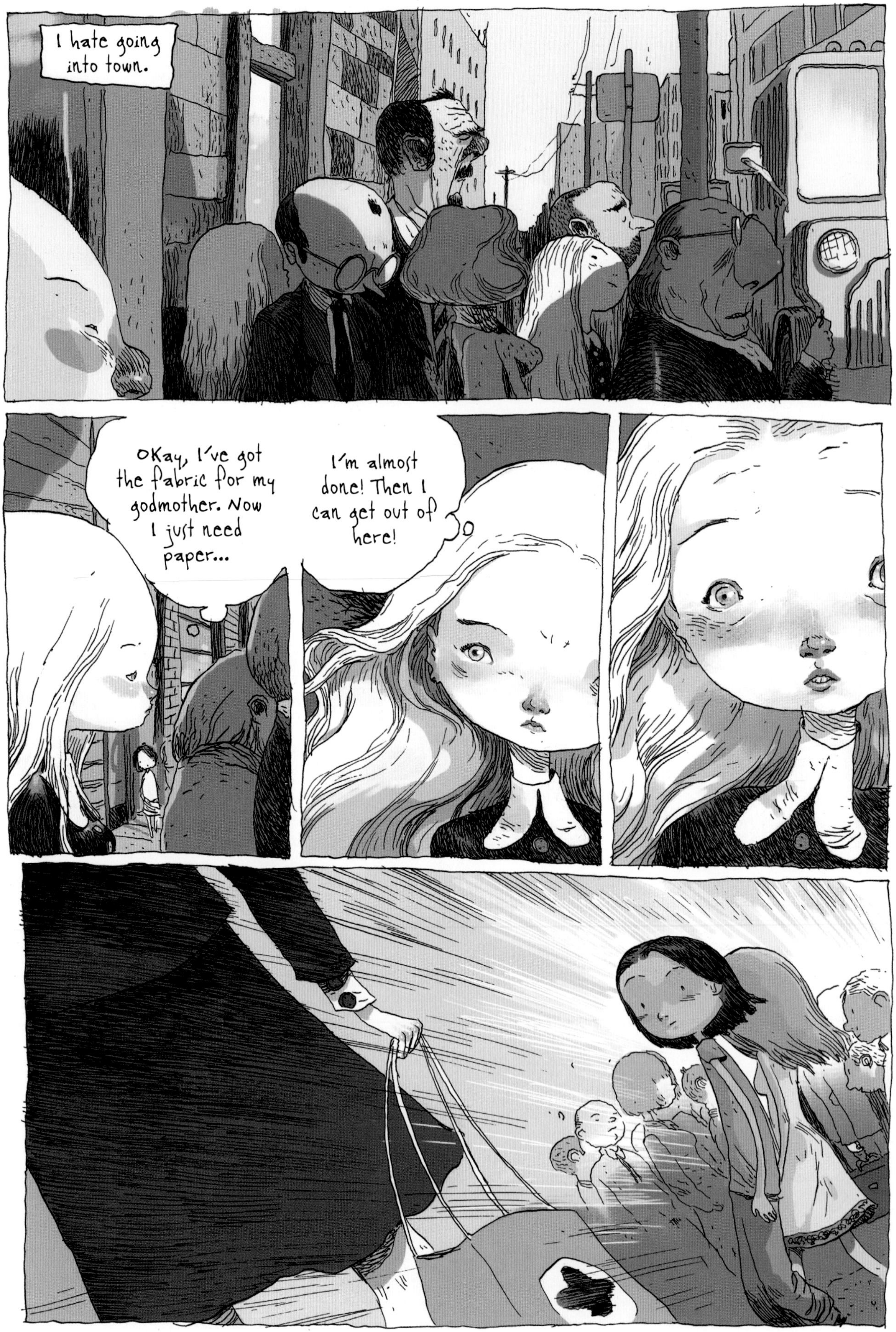
I hate going into town.
Okay, I've got the fabric for my godmother. Now I just need paper...
I'm almost done! Then I can get out of here!

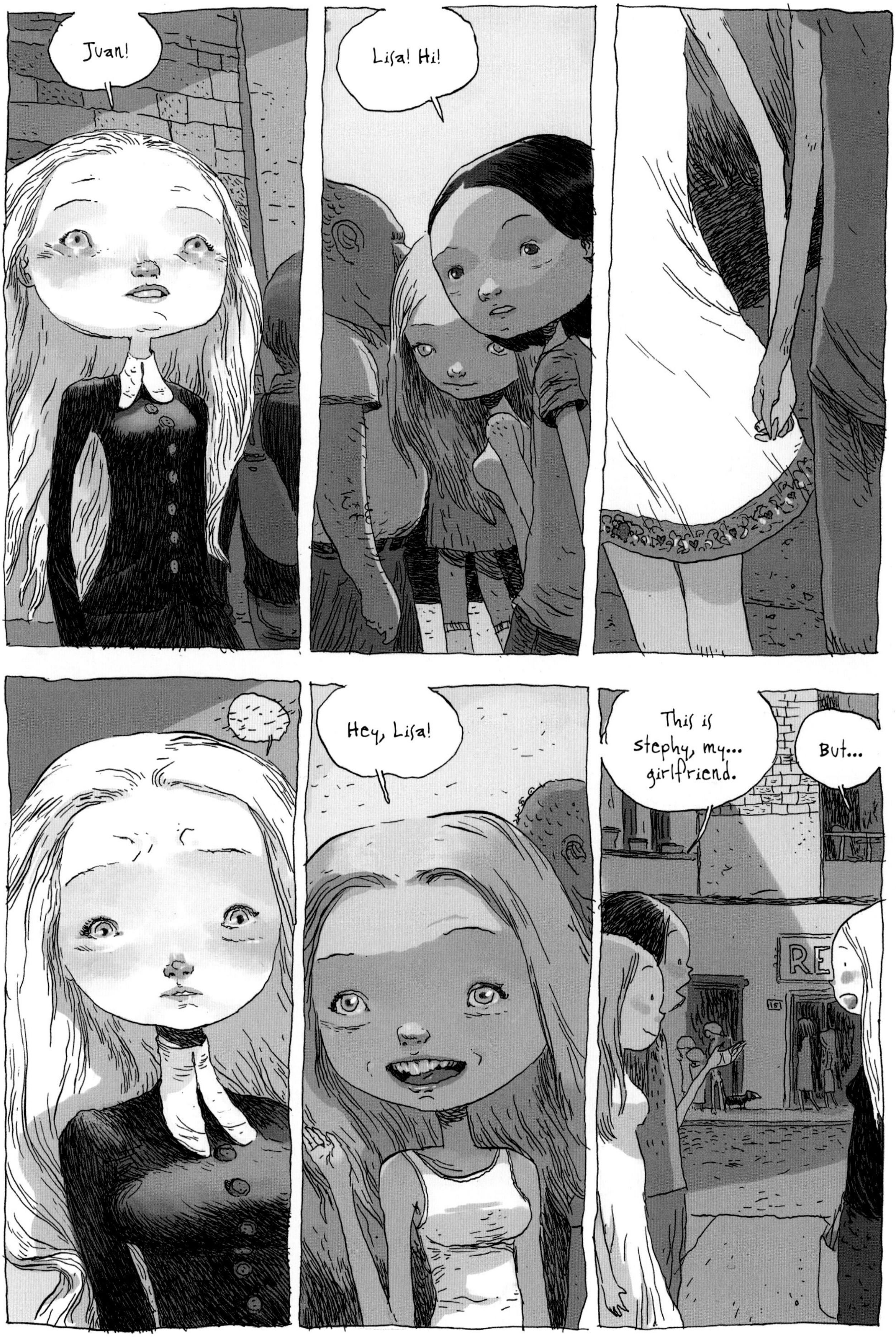
Juan!
Lisa! Hi!
Hey, Lisa!
This is stephy, my... girlfriend.
But...
RE

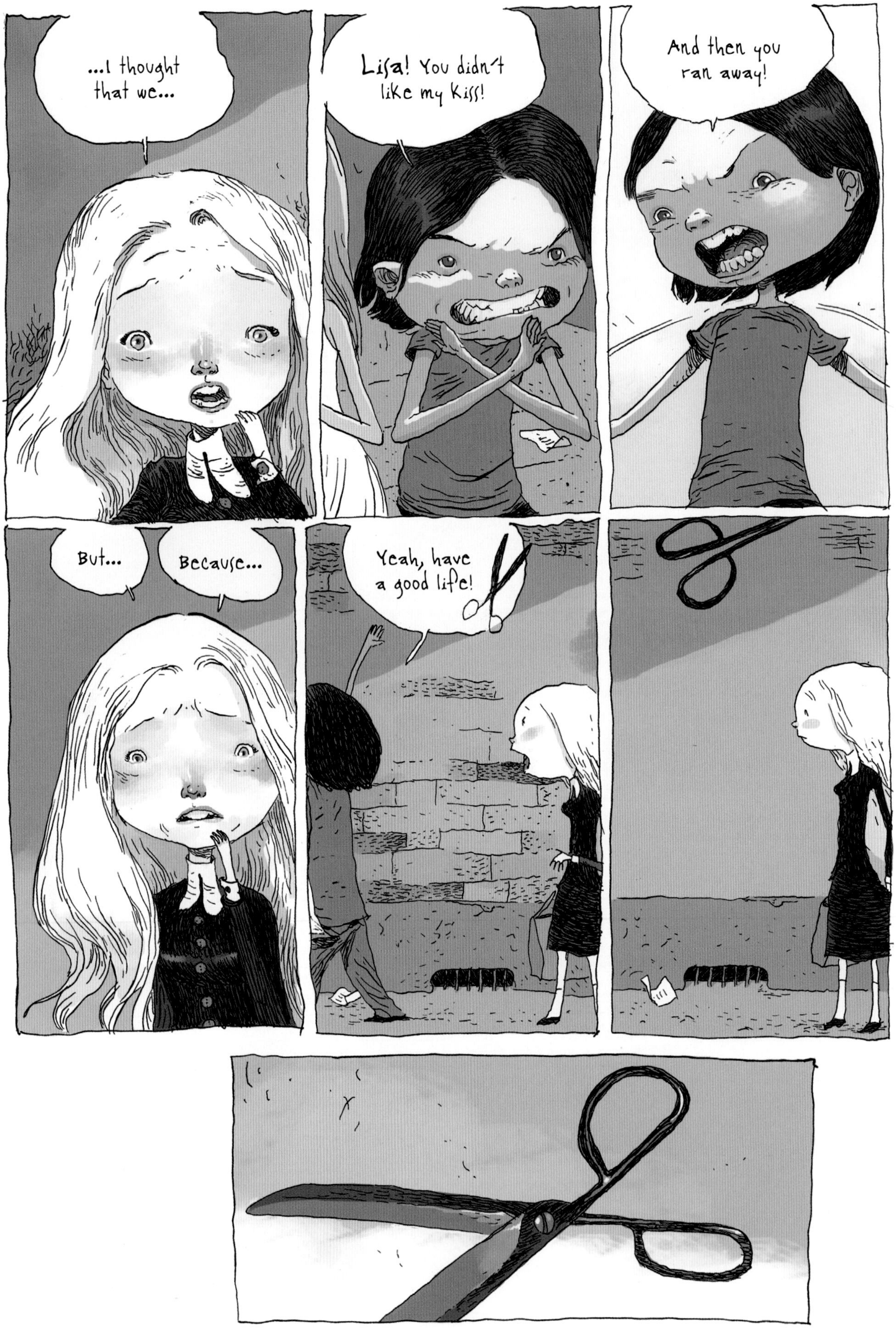
...I thought that we...
Lisa! You didn't like my kiss!
And then you ran away!
But...
Because...
Yeah, have a good life!

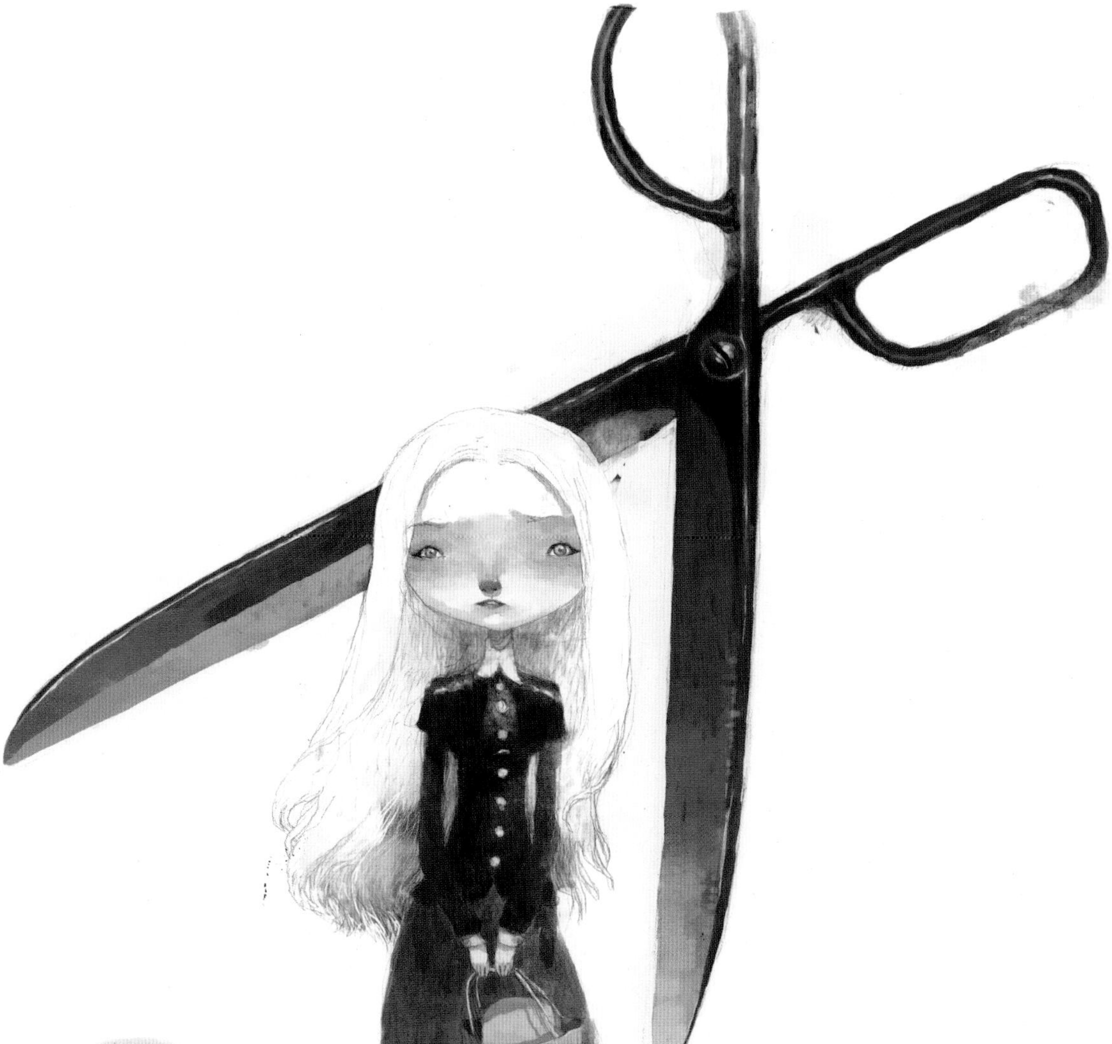

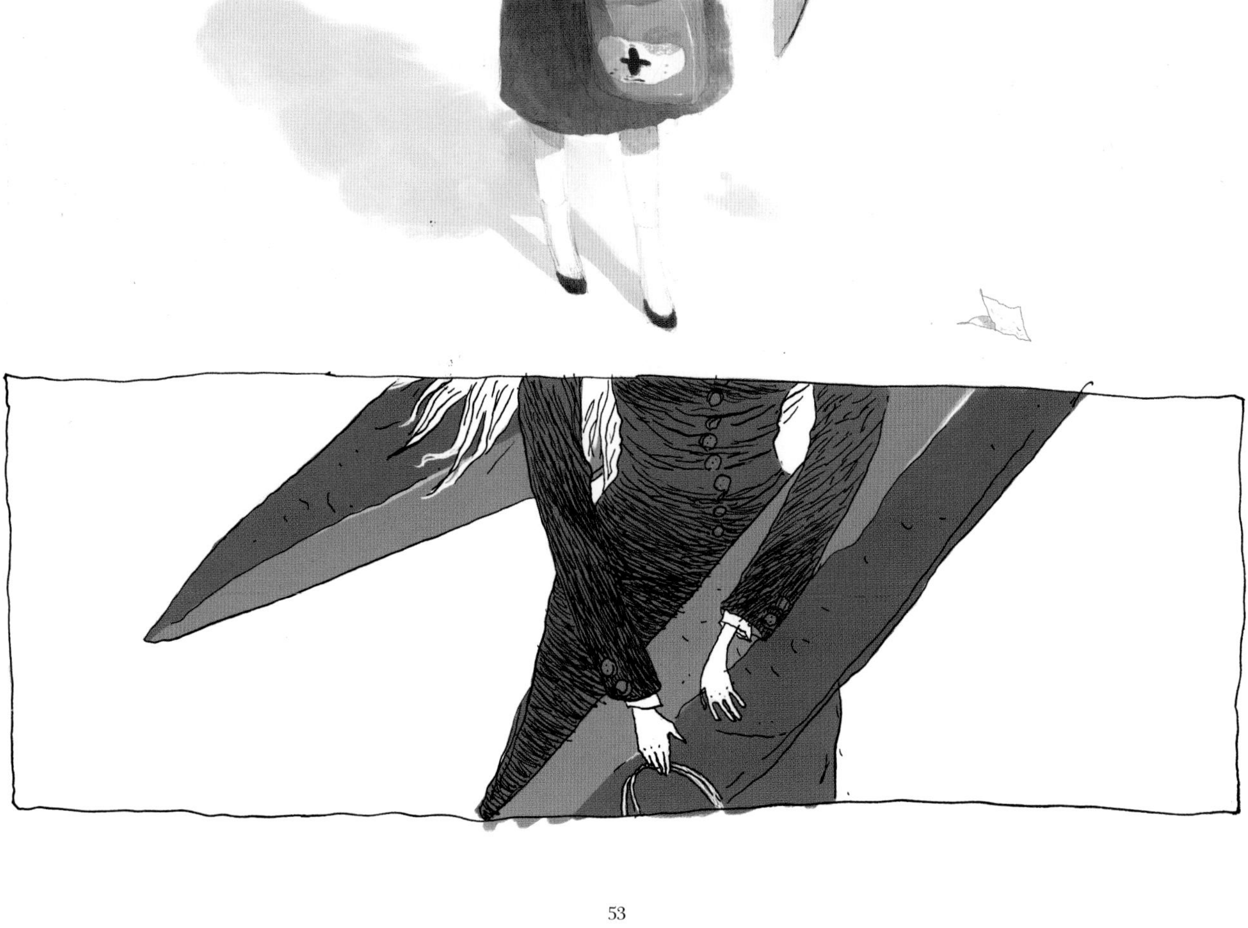

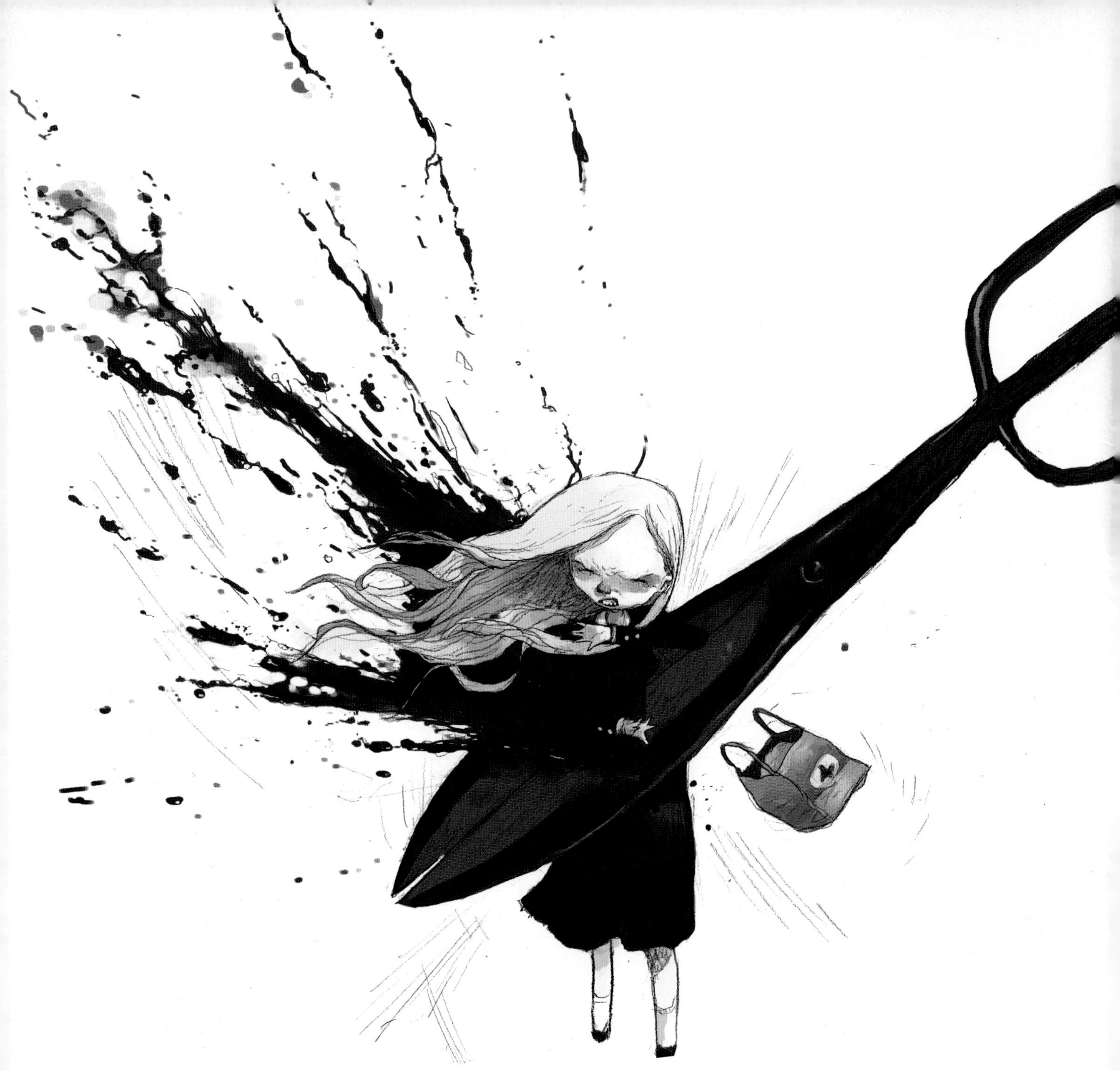

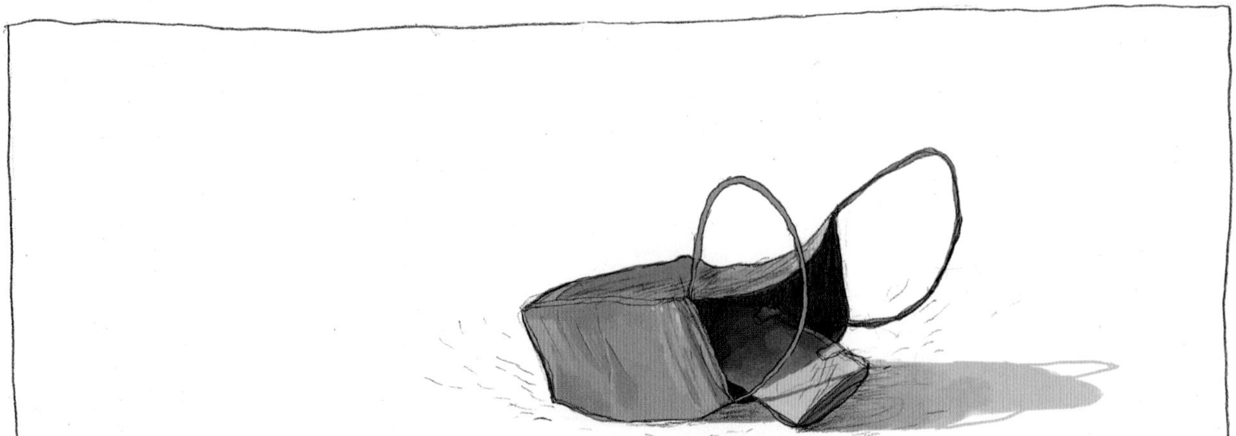

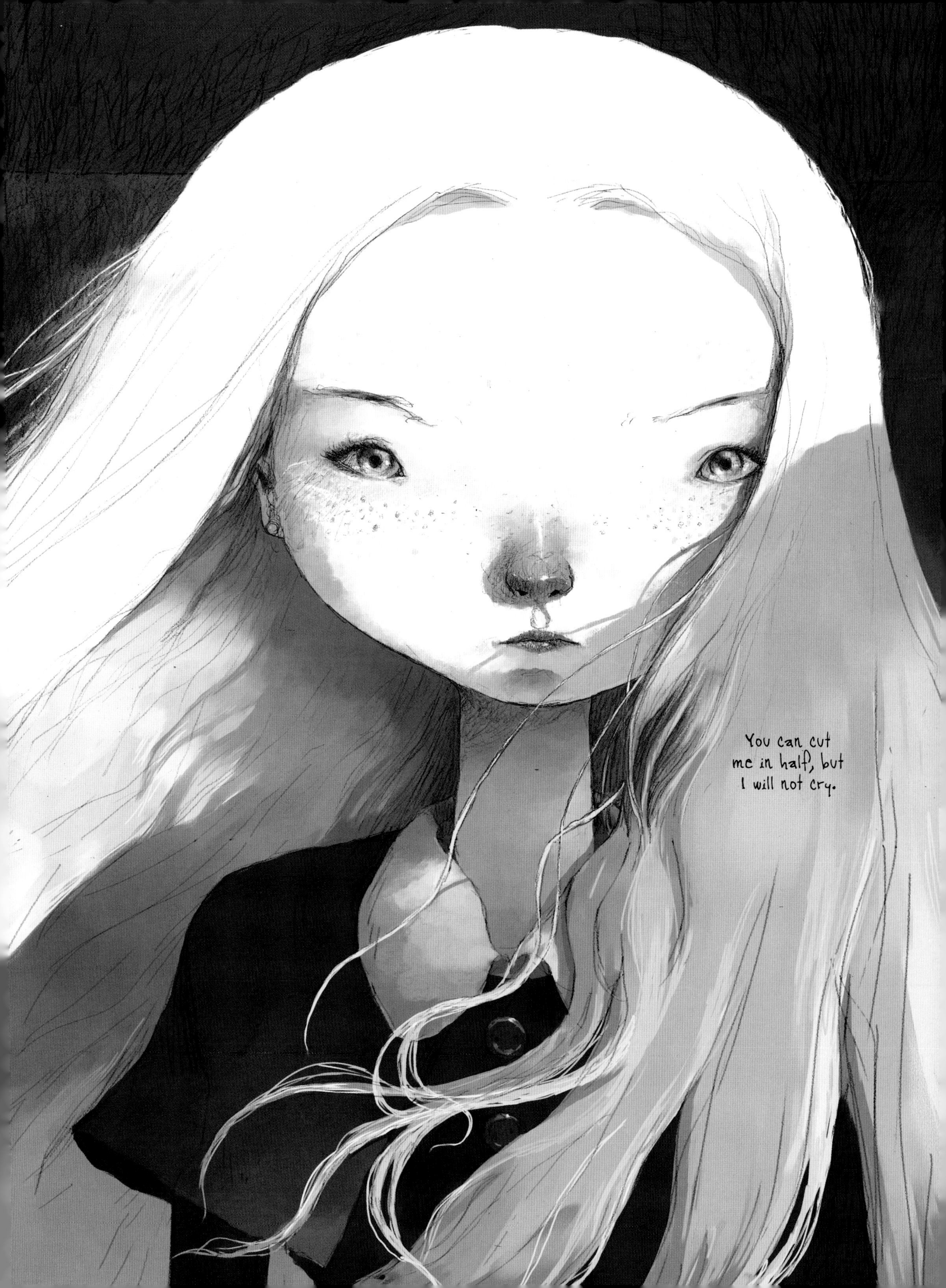
You can cut
me in half, but
I will not cry.

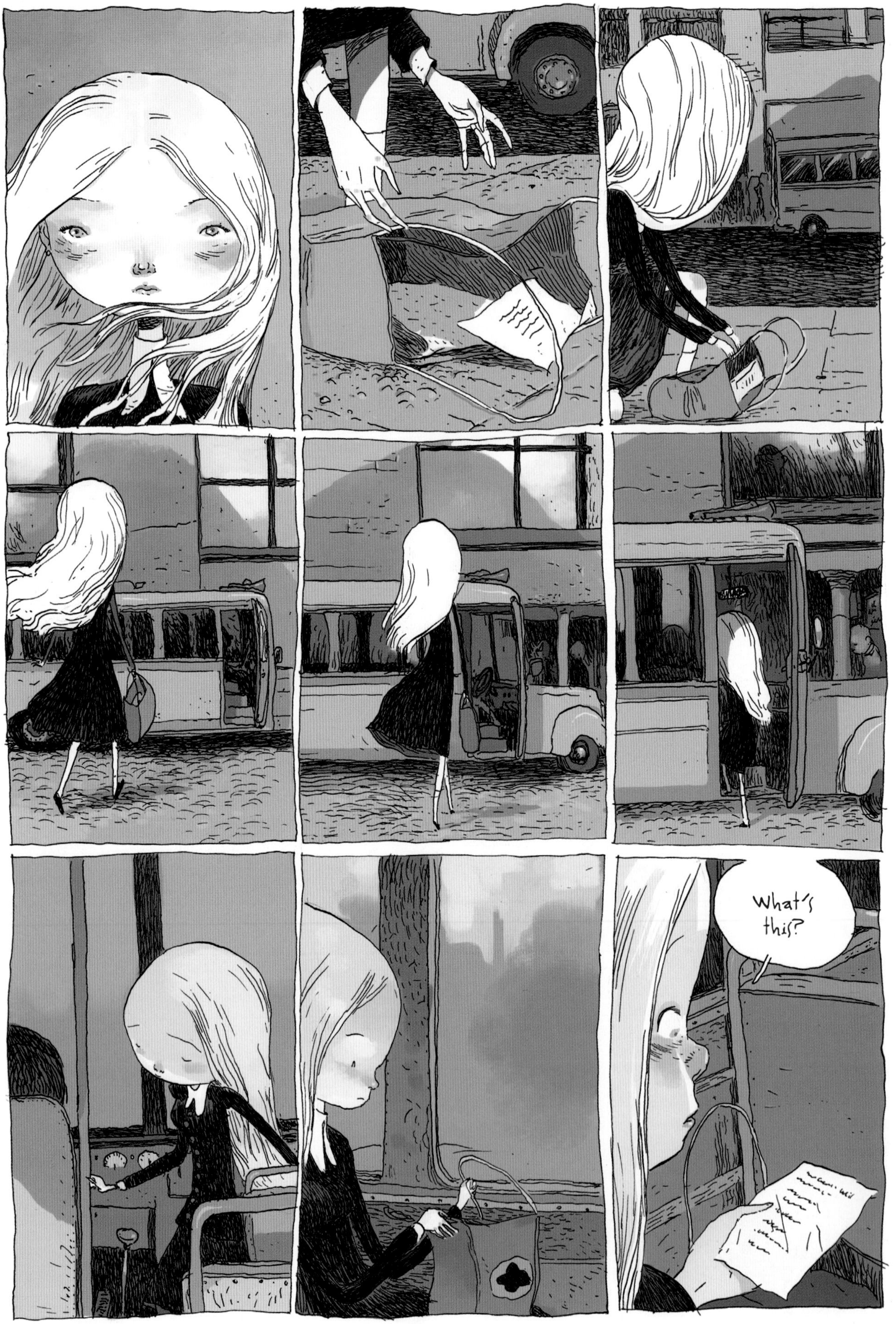
What's this?

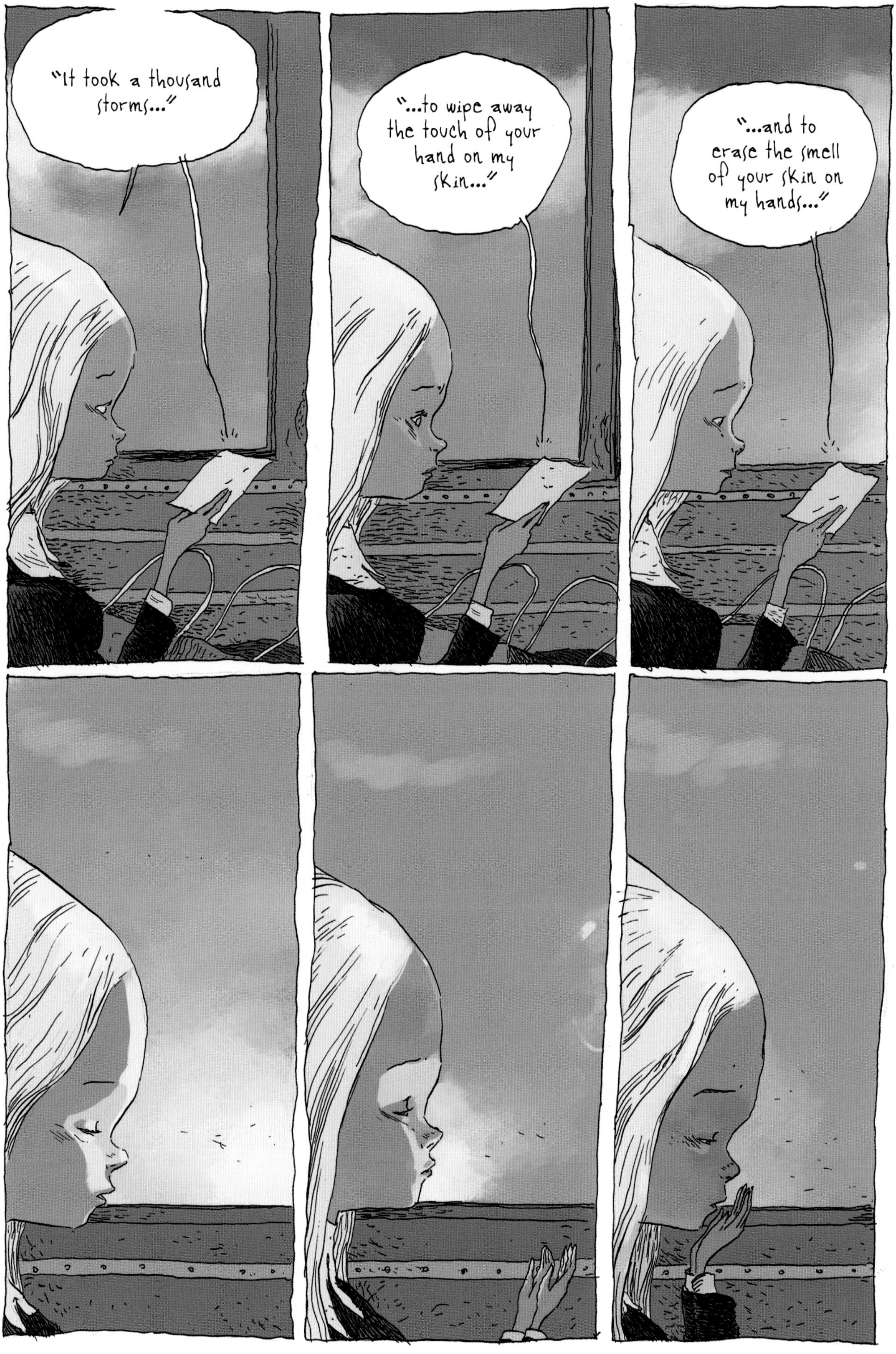
"It took a thousand storms..."
"...to wipe away the touch of your hand on my skin..."
"...and to erase the smell of your skin on my hands..."

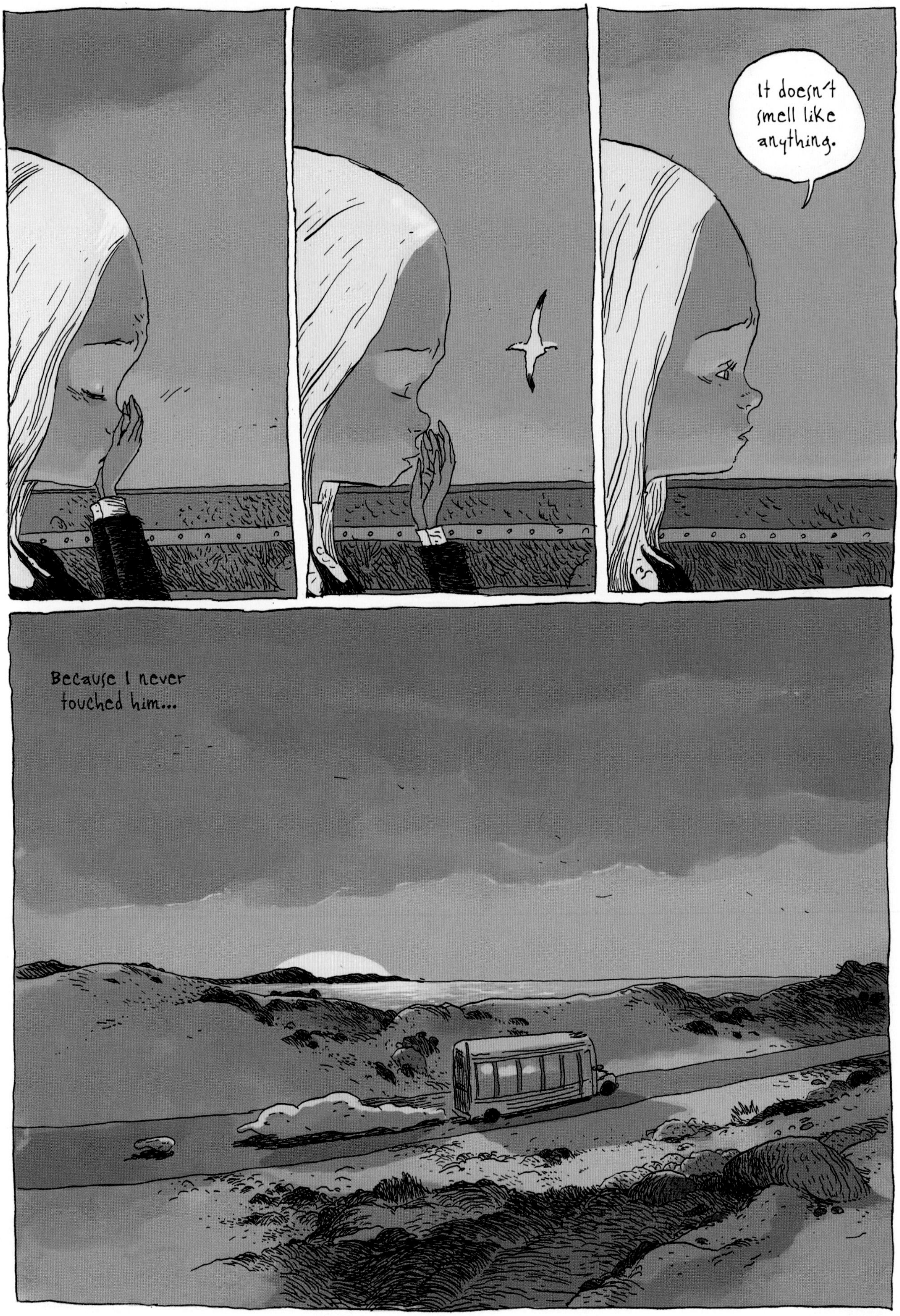
It doesn't smell like anything.
Because I never touched him...

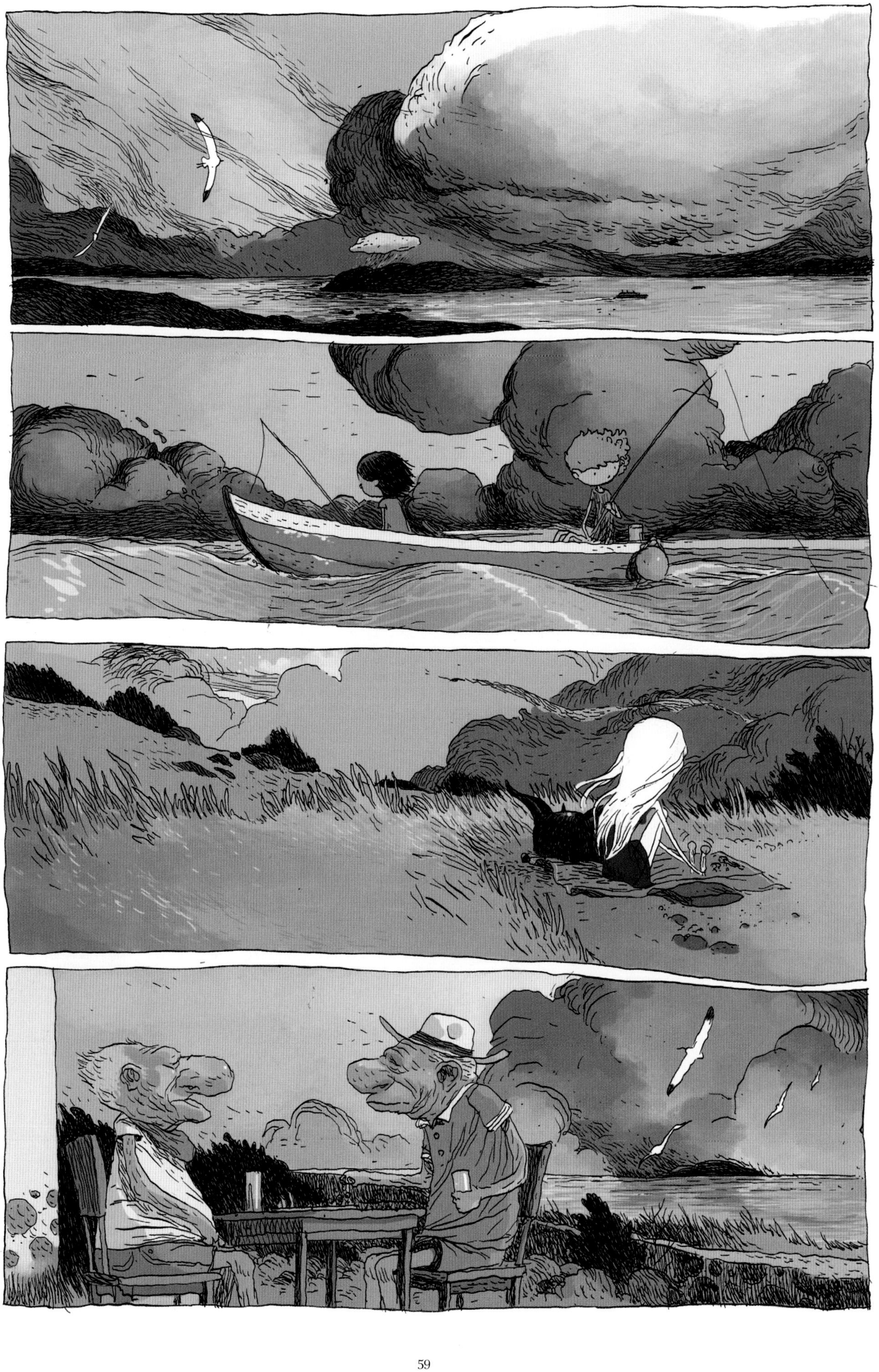

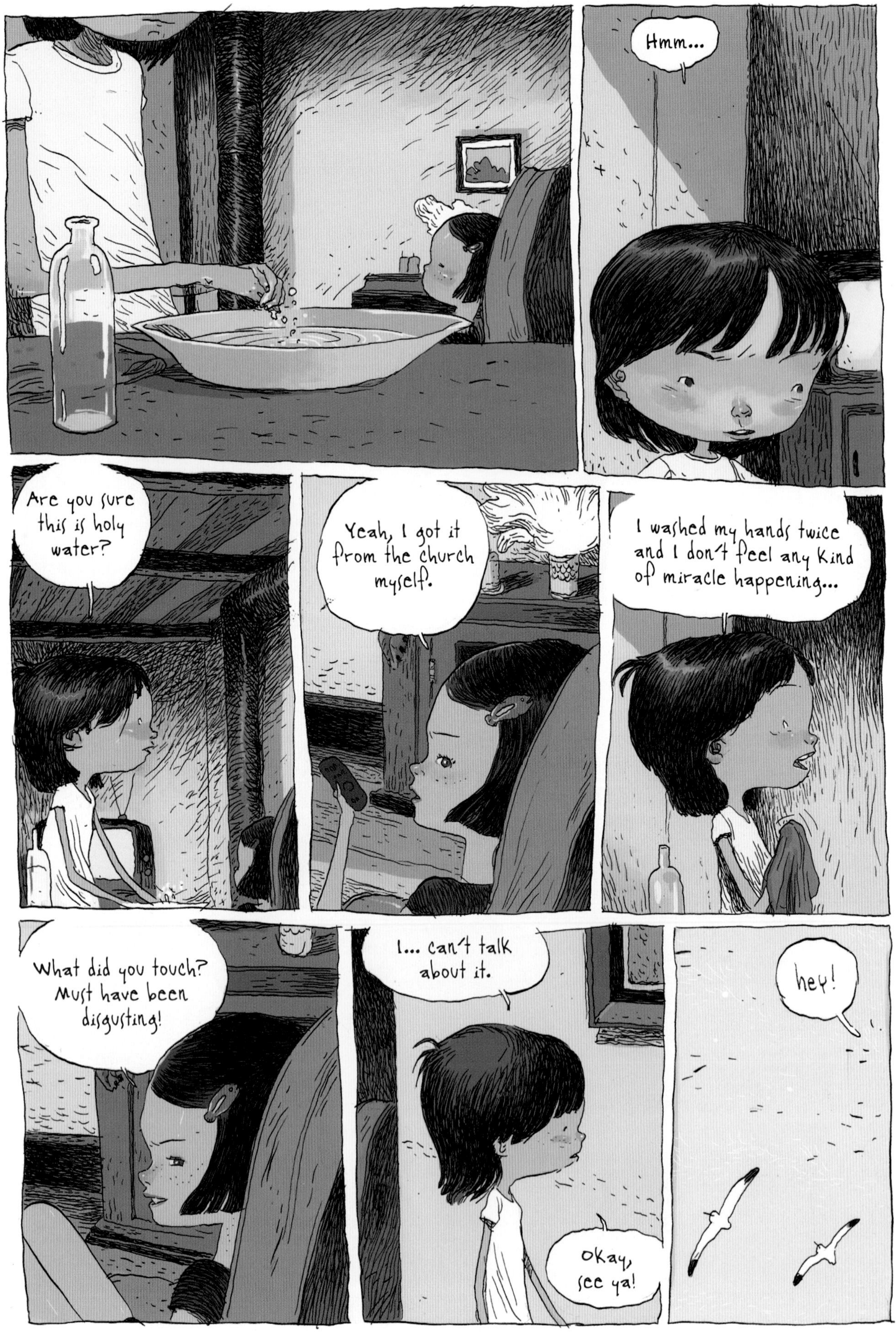
Hmm...
Are you sure this is holy water?
Yeah, I got it from the church myself.
I washed my hands twice and I don't feel any kind of miracle happening...
What did you touch? Must have been disgusting!
I... can't talk about it.
Okay, see ya!
hey!

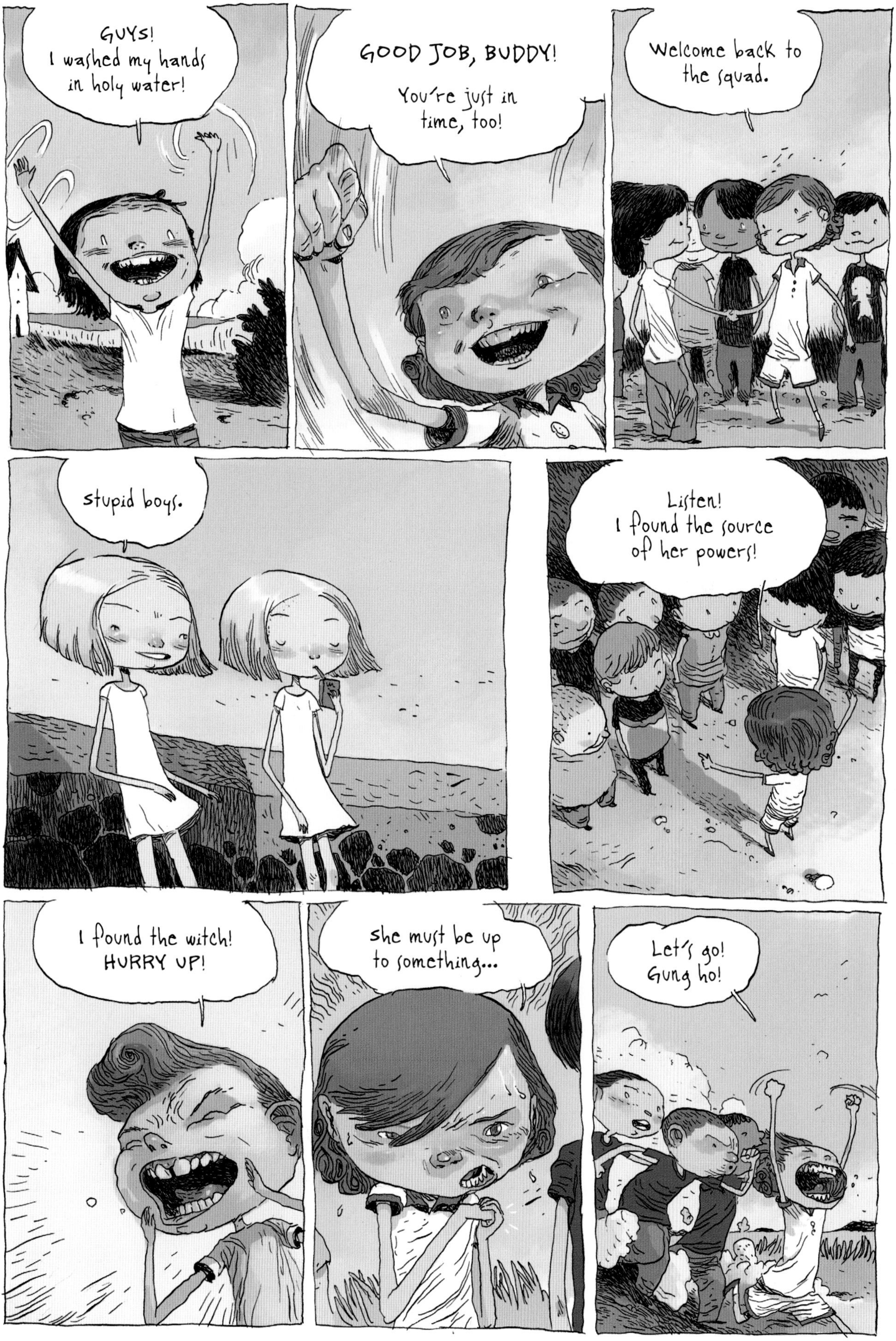
GUYS!
I washed my hands in holy water!
GOOD JOB, BUDDY!
You're just in time, too!
Welcome back to the squad.
stupid boys.
Listen!
I found the source of her powers!
I found the witch!
HURRY UP!
she must be up to something...
Let's go!
Gung ho!

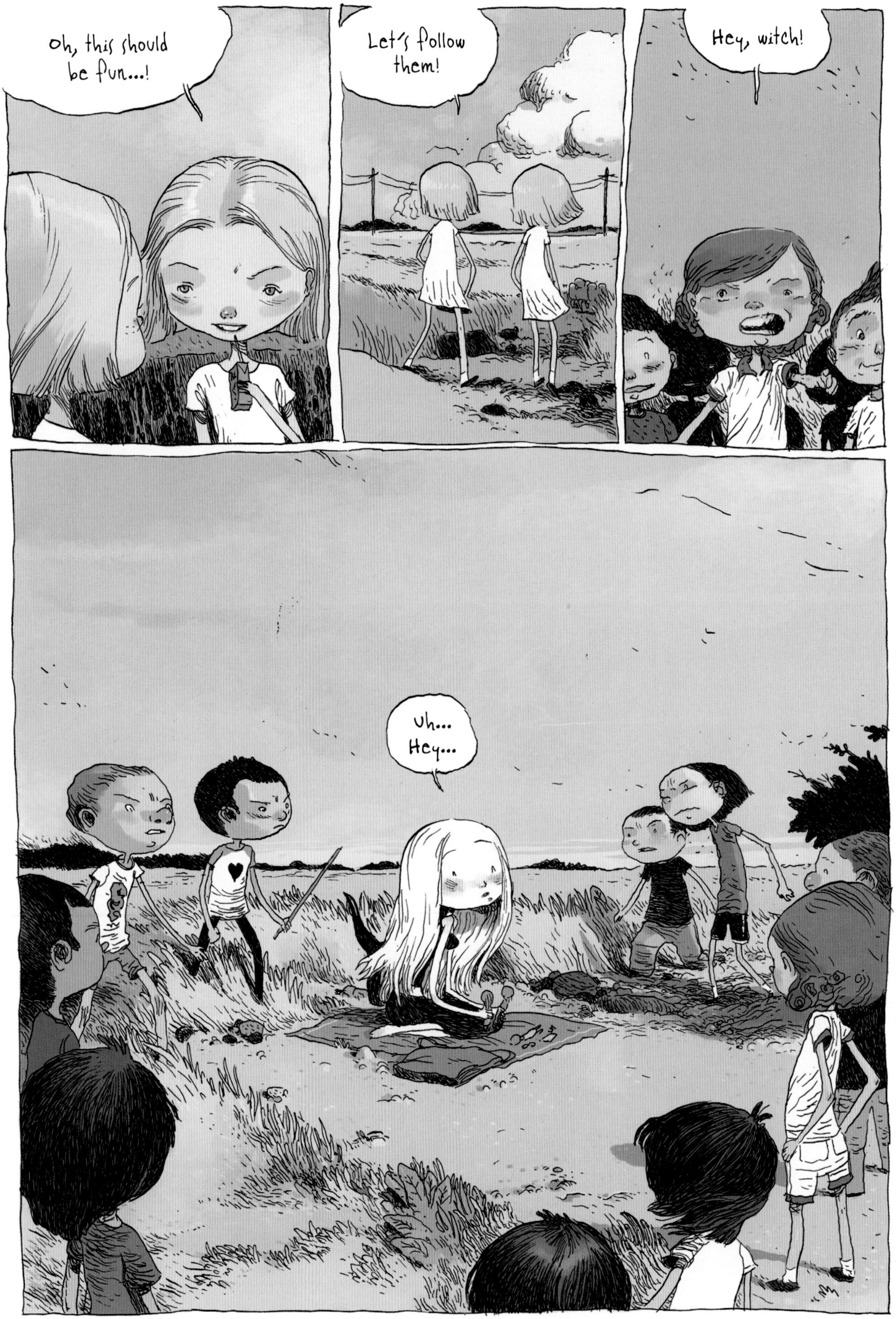
Oh, this should be fun...!
Let's follow them!
Hey, witch!
Uh... Hey...

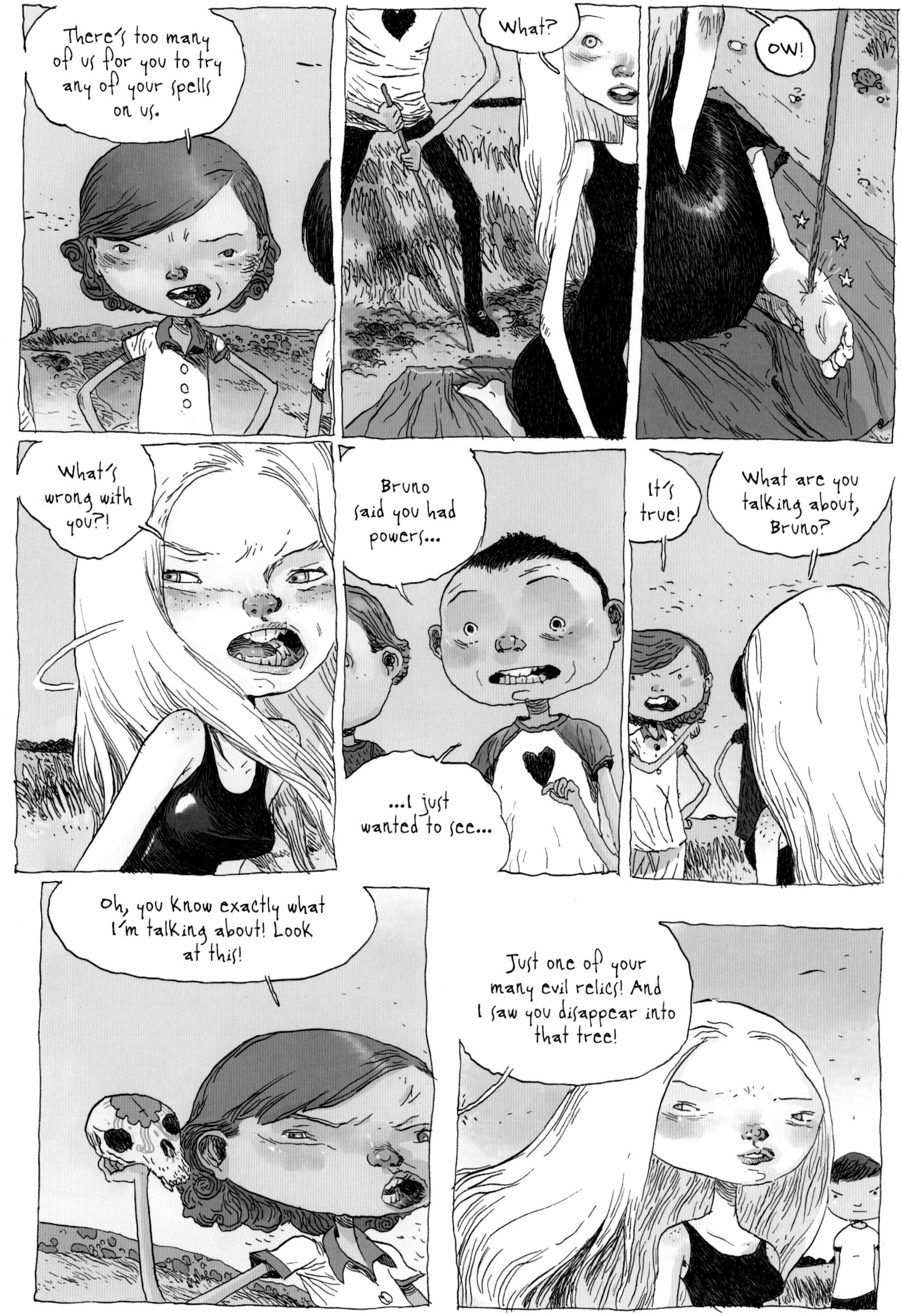
There's too many of us for you to try any of your spells on us.
What?
OW!
What's wrong with you?!
Bruno said you had powers...
...I just wanted to see...
It's true!
What are you talking about, Bruno?
Oh, you know exactly what I'm talking about! Look at this!
Just one of your many evil relics! And I saw you disappear into that tree!

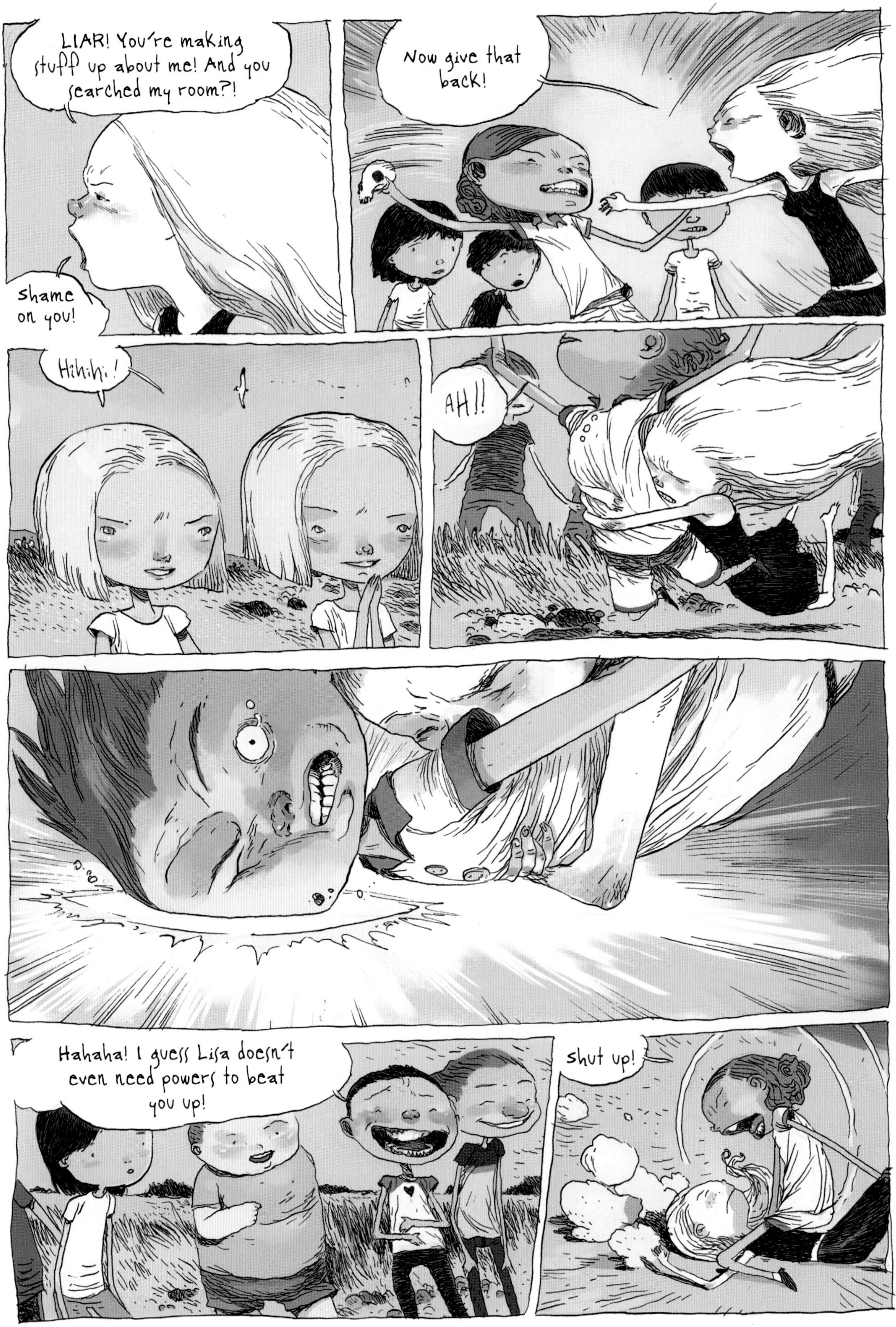
LIAR! You're making stuff up about me! And you searched my room?!
shame on you!
Now give that back!
Hihihi!
AH!!
Hahaha! I guess Lisa doesn't even need powers to beat you up!
shut up!

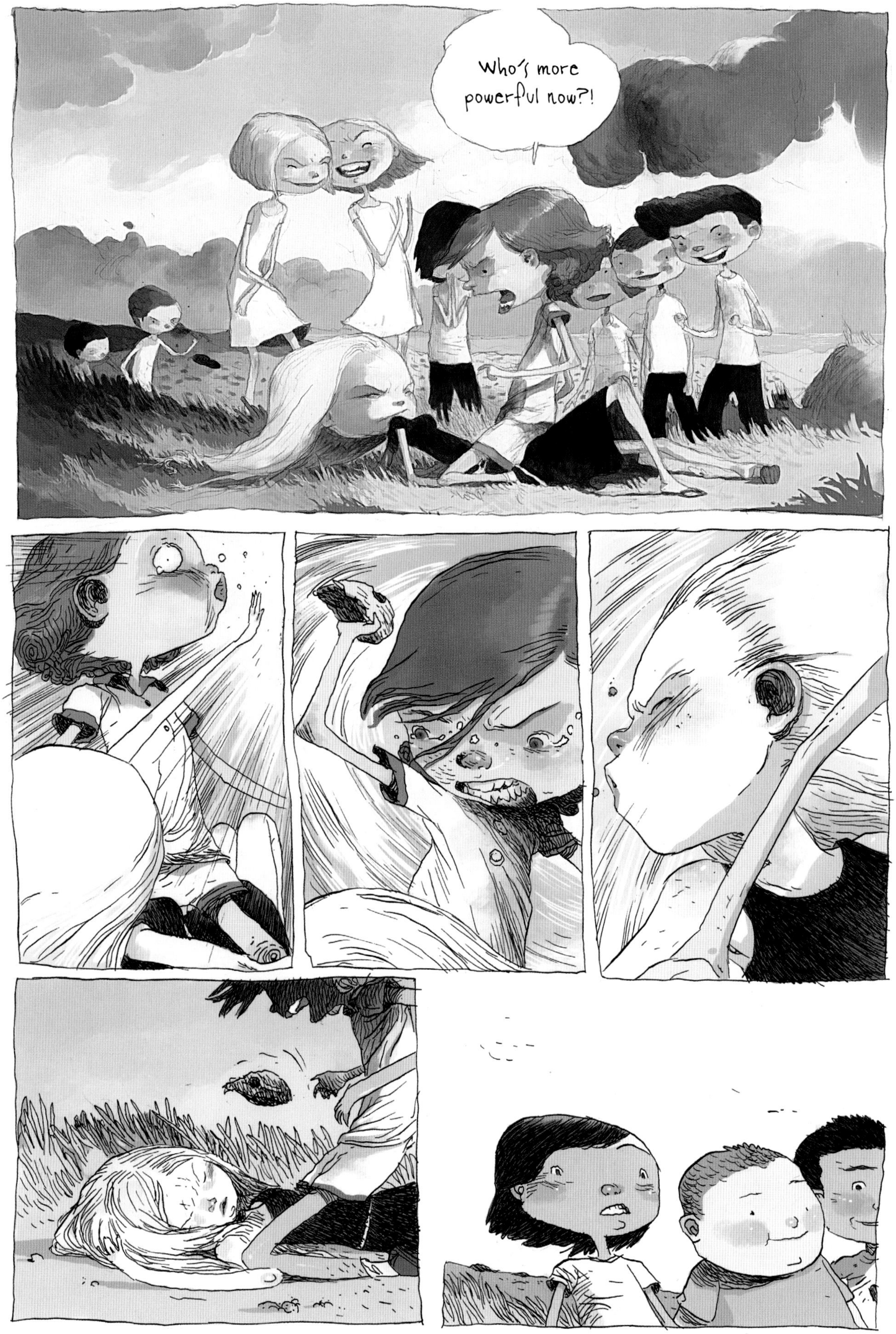
Who's more
powerful now?!

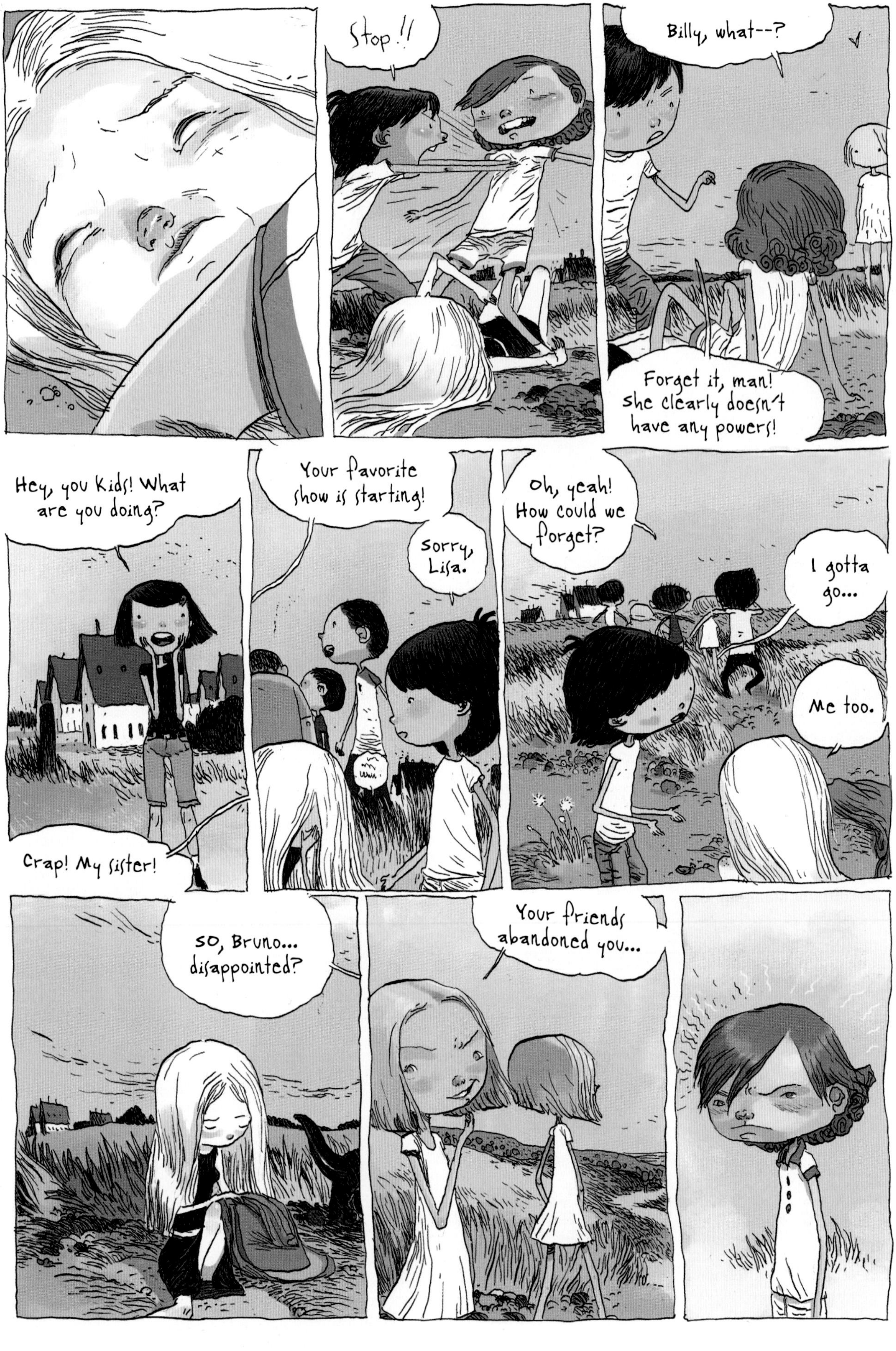
Stop!!
Billy, what--?
Forget it, man! she clearly doesn't have any powers!
Hey, you kids! What are you doing?
Crap! My sister!
Your favorite show is starting!
Sorry, Lisa.
Oh, yeah! How could we forget?
I gotta go...
Me too.
So, Bruno... disappointed?
Your friends abandoned you...

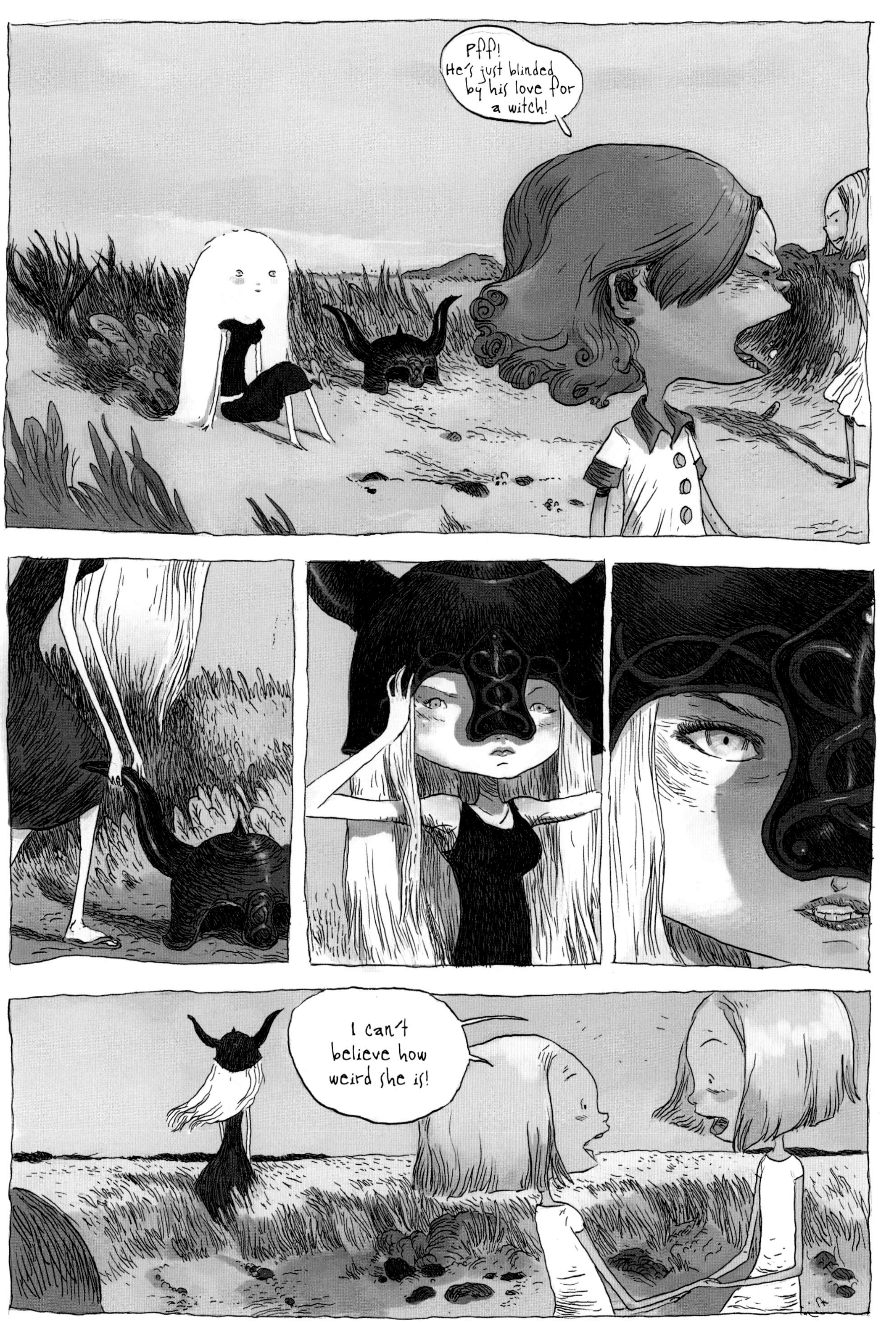
Pff!
He's just blinded by his love for a witch!
I can't believe how weird she is!

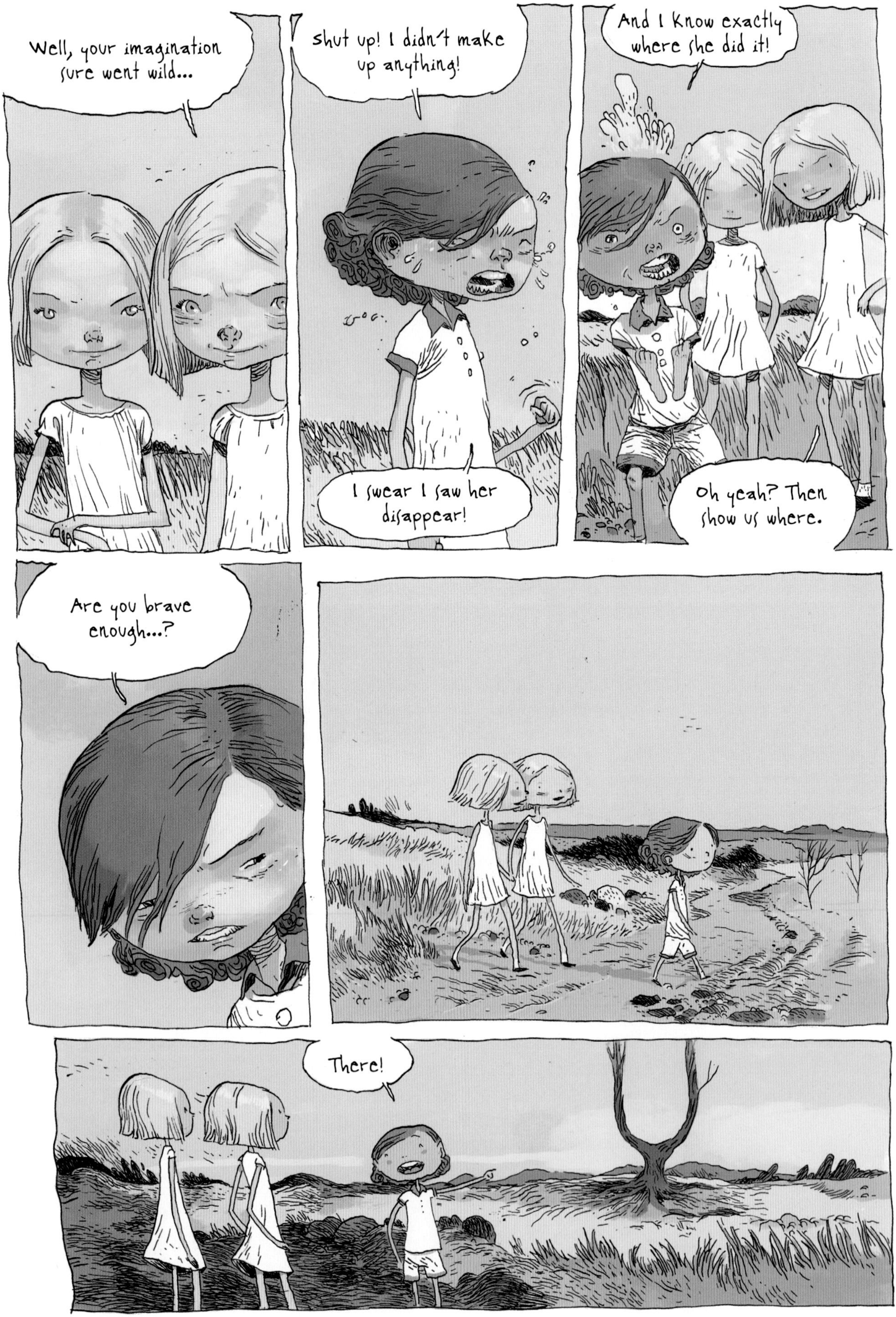
Well, your imagination sure went wild...
Shut up! I didn't make up anything!
I swear I saw her disappear!
And I know exactly where she did it!
Oh yeah? Then show us where.
Are you brave enough...?
There!

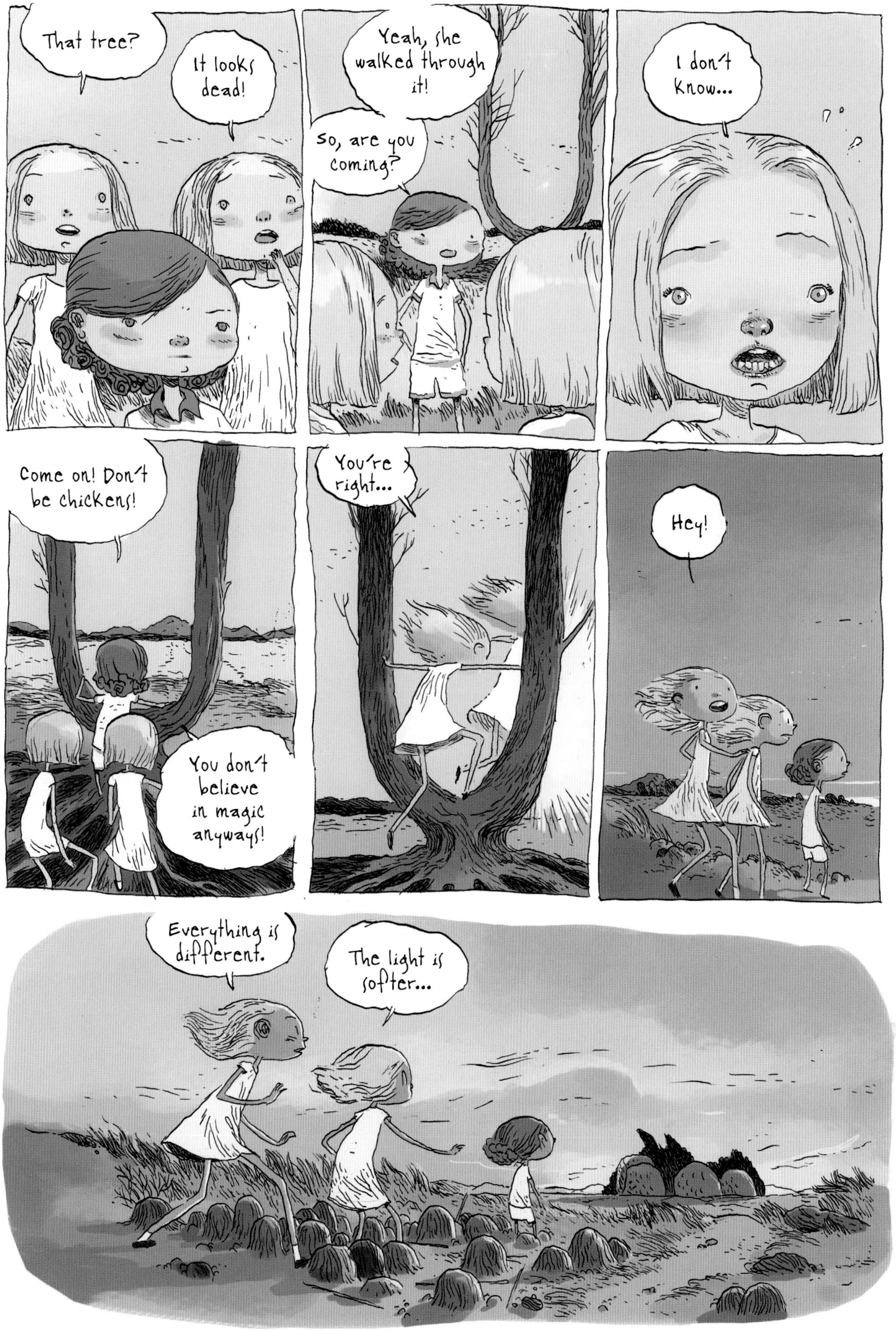
That tree?
It looks dead!
Yeah, she walked through it!
So, are you coming?
I don't know...
Come on! Don't be chickens!
You don't believe in magic anyways!
You're right...
Hey!
Everything is different.
The light is softer...

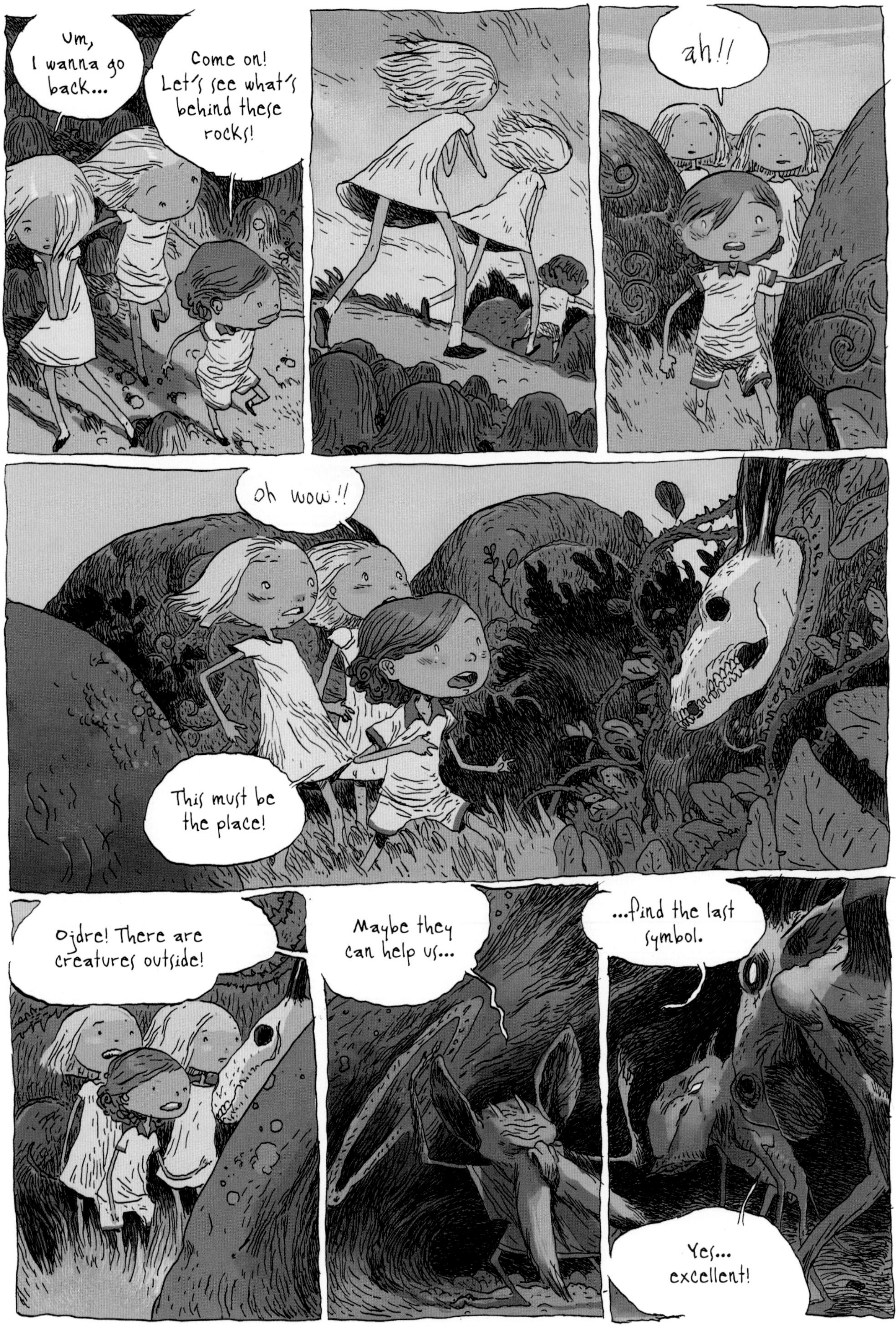
Um, I wanna go back...
Come on! Let's see what's behind these rocks!
ah!!
oh wow!!
This must be the place!
Ojdre! There are creatures outside!
Maybe they can help us...
...find the last symbol.
Yes... excellent!

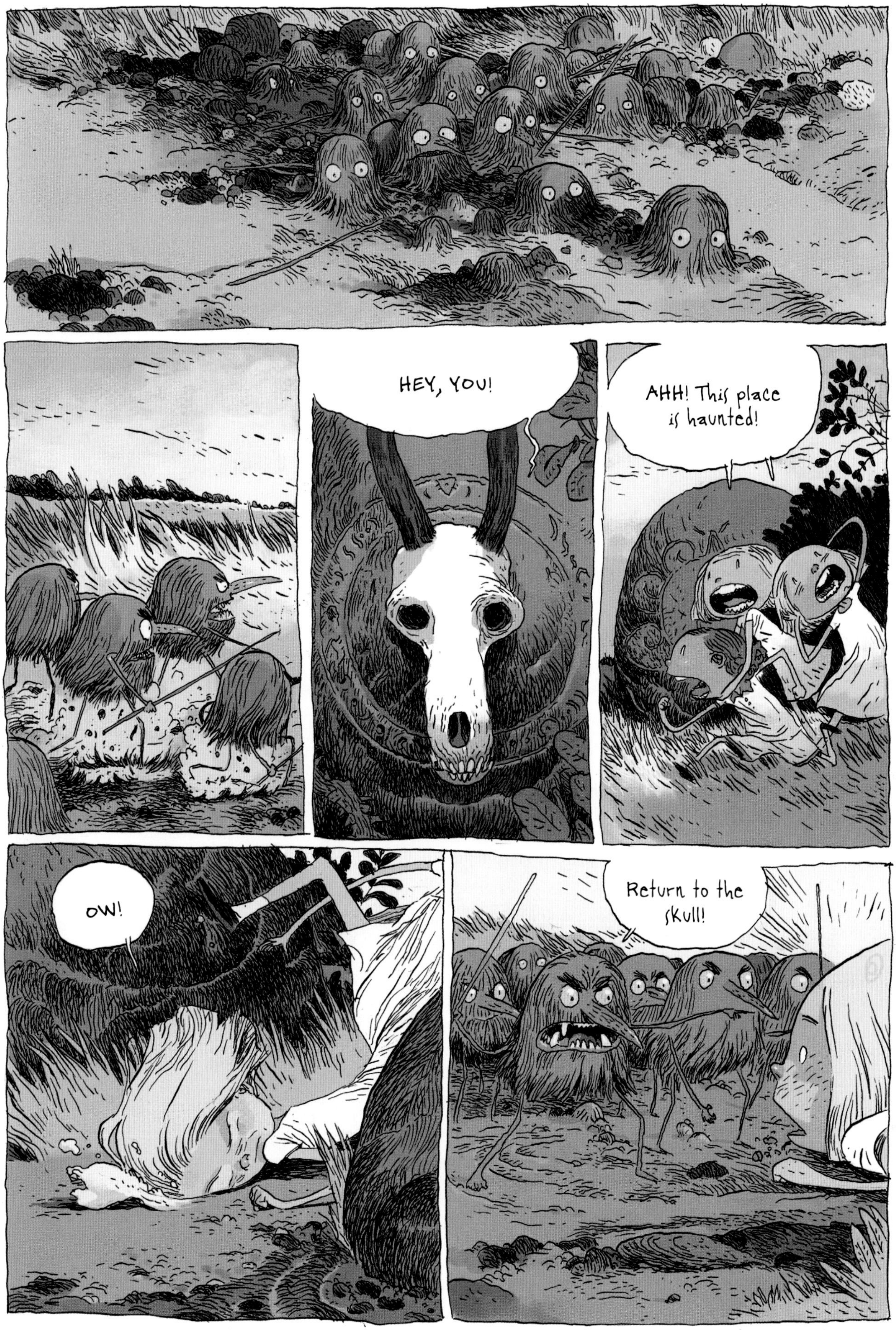
HEY, YOU!
AHH! This place is haunted!
OW!
Return to the skull!

WHAT ARE THOSE LITTLE THINGS?!

Little things...?

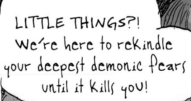

LITTLE THINGS?! We're here to rekindle your deepest demonic fears until it kills you!

Please! Don't kill us!

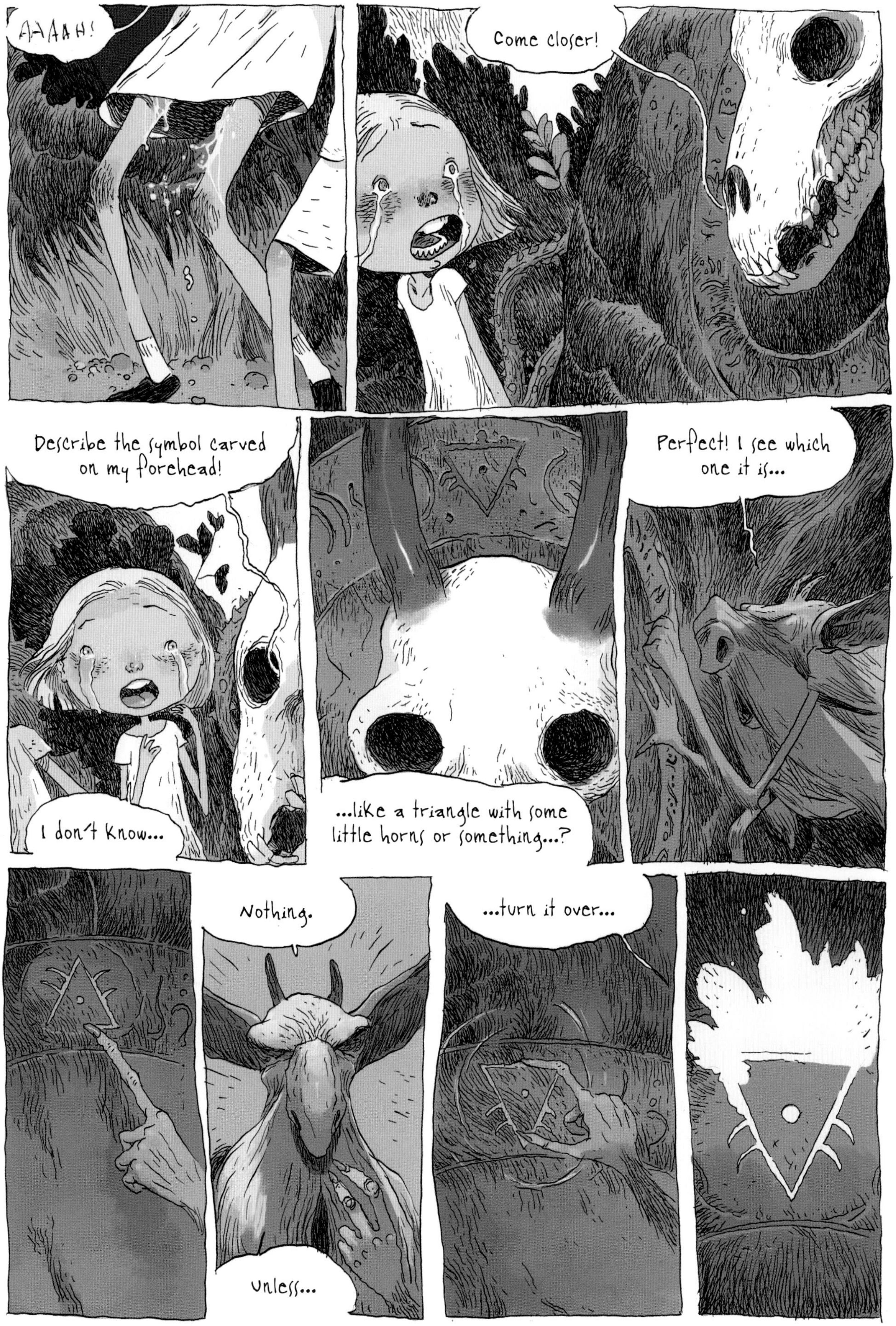
AAAAH!
Come closer!
Describe the symbol carved on my forehead!
I don't know...
...like a triangle with some little horns or something...?
Perfect! I see which one it is...
Nothing.
Unless...
...turn it over...

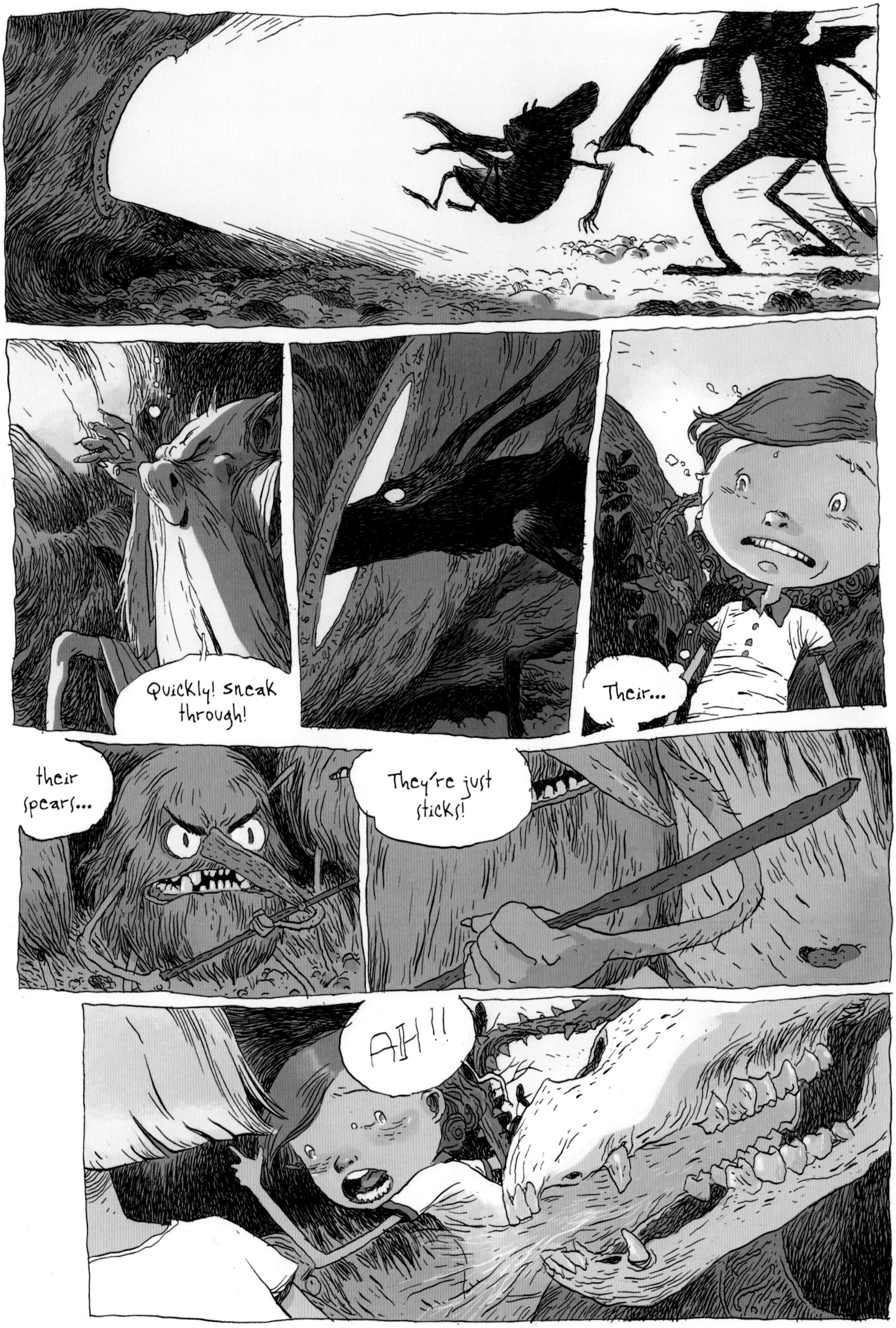
Quickly! sneak through!
Their...
their spears...
They're just sticks!
AH!!

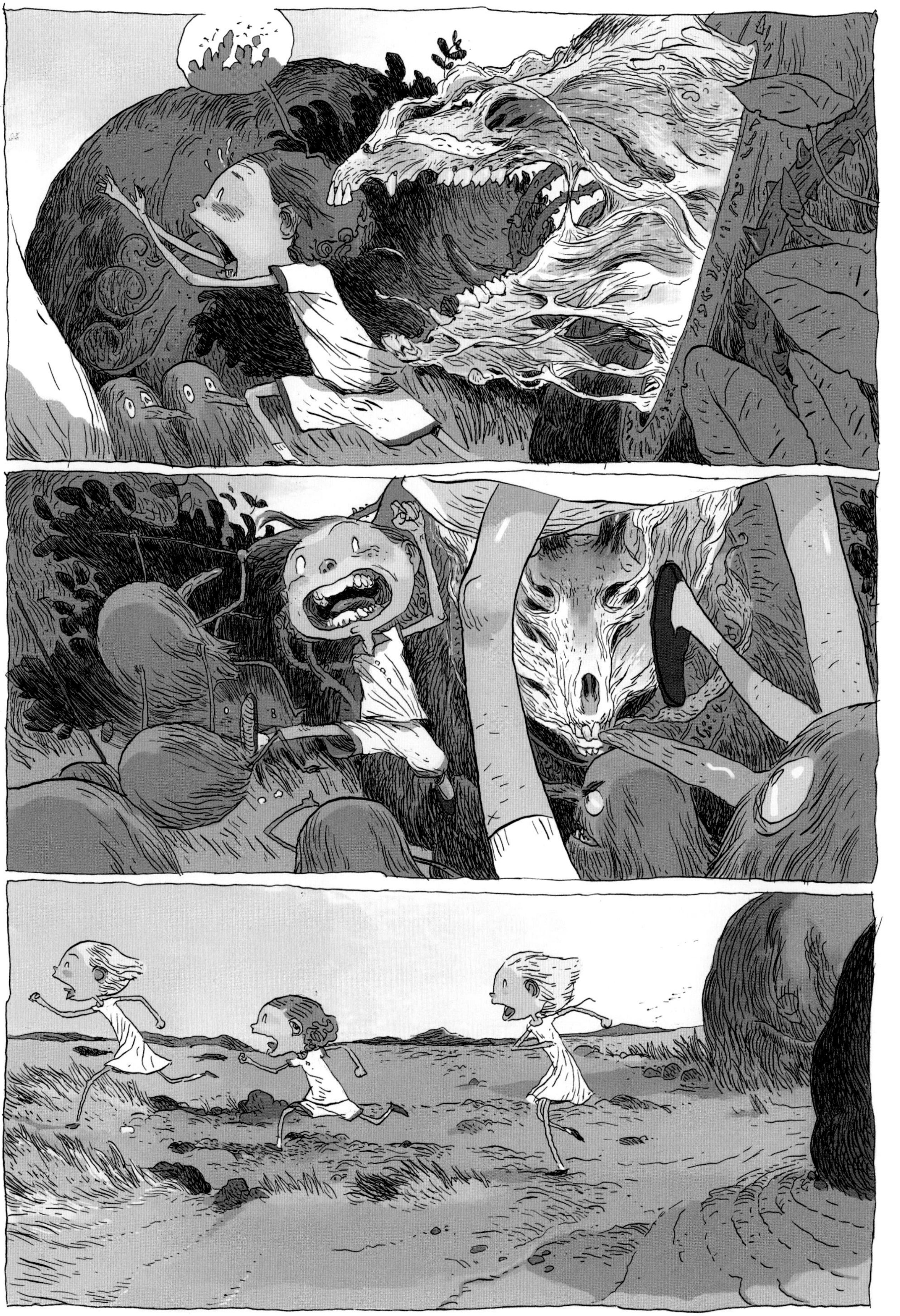

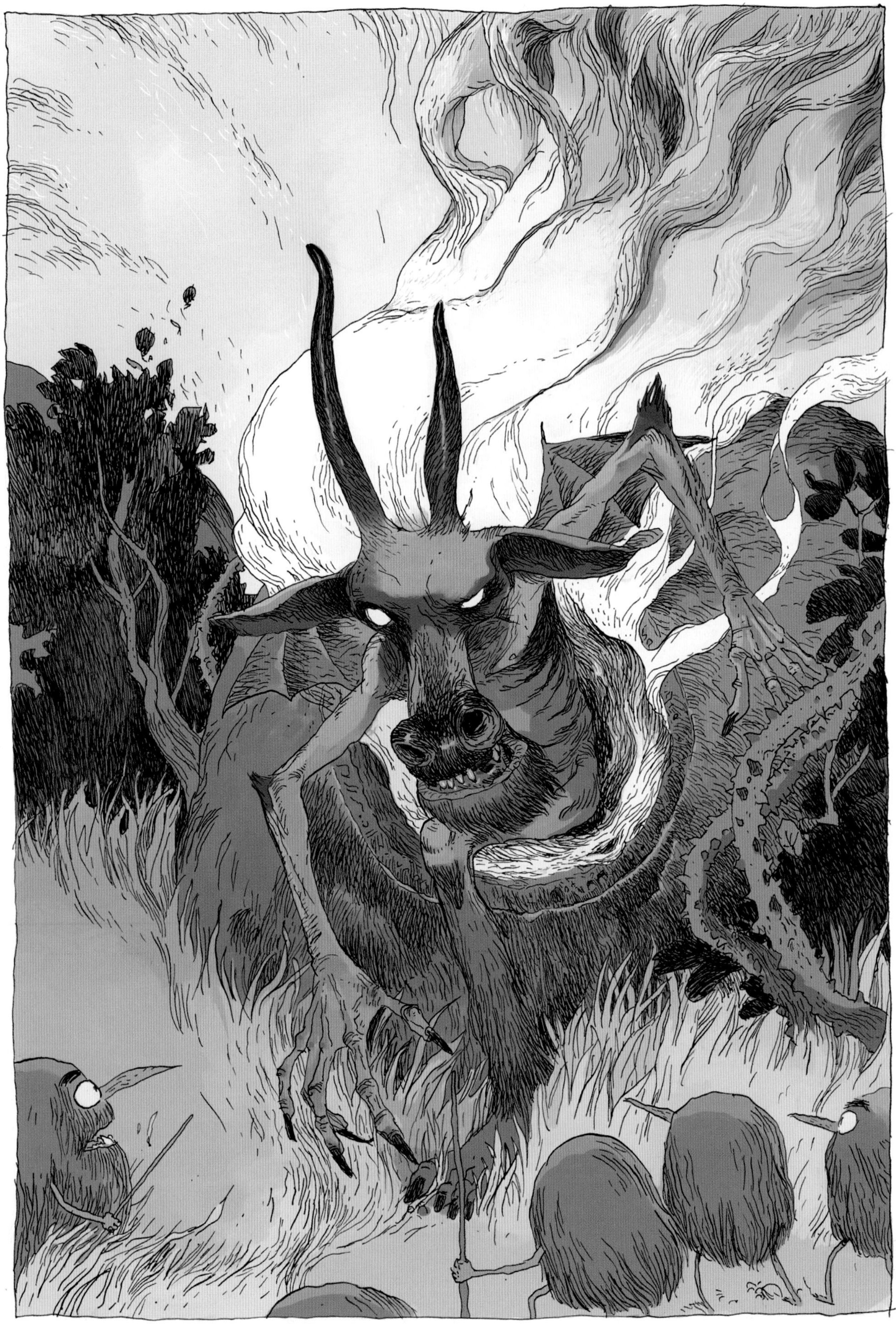

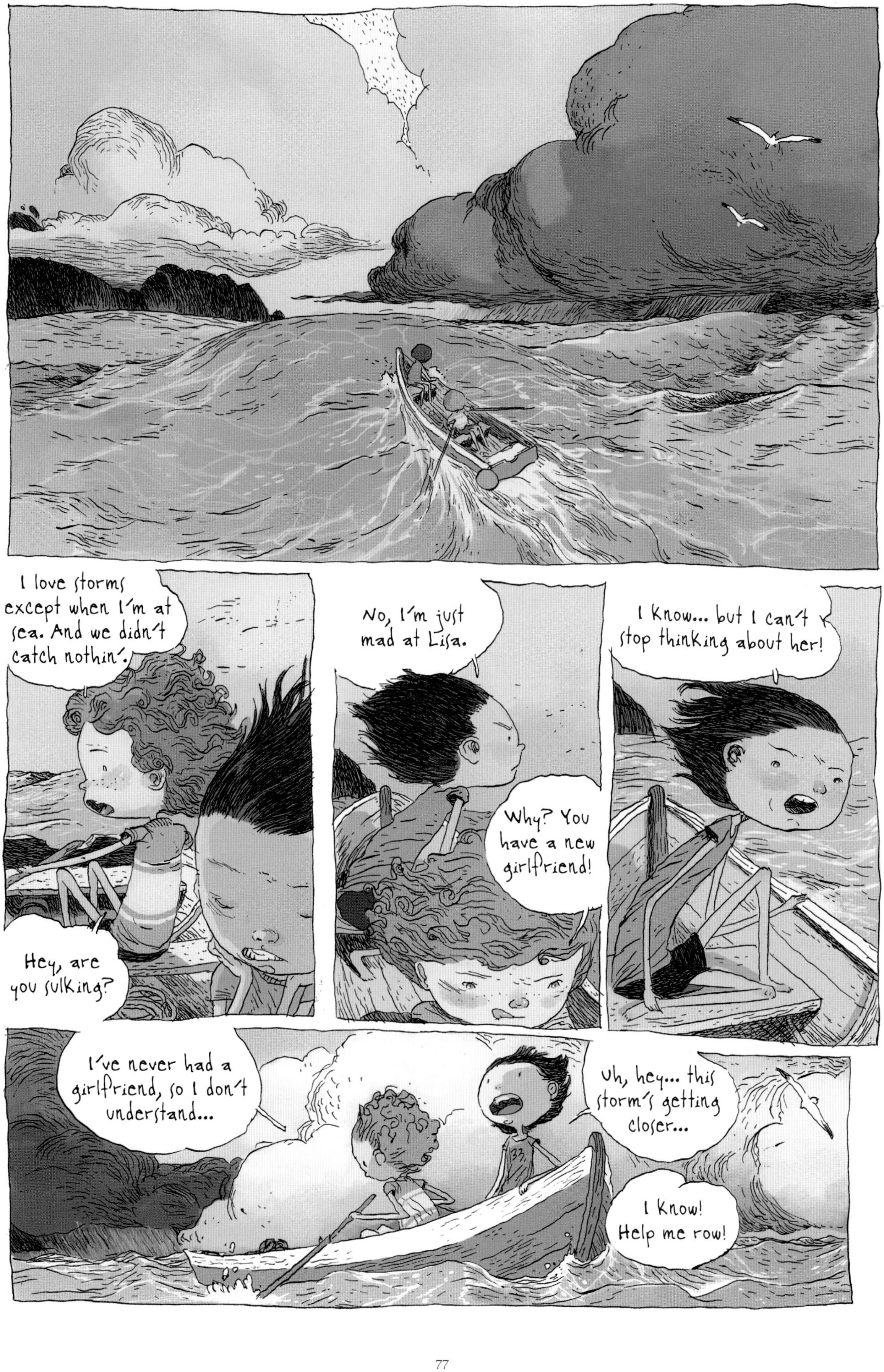
I love storms except when I'm at sea. And we didn't catch nothin'.
Hey, are you sulking?
No, I'm just mad at Lisa.
Why? You have a new girlfriend!
I know... but I can't stop thinking about her!
I've never had a girlfriend, so I don't understand...
Uh, hey... this storm's getting closer...
I know! Help me row!

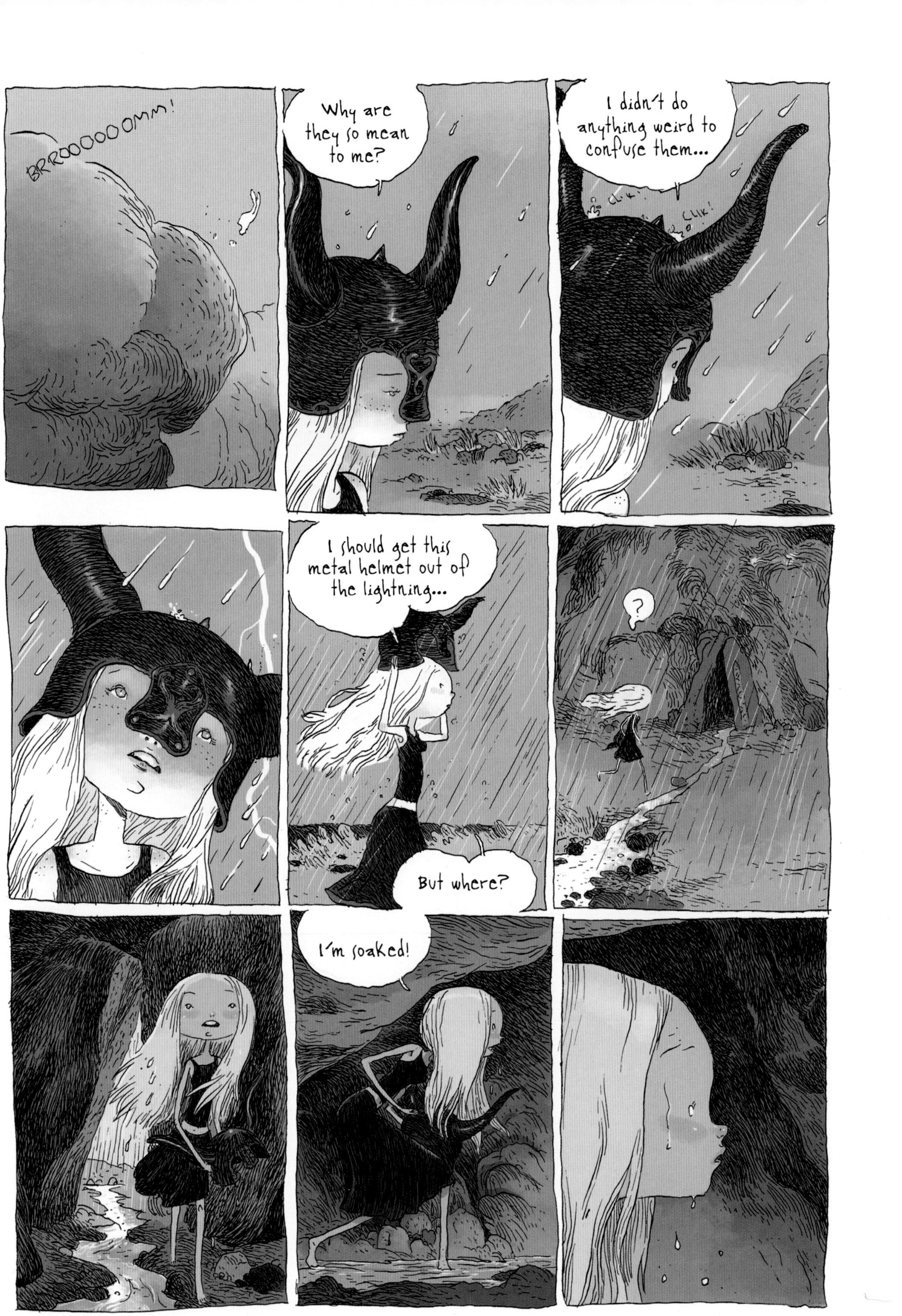
BRROOOOOOOMM!
Why are they so mean to me?
I didn't do anything weird to confuse them...
CLIK!
CLIK!
I should get this metal helmet out of the lightning...
But where?
?
I'm soaked!

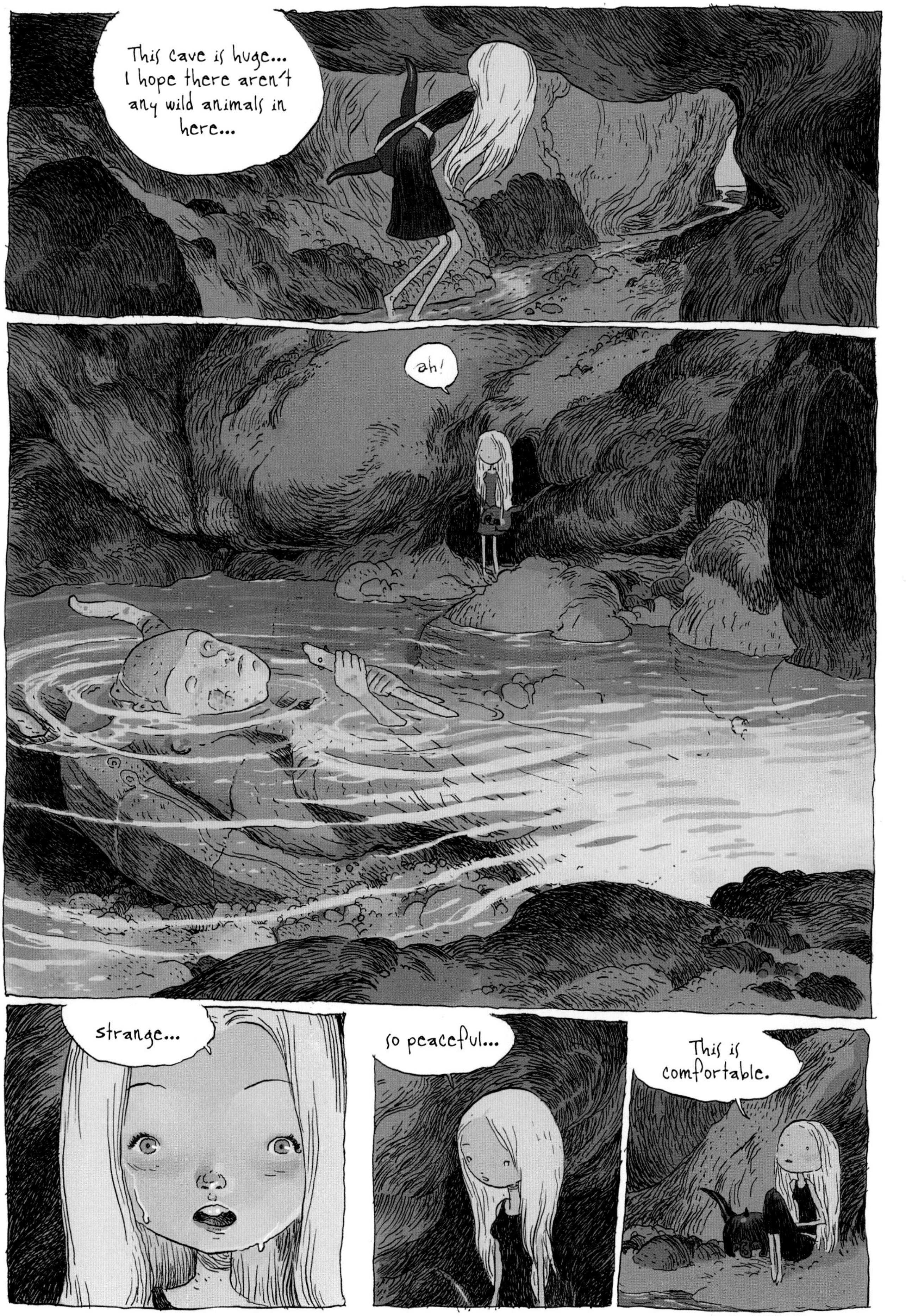
This is cave is huge... I hope there aren't any wild animals in here...
ah!
strange...
so peaceful...
This is comfortable.

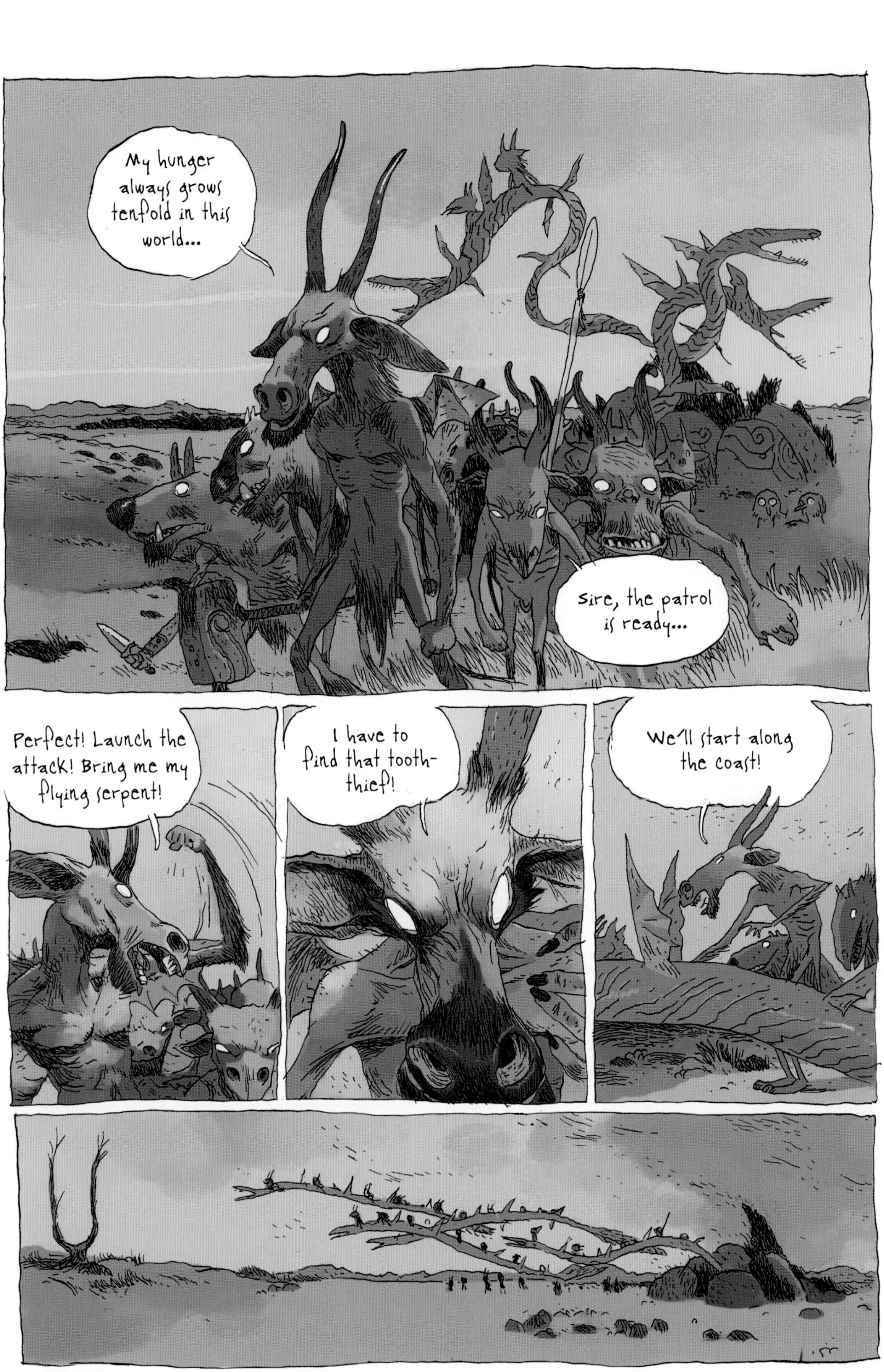
My hunger always grows tenfold in this world...
Sire, the patrol is ready...
Perfect! Launch the attack! Bring me my flying serpent!
I have to find that tooth-thief!
We'll start along the coast!

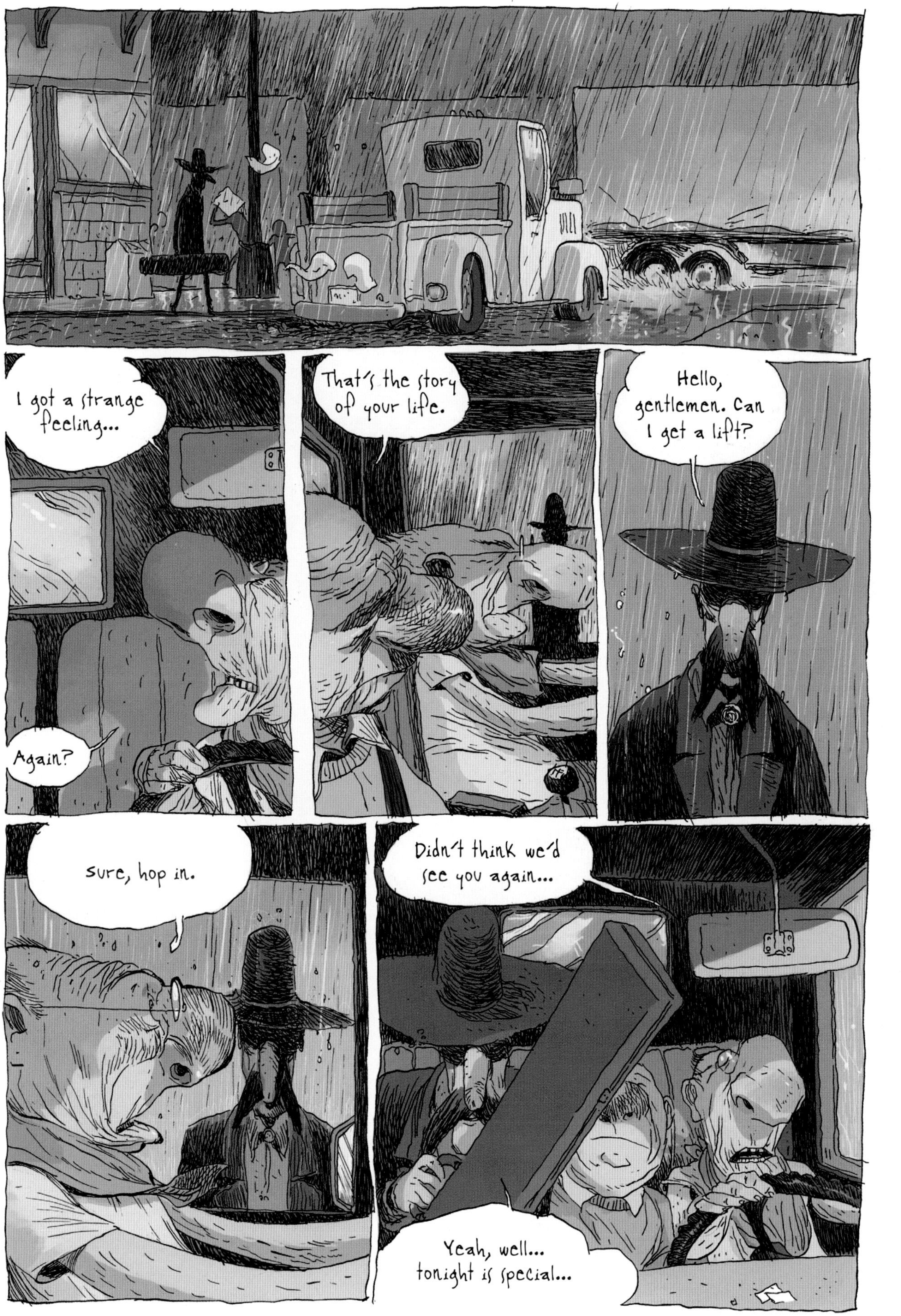
I got a strange feeling...
Again?
That's the story of your life.
Hello, gentlemen. Can I get a lift?
Sure, hop in.
Didn't think we'd see you again...
Yeah, well... tonight is special...

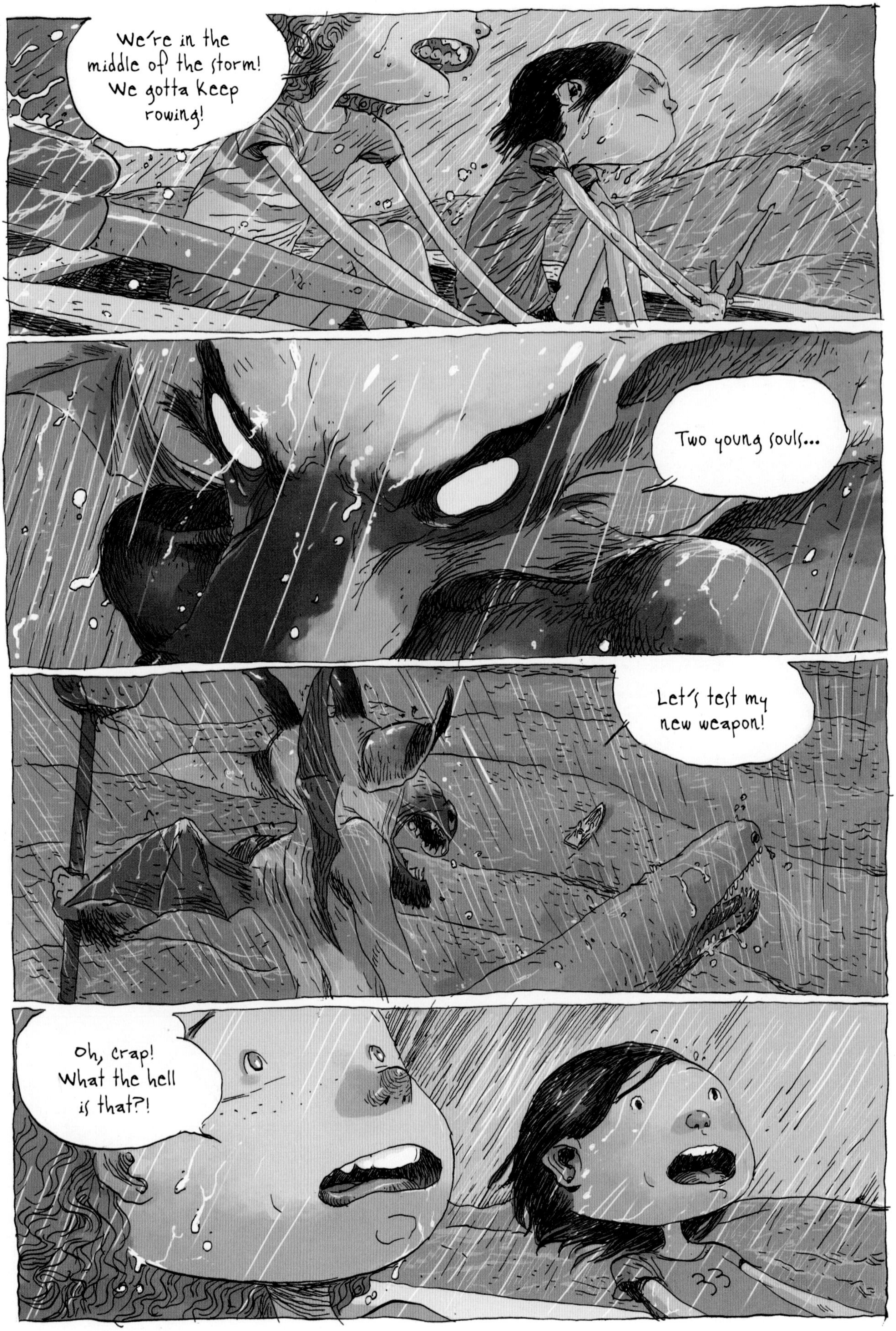
We're in the middle of the storm! We gotta keep rowing!
Two young souls...
Let's test my new weapon!
Oh, crap! What the hell is that?!

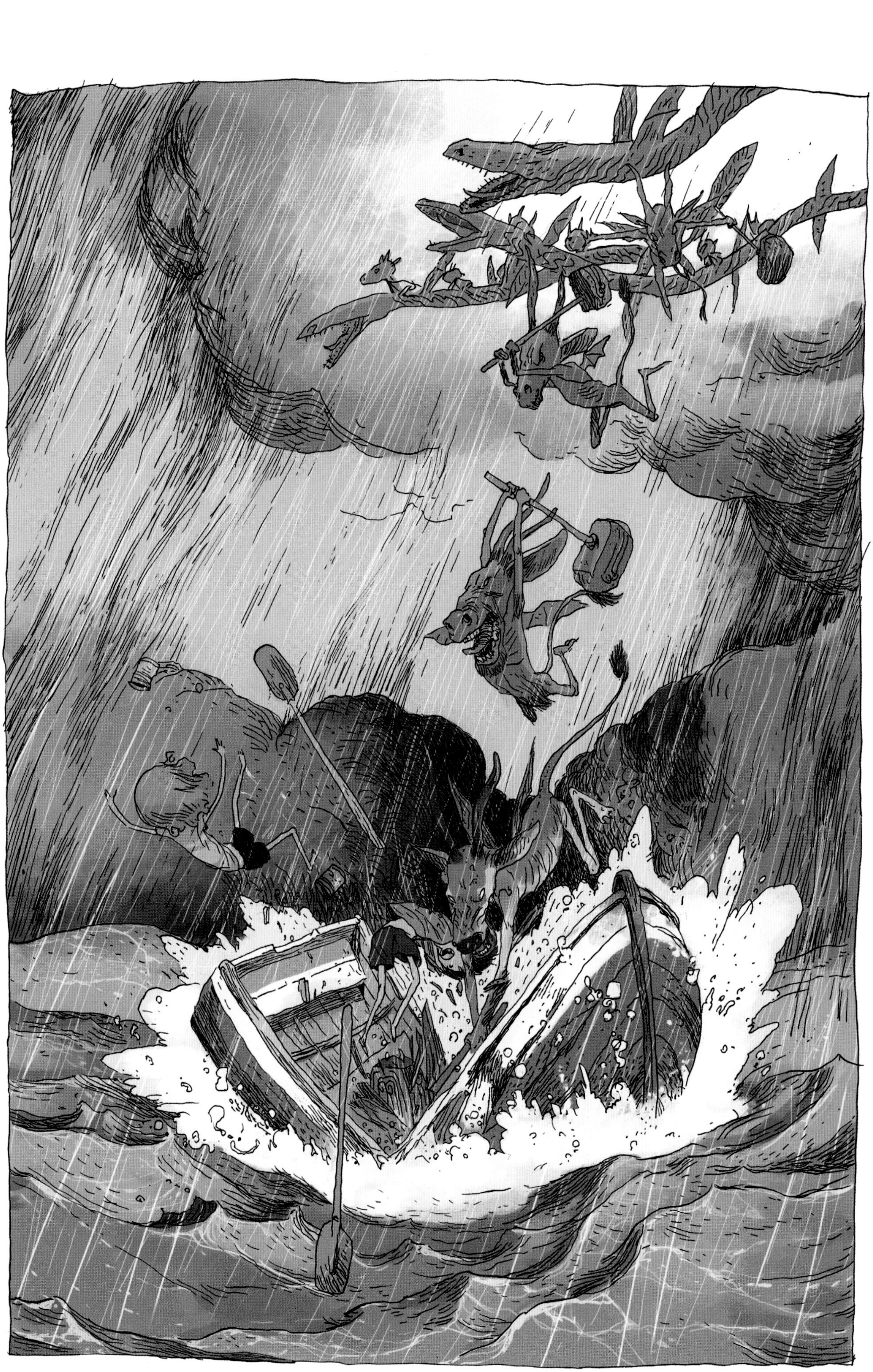

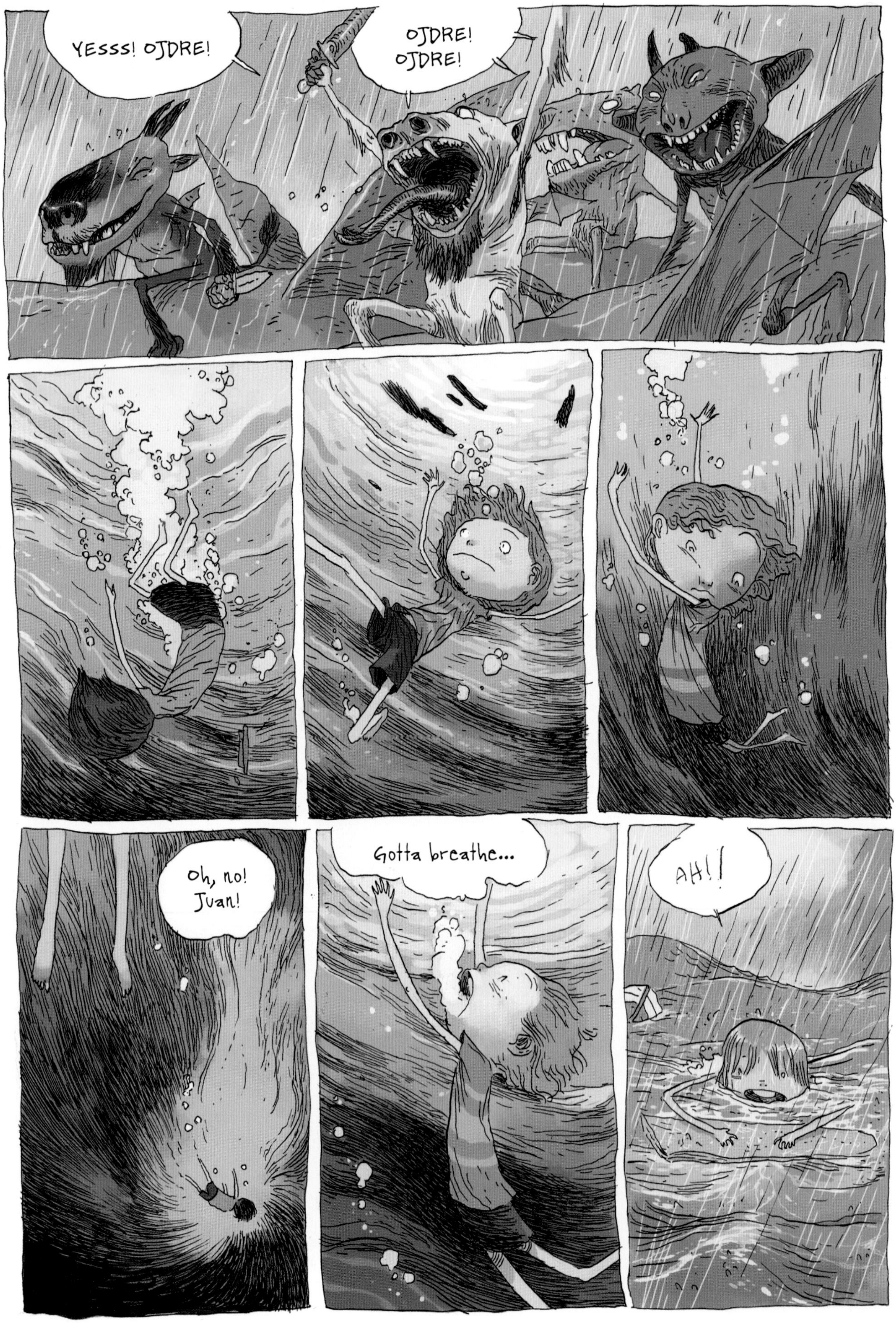
YESSS! OJDRE!
OJDRE! OJDRE!
Oh, no! Juan!
Gotta breathe...
AH!!

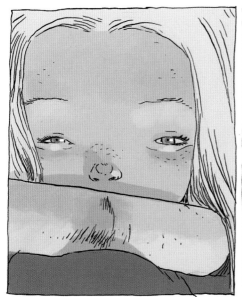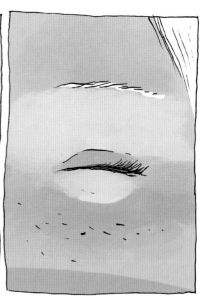

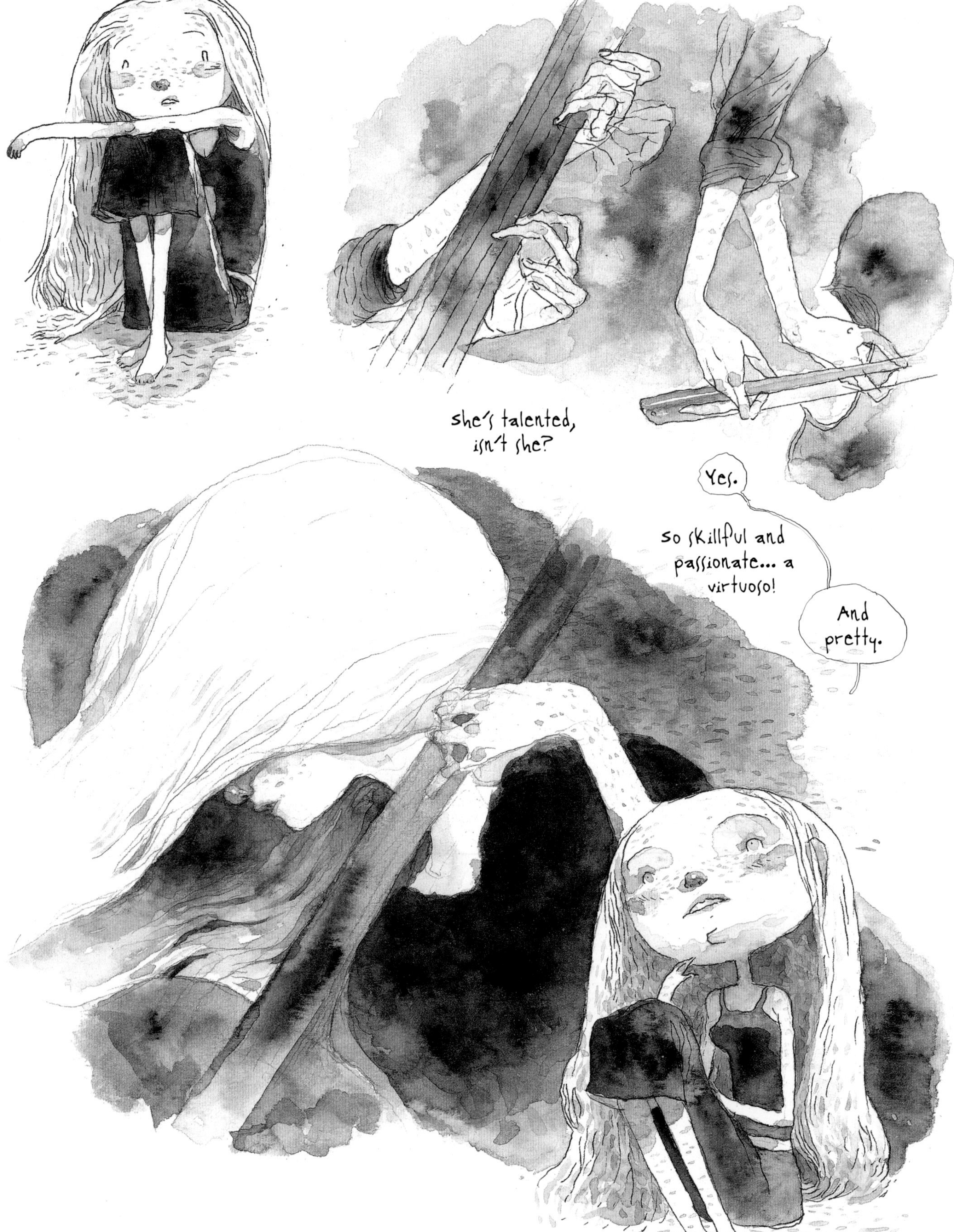
She's talented, isn't she?
Yes.
So skillful and passionate... a virtuoso!
And pretty.

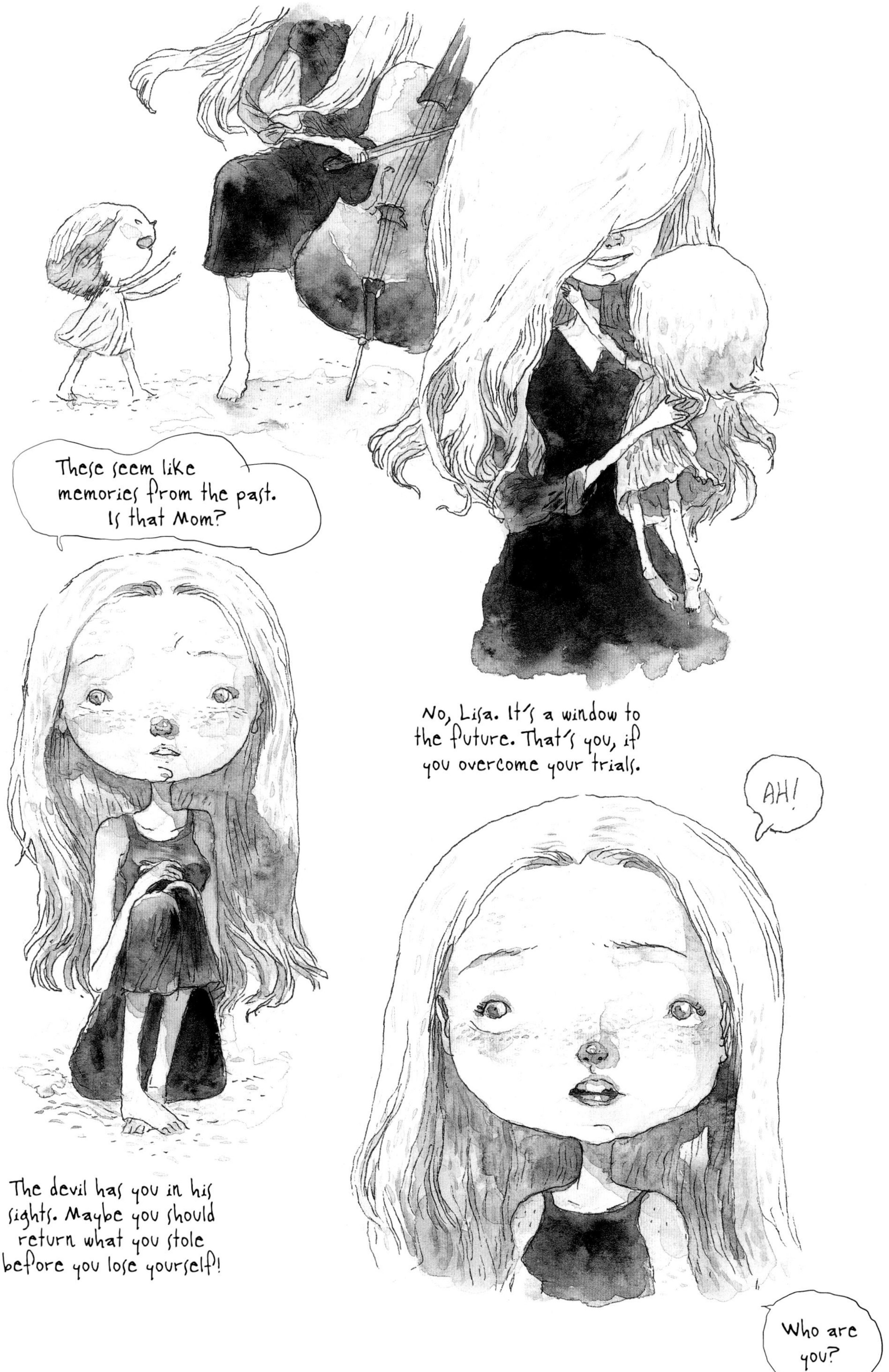
These seem like memories from the past. Is that Mom?
No, Lisa. It's a window to the future. That's you, if you overcome your trials.
AH!
The devil has you in his sights. Maybe you should return what you stole before you lose yourself!
Who are you?

I am a soul who has been wandering since the dawn
of time. My people have confused you for me.
Return home now. Fulfill your destiny.

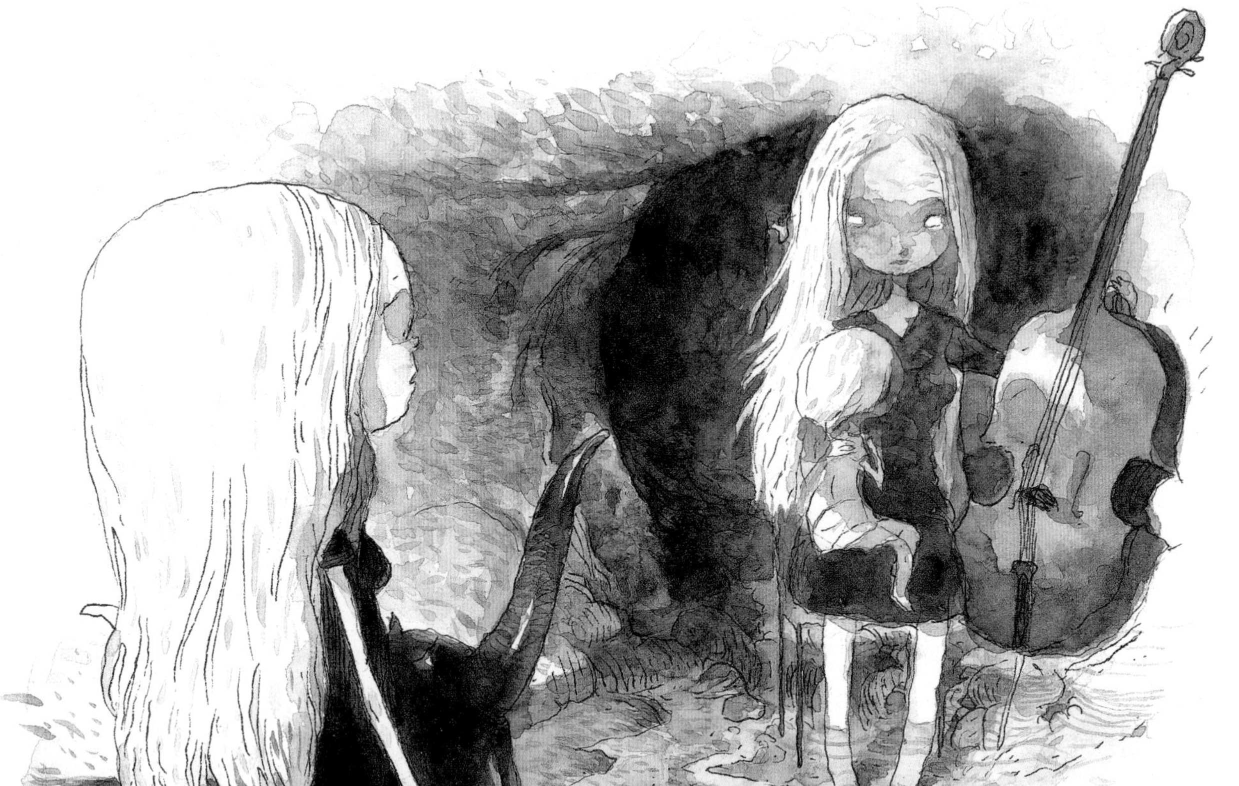

I salute you, Lisa!
Angel and Demon...

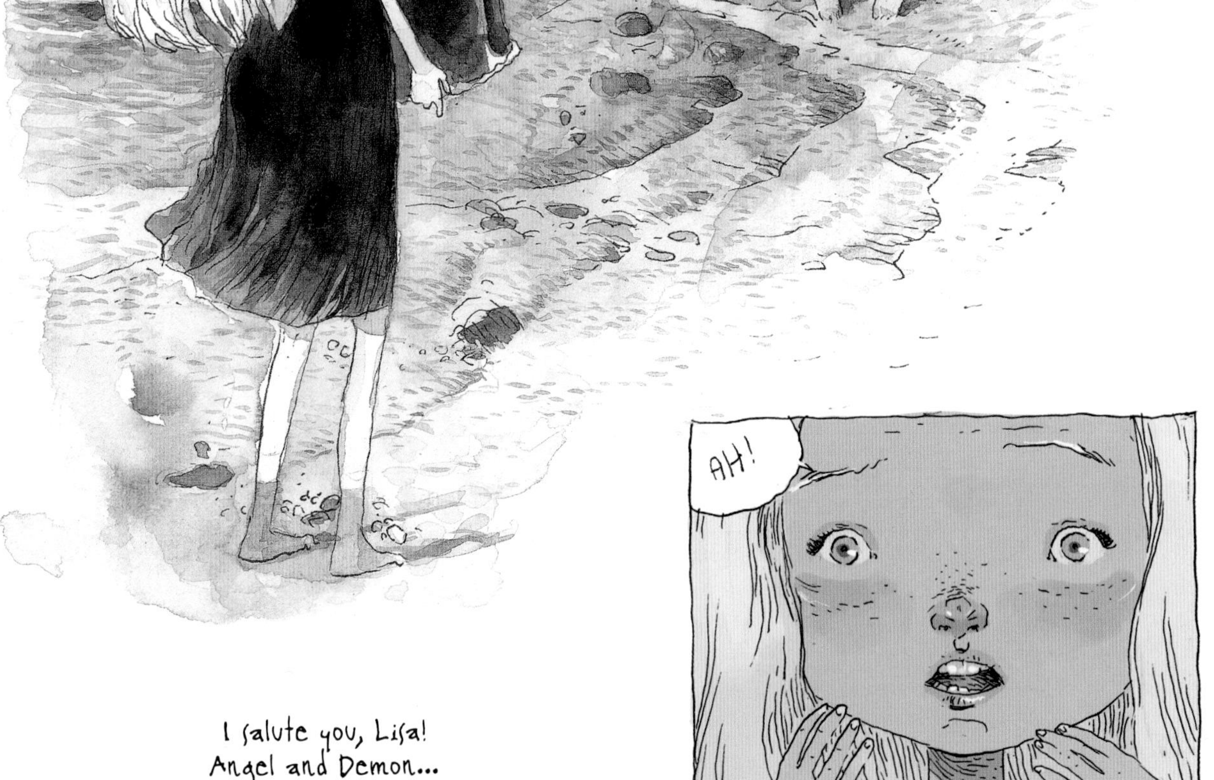
AH!

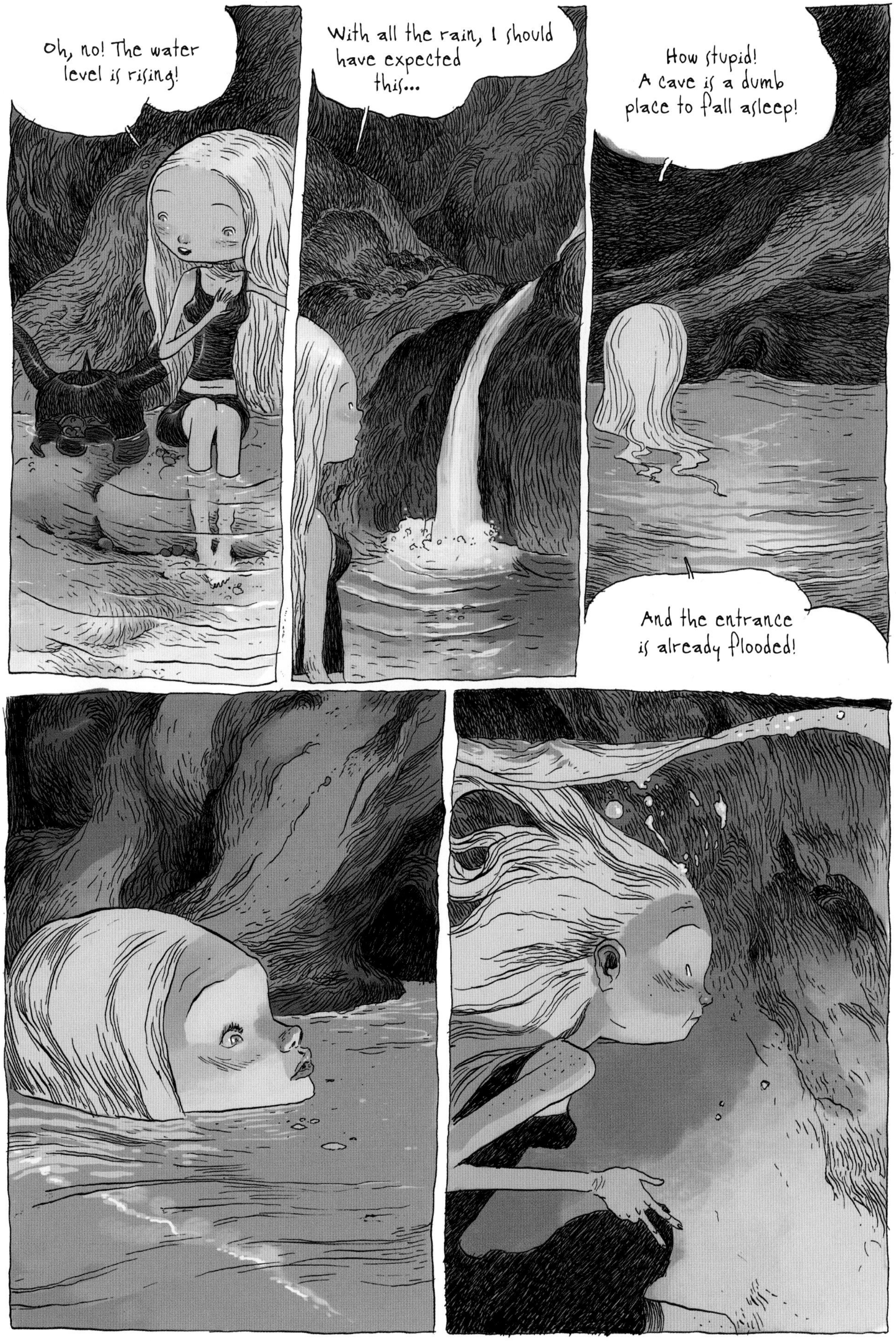
Oh, no! The water level is rising!
With all the rain, I should have expected this...
How stupid! A cave is a dumb place to fall asleep!
And the entrance is already flooded!

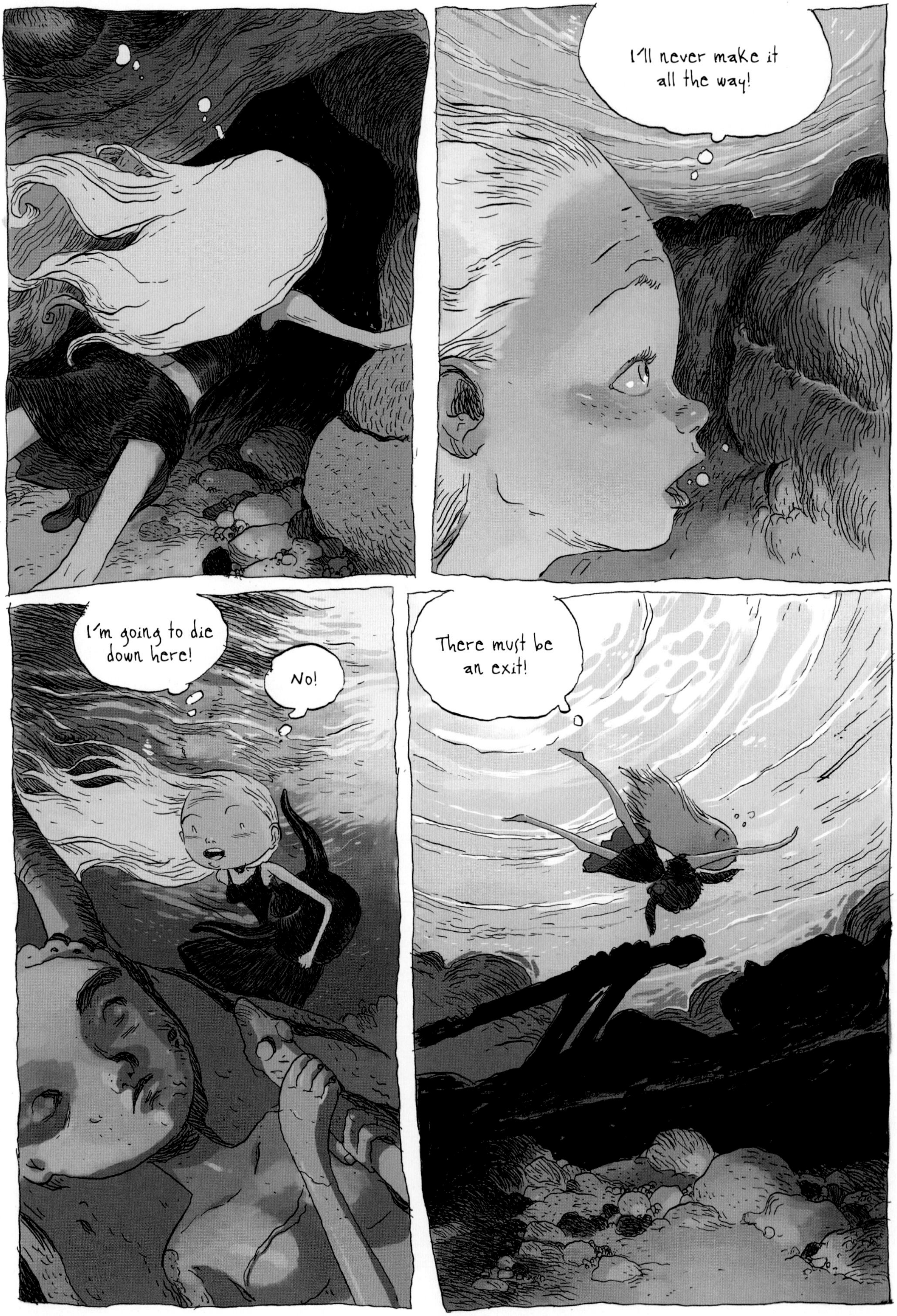
I'll never make it all the way!
I'm going to die down here!
No!
There must be an exit!

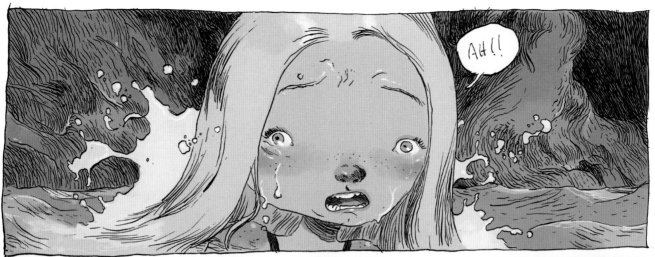

AH!!

?

I can't give up...

This staircase is like the start of a new life...

...time to discover my destiny!

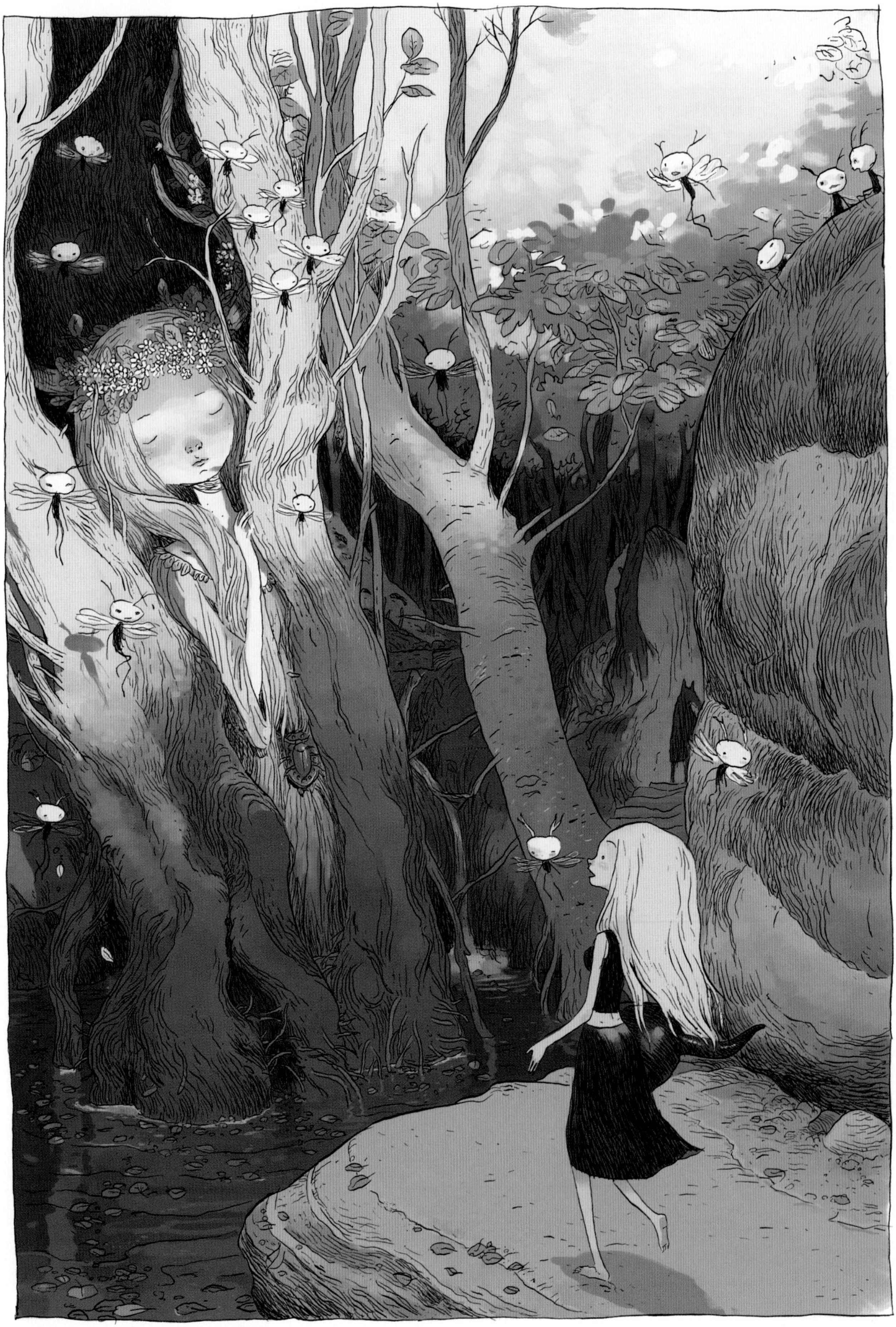

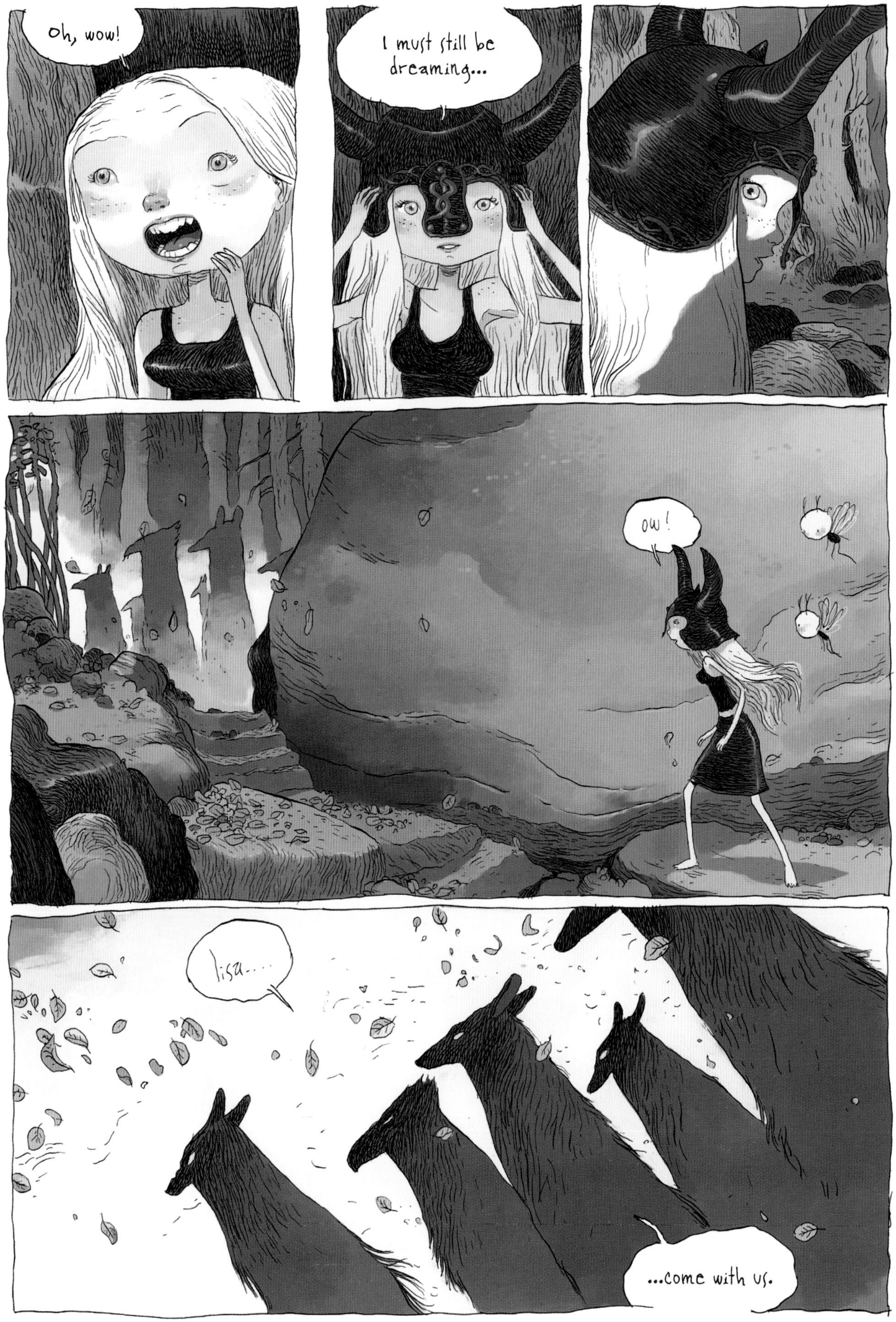
Oh, wow!
I must still be dreaming...
ow!
lisa....
...come with us.

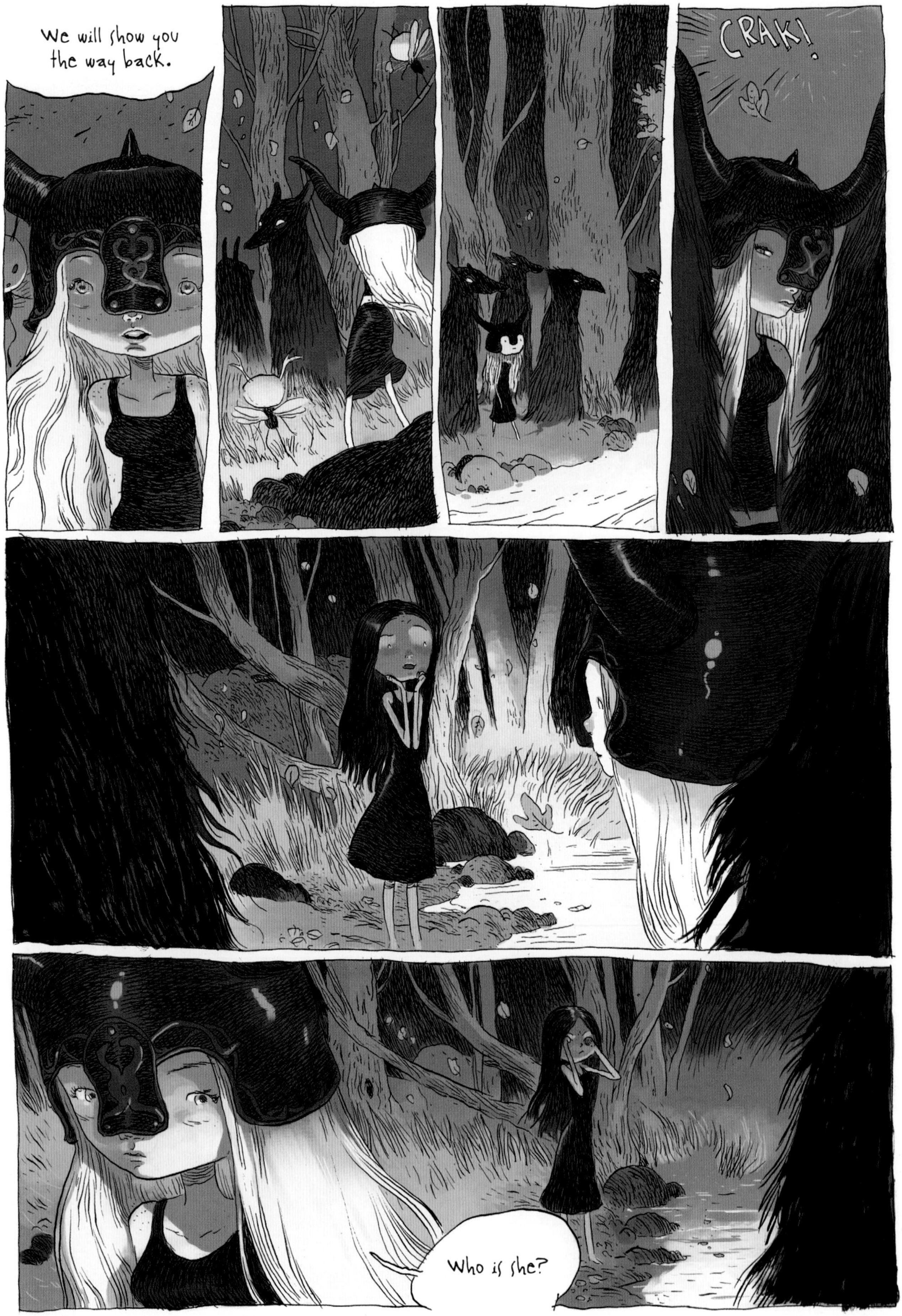
We will show you the way back.
CRAK!
Who is she?

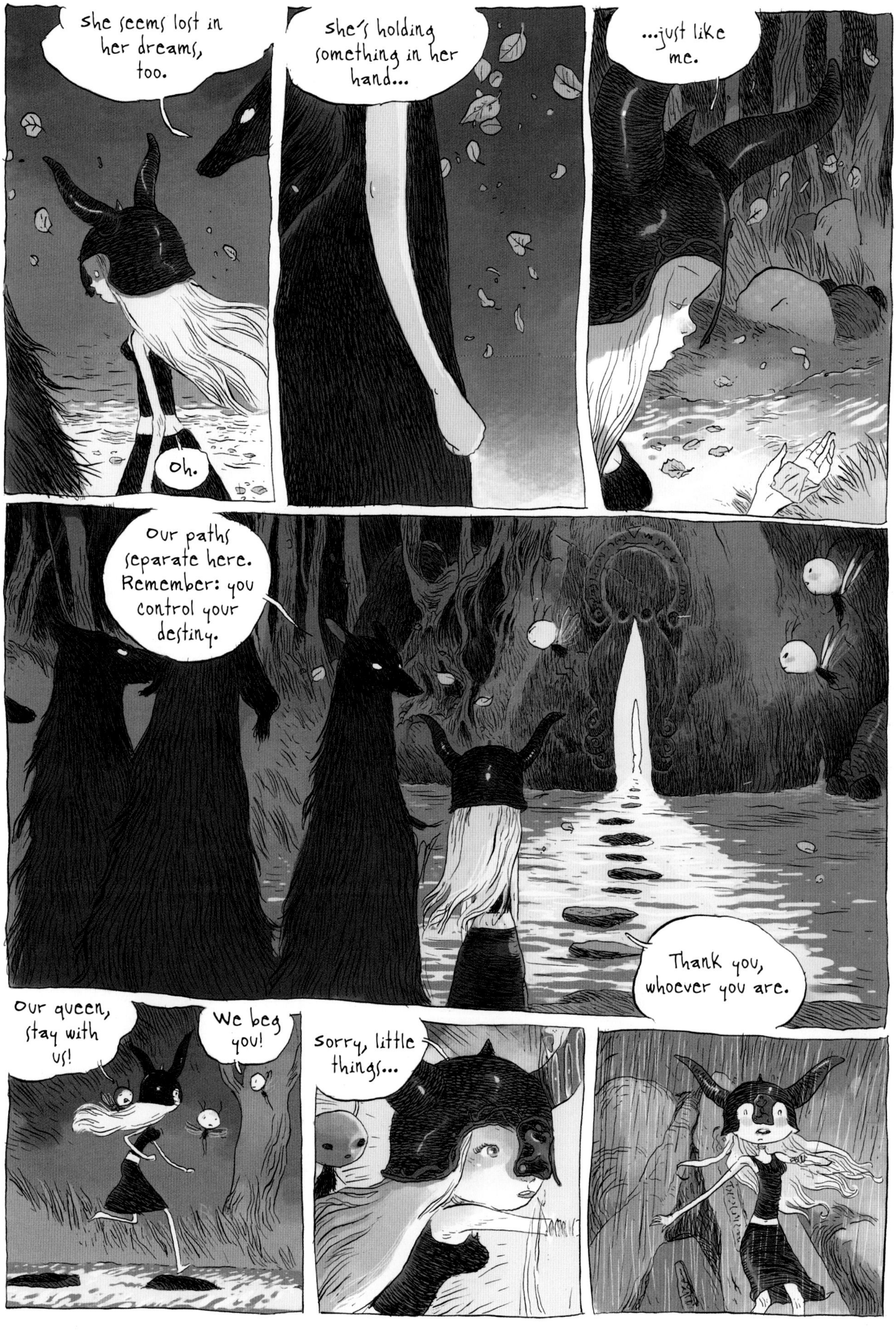

she seems lost in her dreams, too.
Oh.
she's holding something in her hand...
...just like me.
Our paths separate here. Remember: you control your destiny.
Thank you, whoever you are.
Our queen, stay with us!
We beg you!
Sorry, little things...

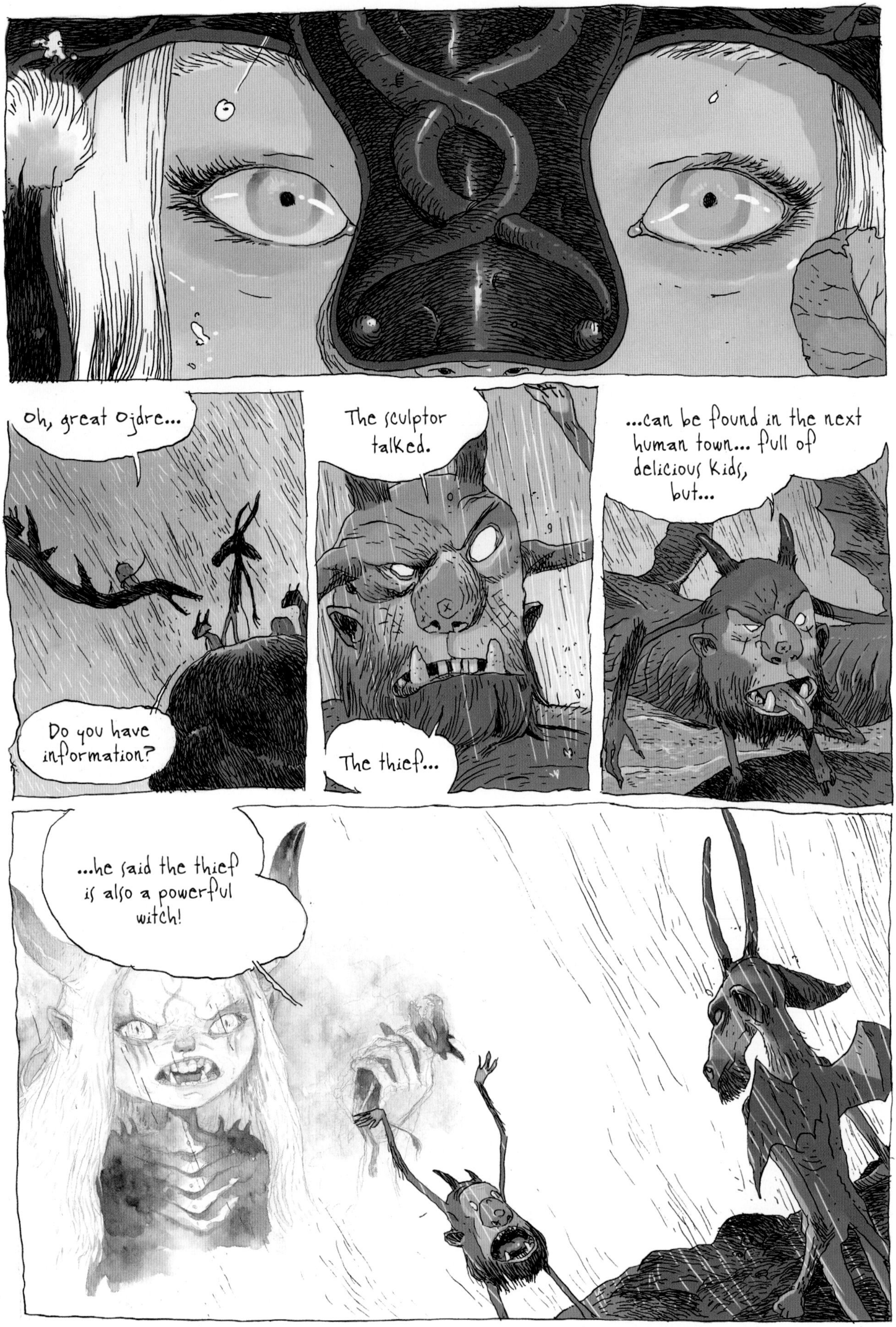
Oh, great Ojdre...
Do you have information?
The sculptor talked.
The thief...
...can be found in the next human town... full of delicious kids, but...
...he said the thief is also a powerful witch!

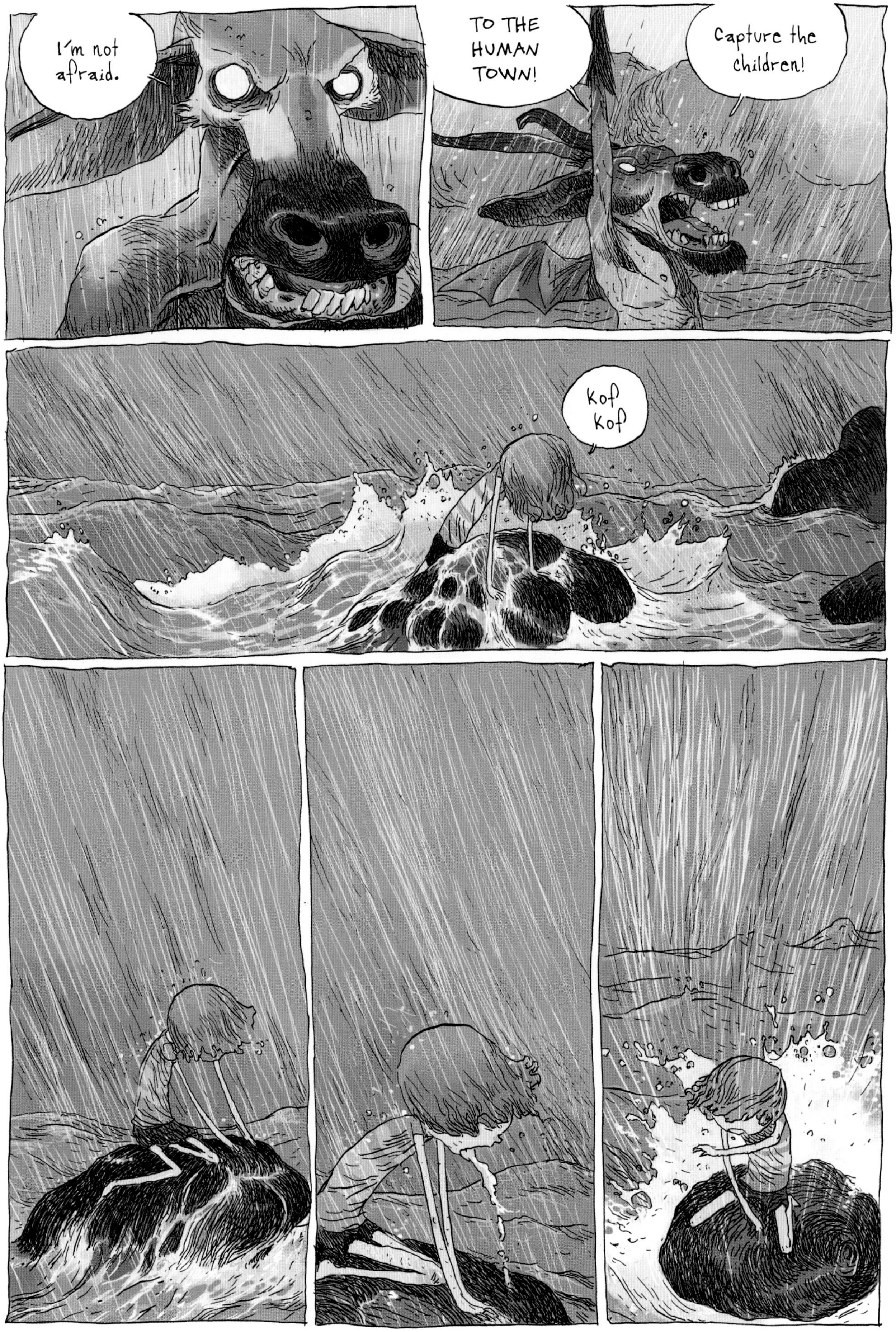
I'm not afraid.
TO THE HUMAN TOWN!
Capture the children!
Kof kof

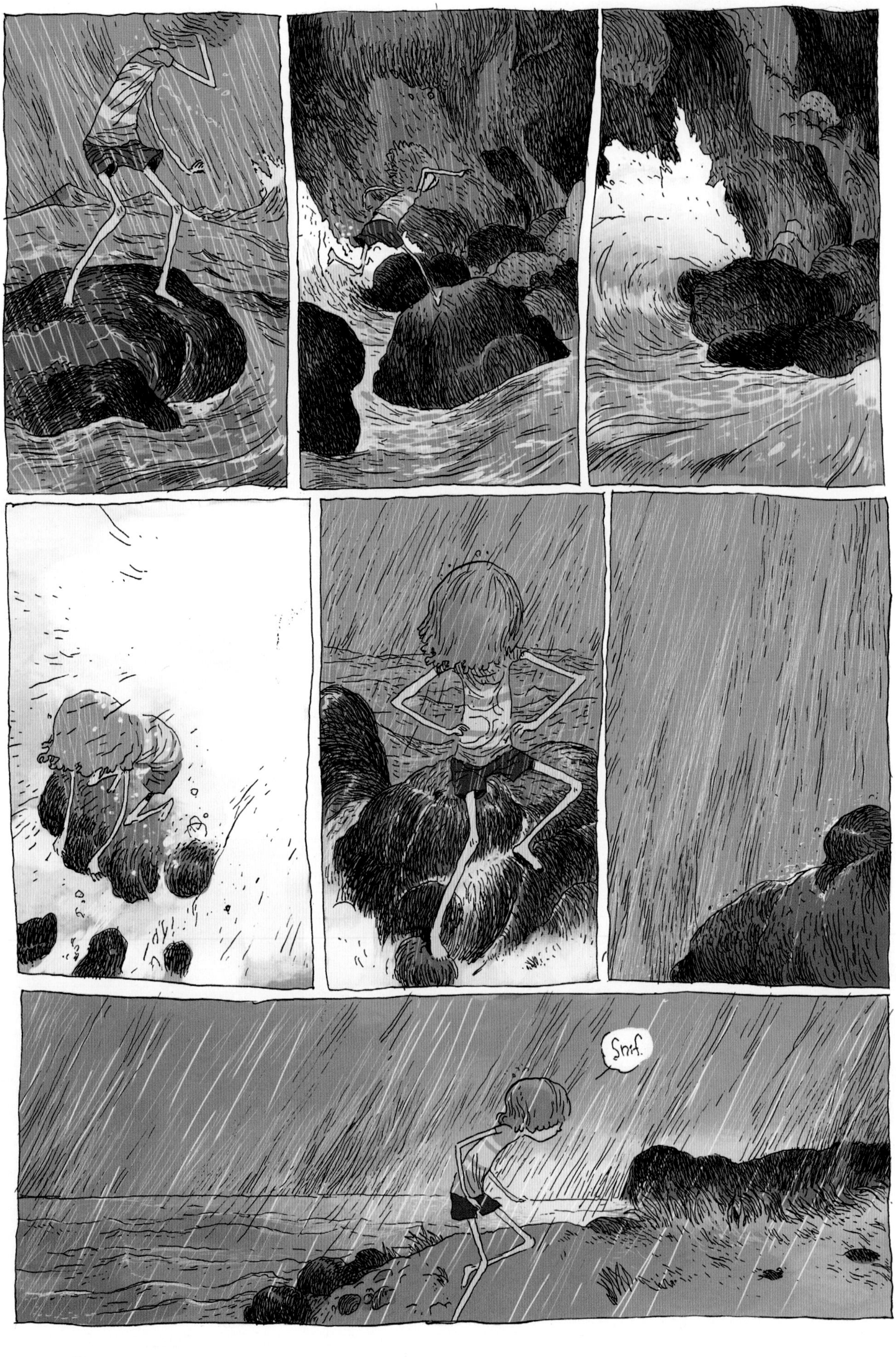
Snif.

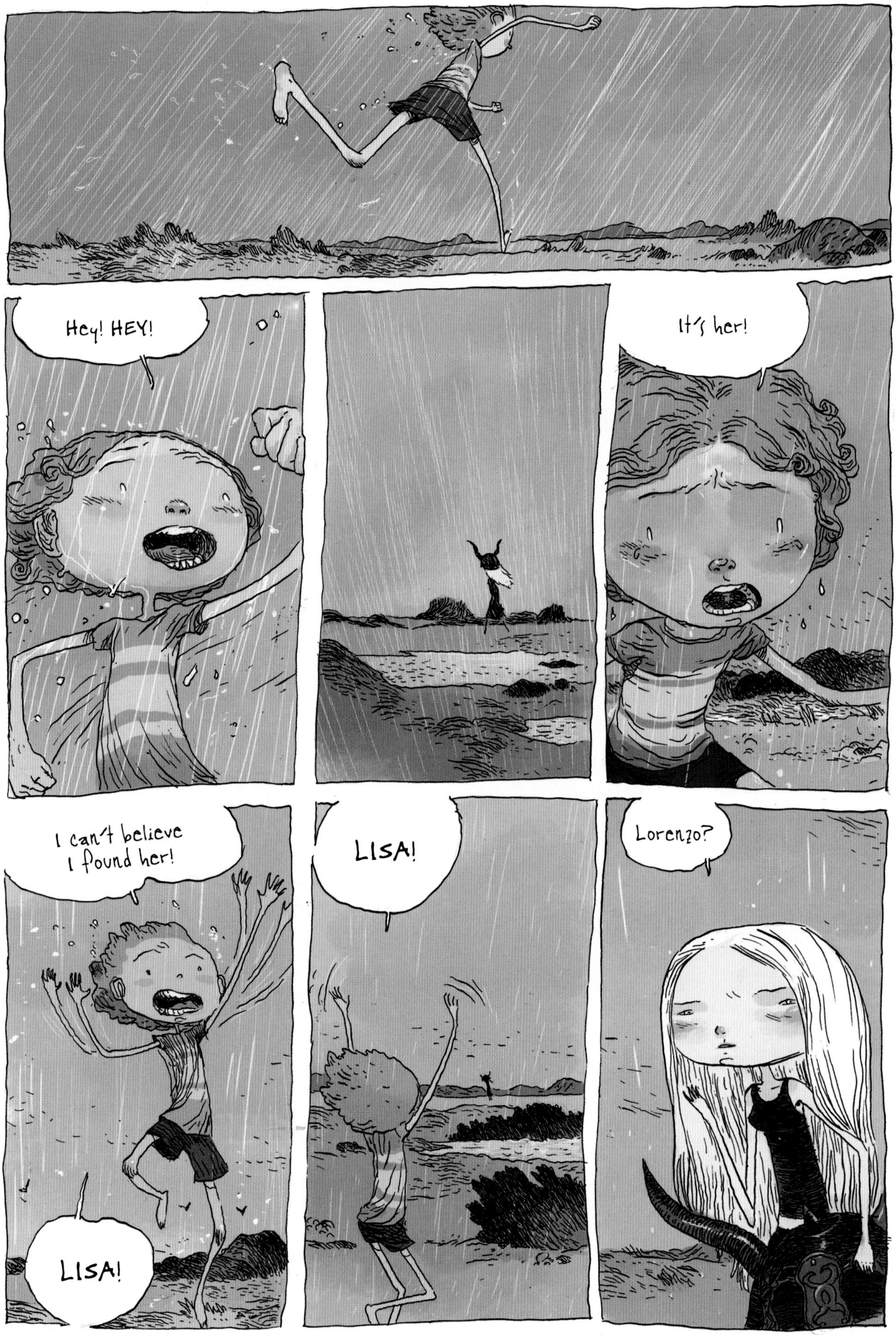
Hey! HEY!
It's her!
I can't believe
I found her!
LISA!
LISA!
Lorenzo?

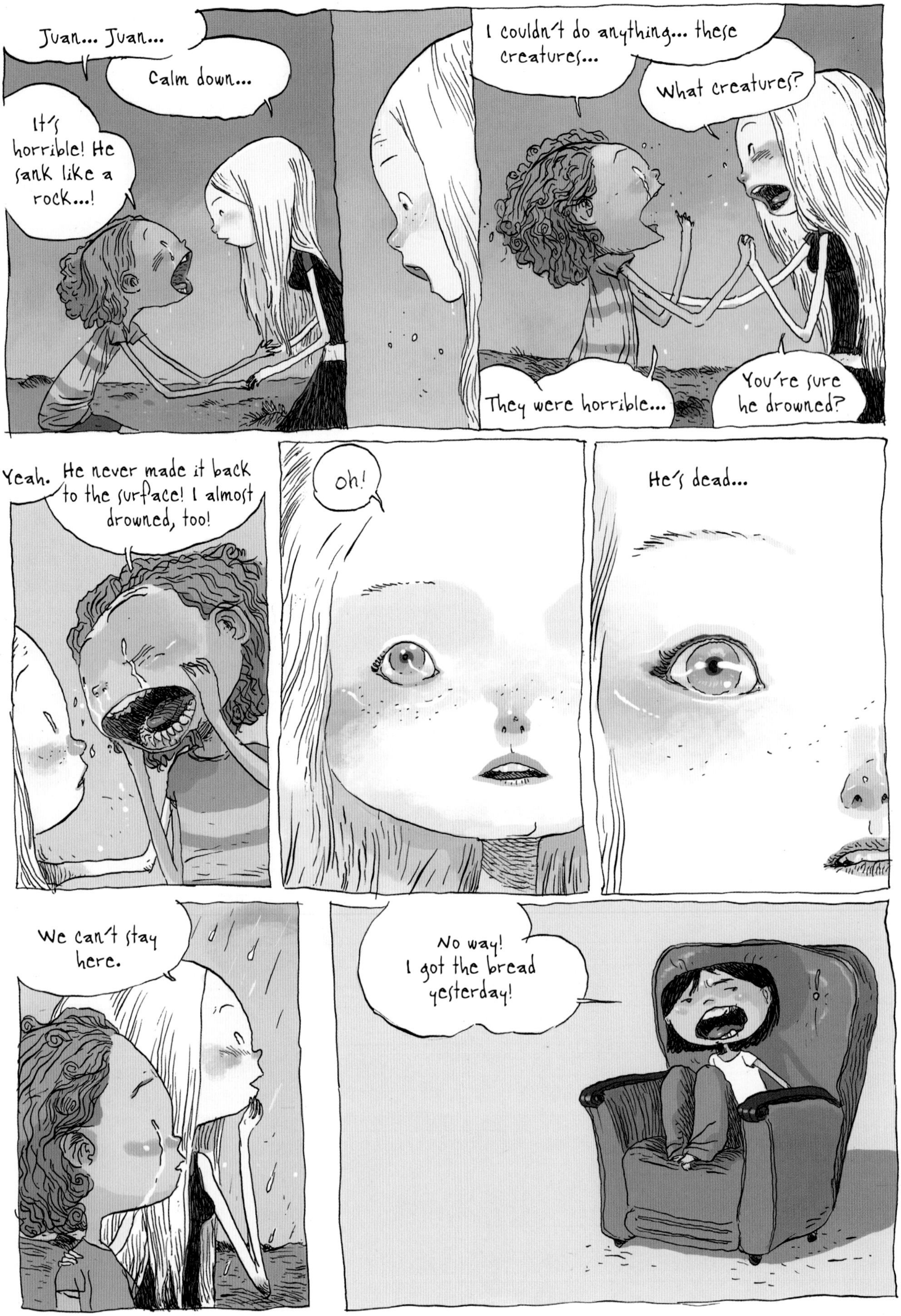
Juan... Juan...
Calm down...
It's horrible! He sank like a rock...!
I couldn't do anything... these creatures...
What creatures?
They were horrible...
You're sure he drowned?
Yeah.
He never made it back to the surface! I almost drowned, too!
Oh!
He's dead...
We can't stay here.
No way! I got the bread yesterday!

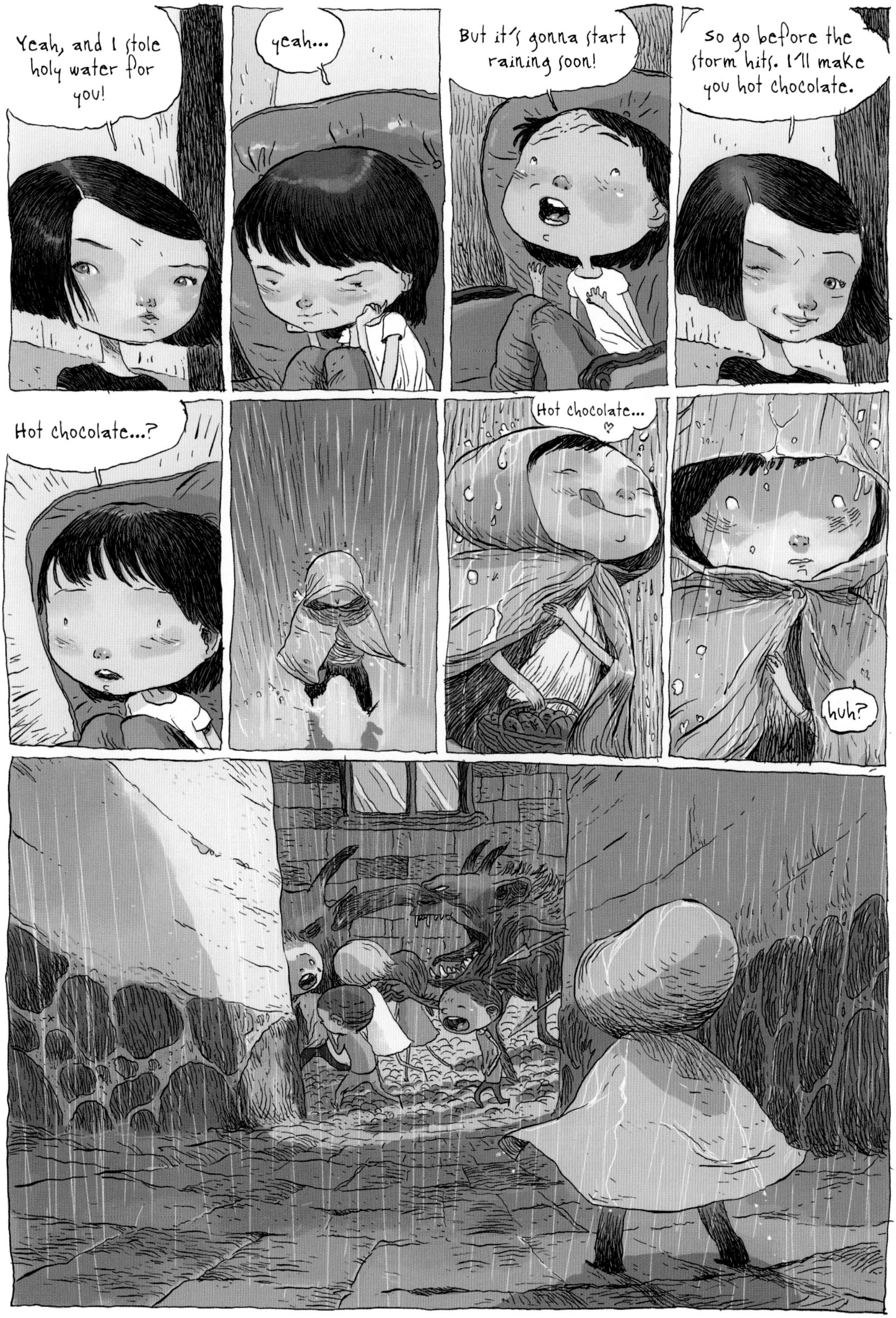
Yeah, and I stole holy water for you!
yeah...
But it's gonna start raining soon!
So go before the storm hits. I'll make you hot chocolate.
Hot chocolate...?
Hot chocolate...
huh?

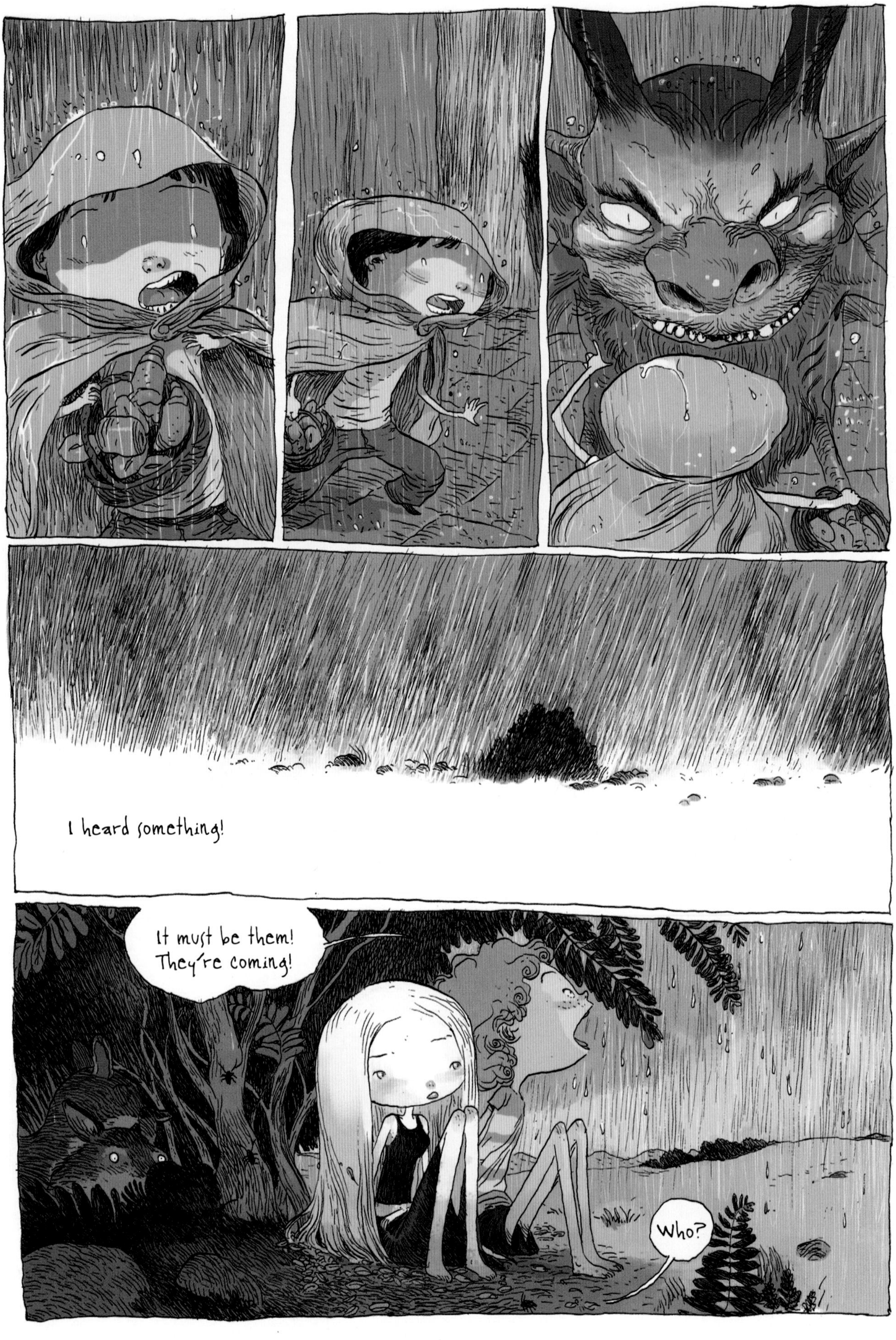
I heard something!
It must be them! They're coming!
Who?

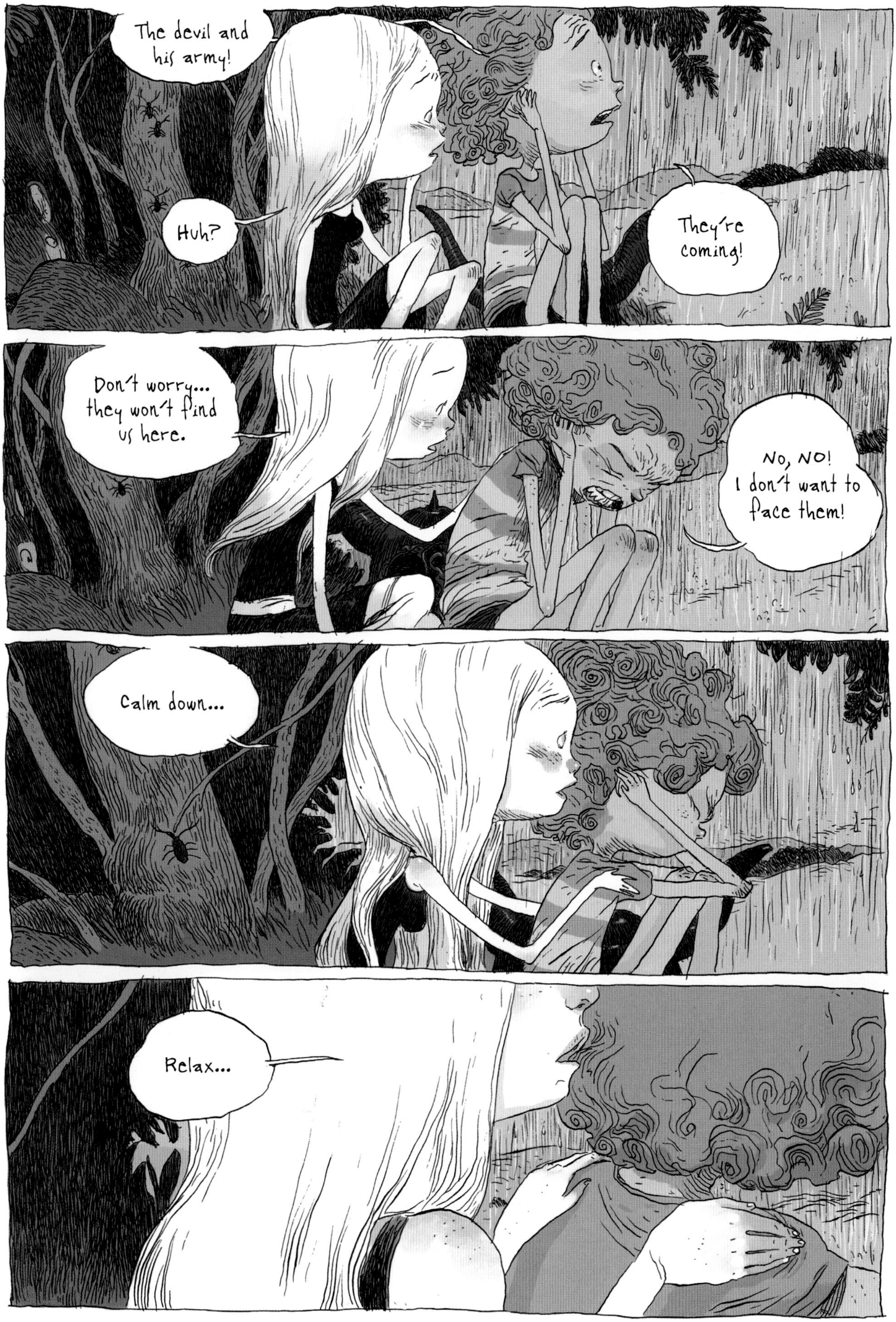
The devil and his army!
Huh?
They're coming!
Don't worry... they won't find us here.
No, NO! I don't want to face them!
Calm down...
Relax...

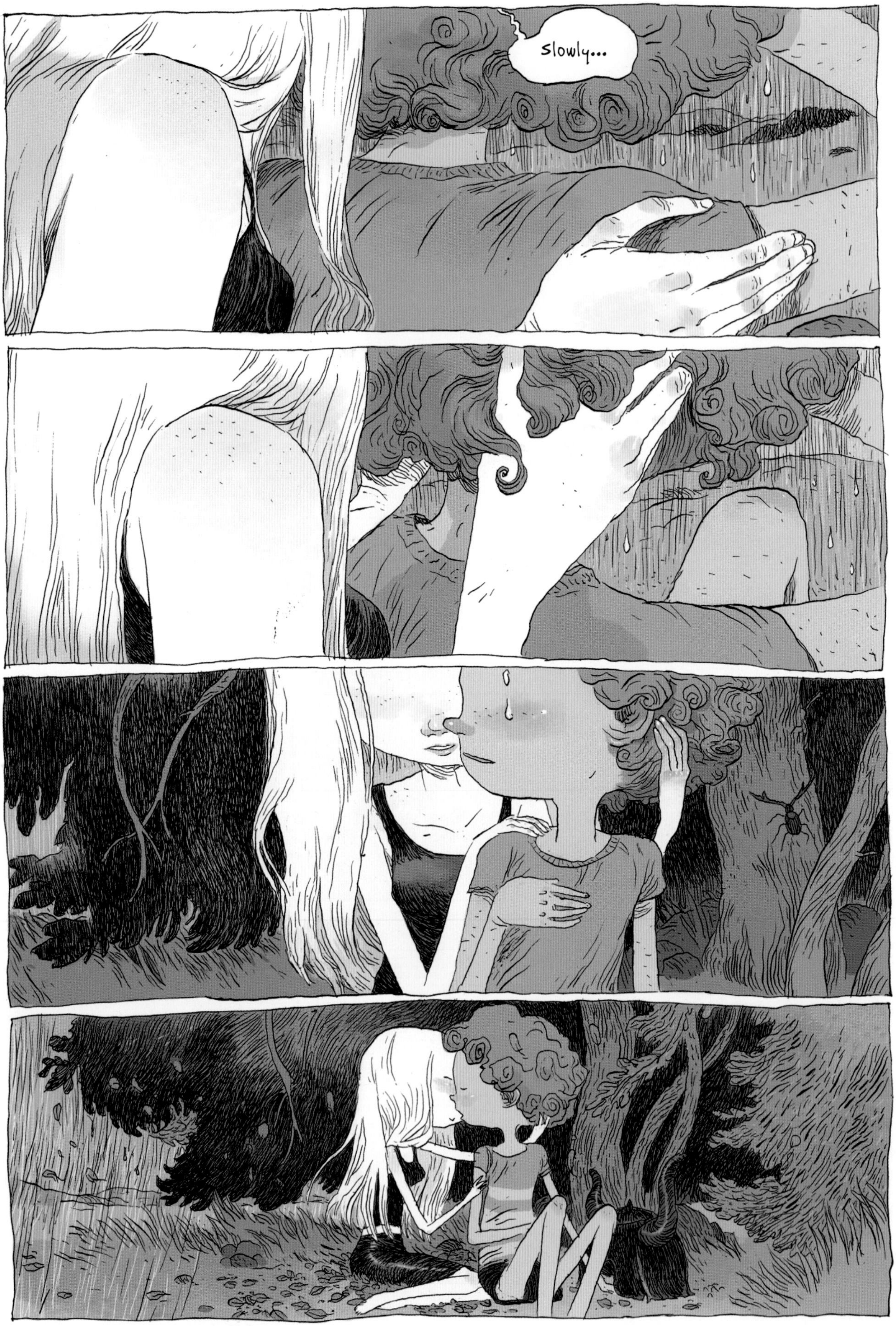
slowly...

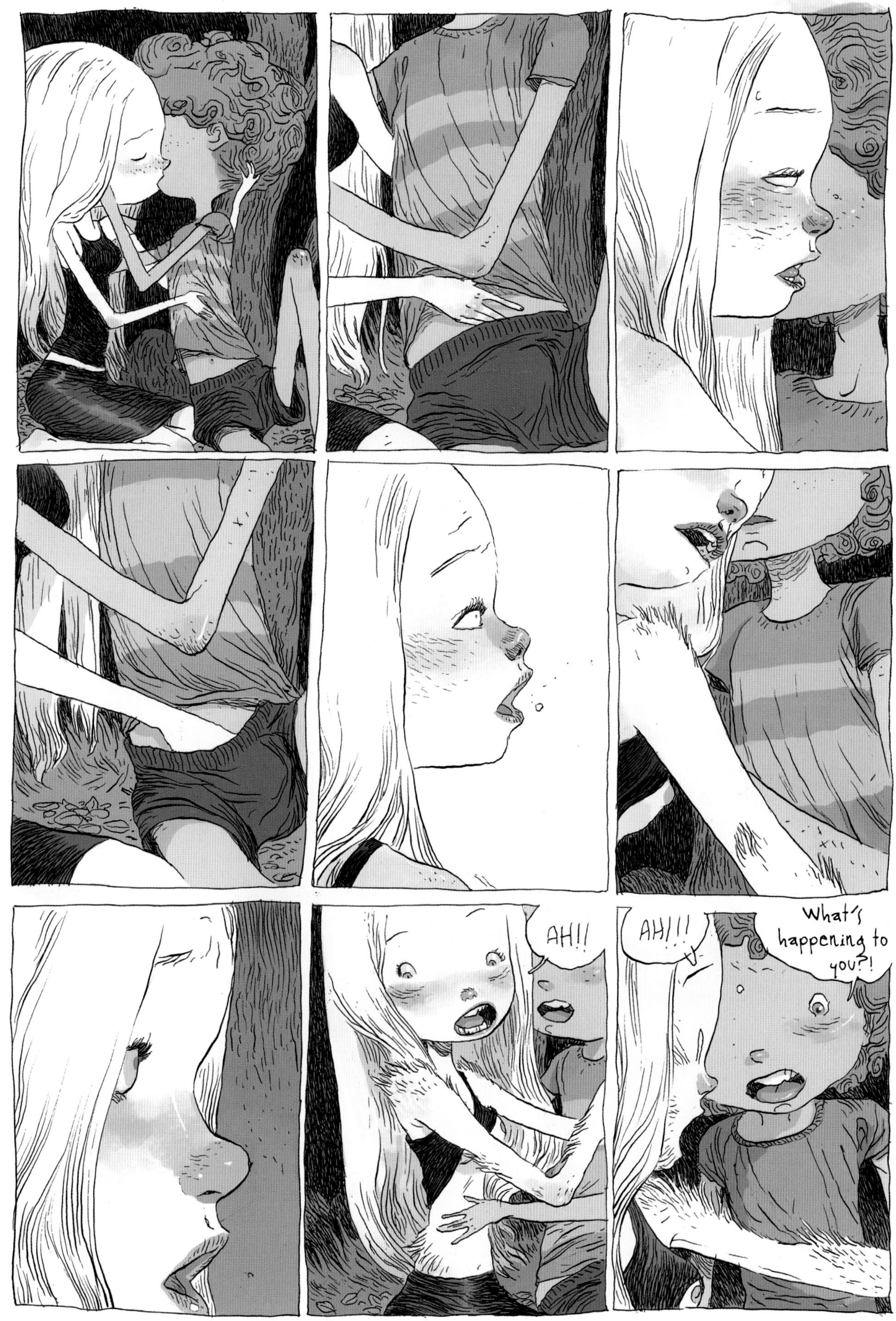
AH!!
AH!!!
What's happening to you?!

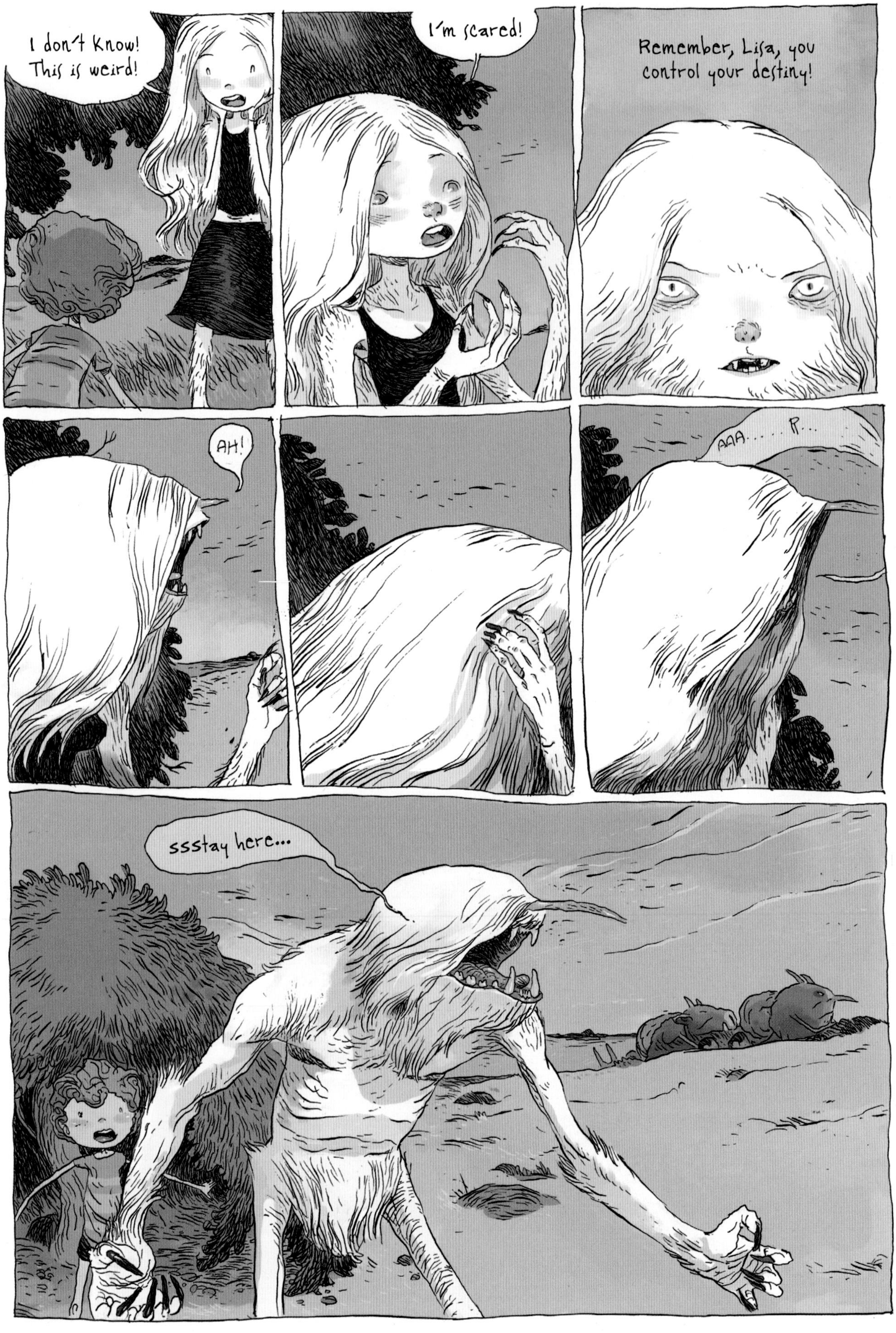
I don't Know! This is weird!
I'm scared!
Remember, Lisa, you control your destiny!
AH!
AAA...... P...
ssstay here...

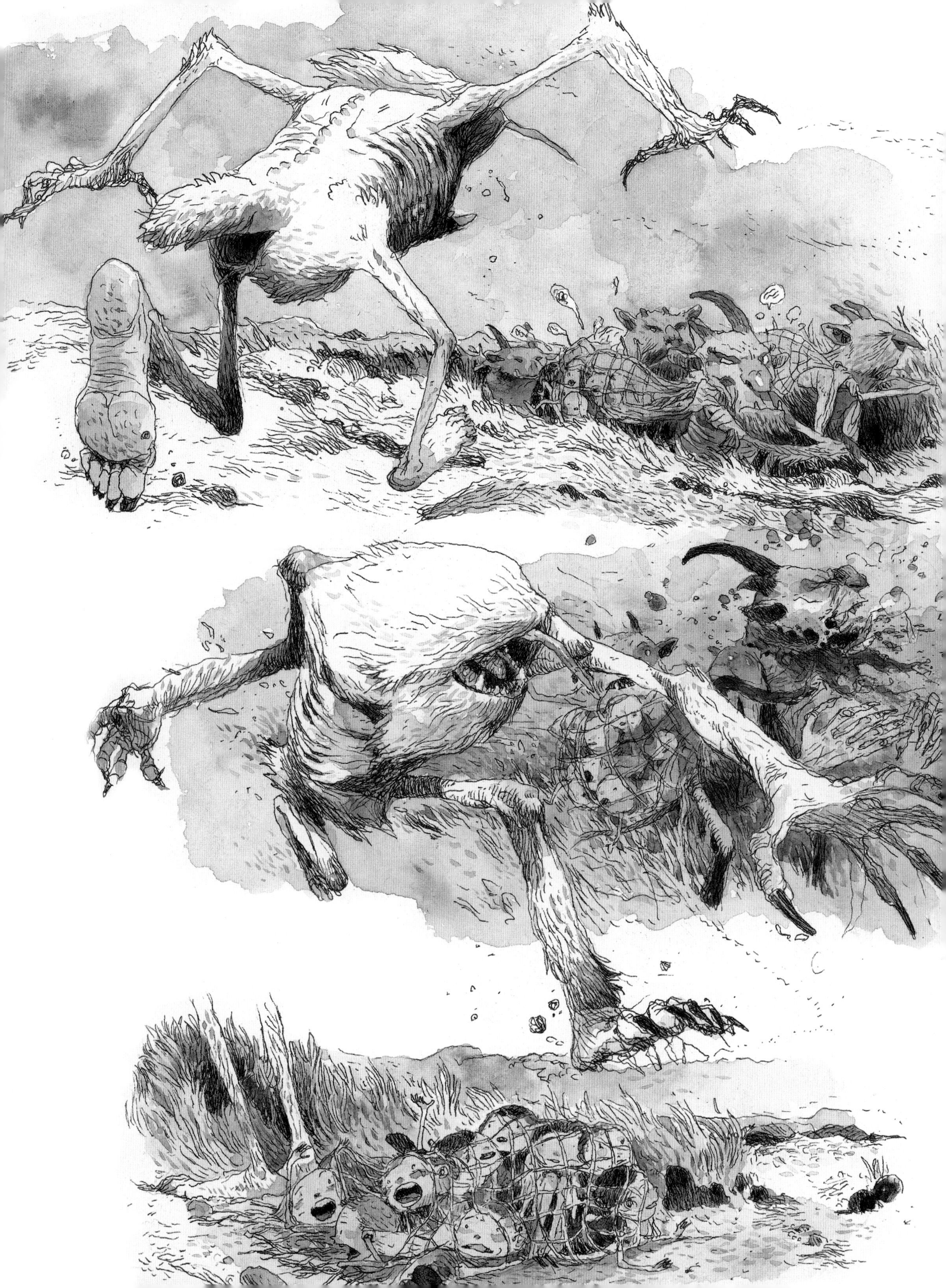

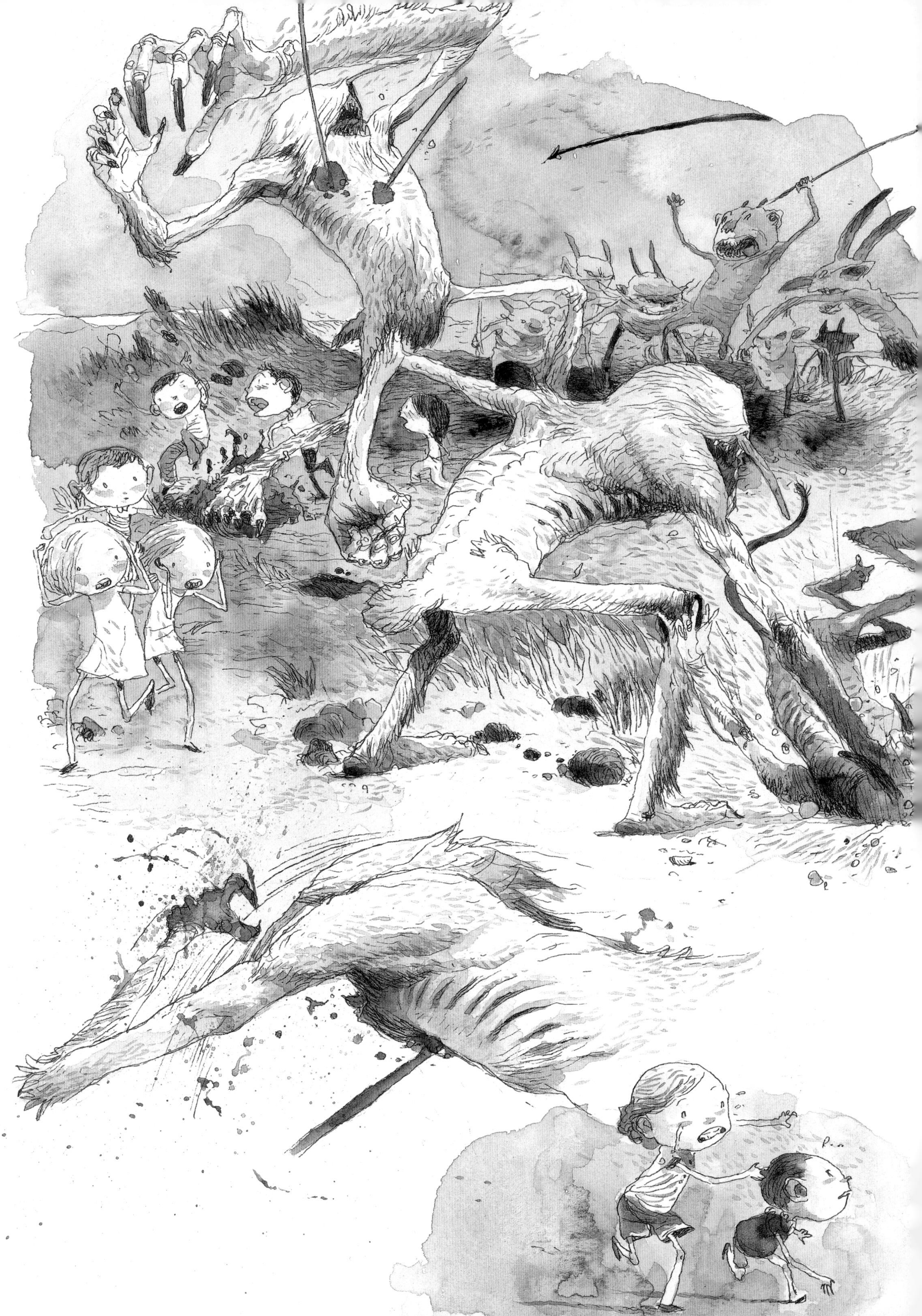

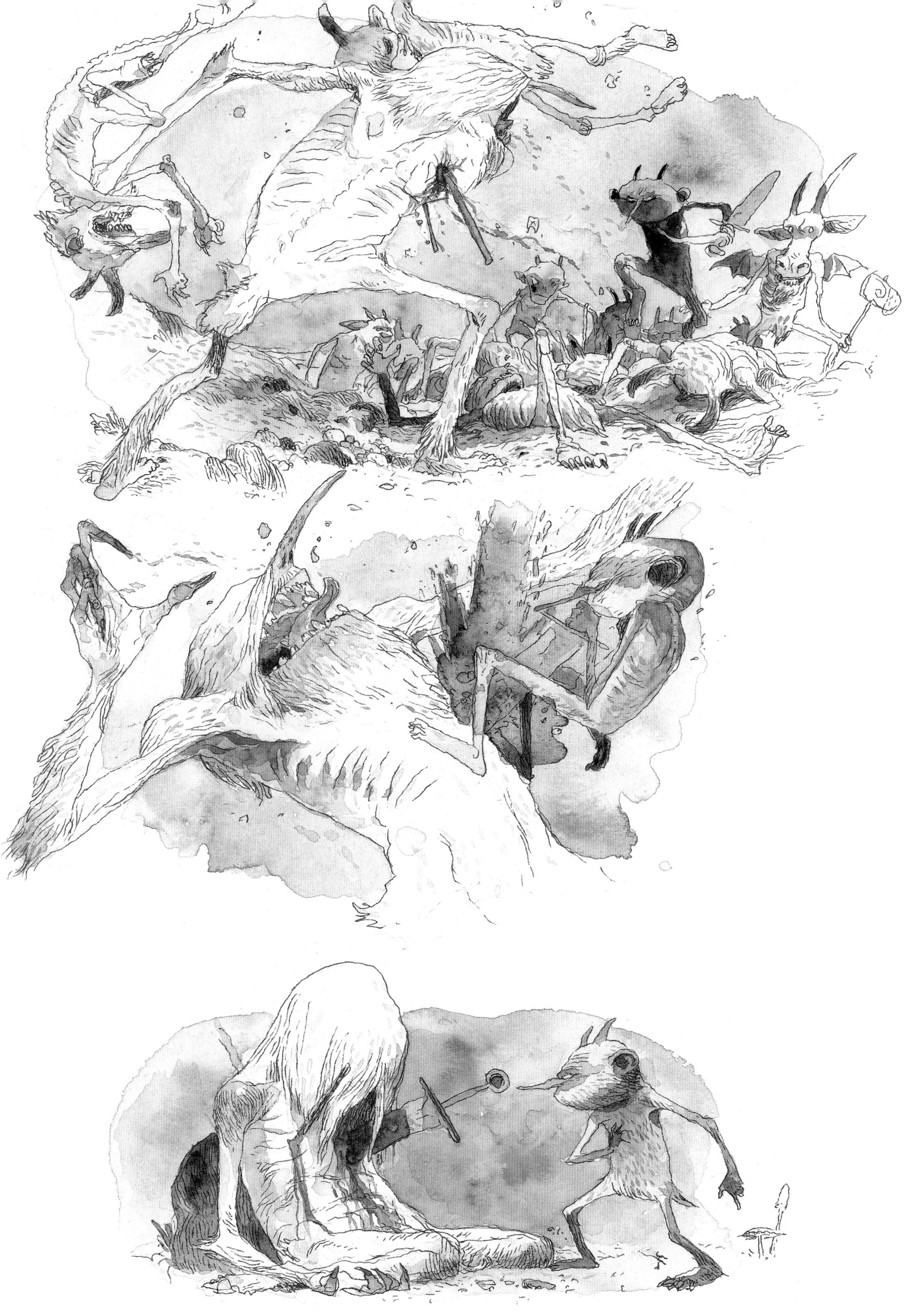

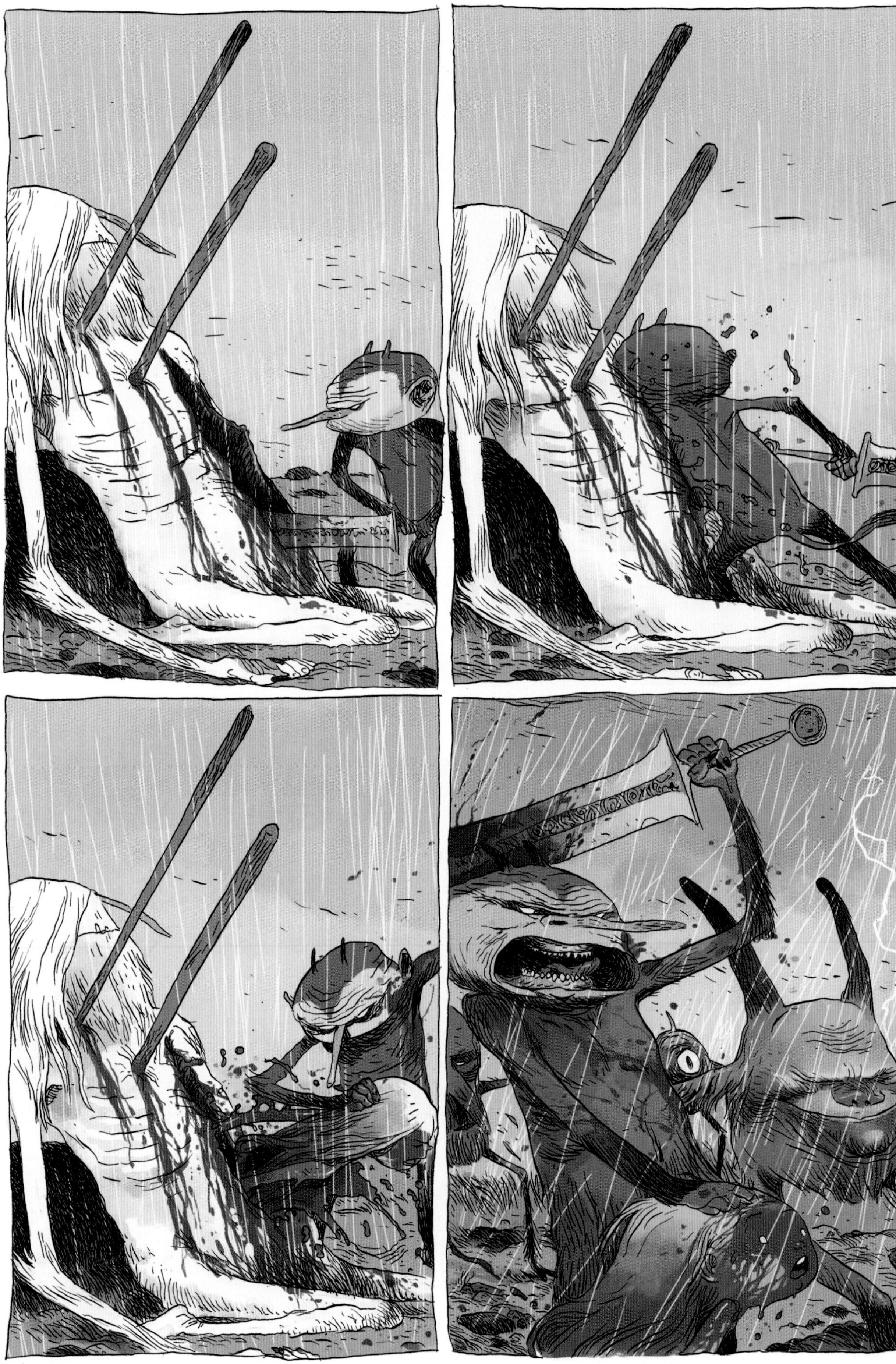

ZWIK!
BAM!
BLAM!

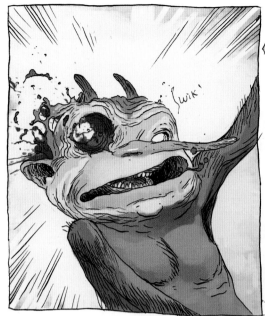

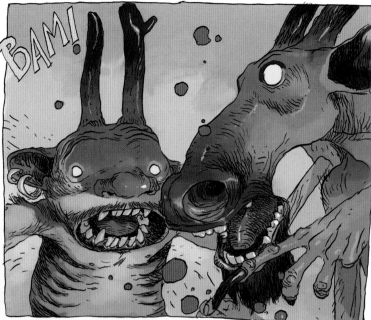

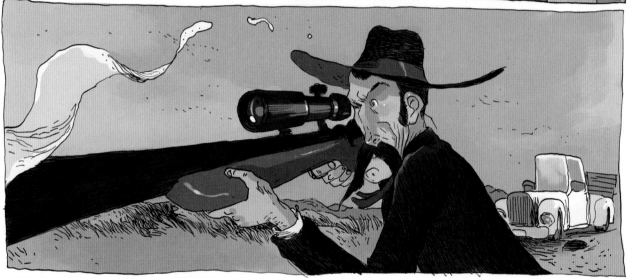

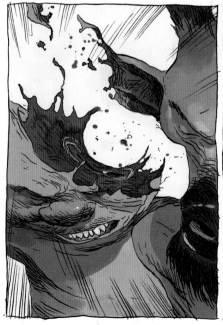

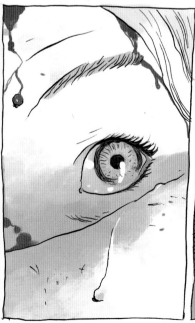

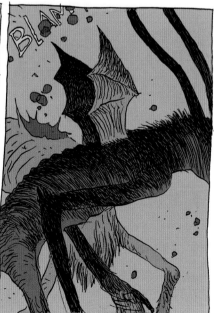

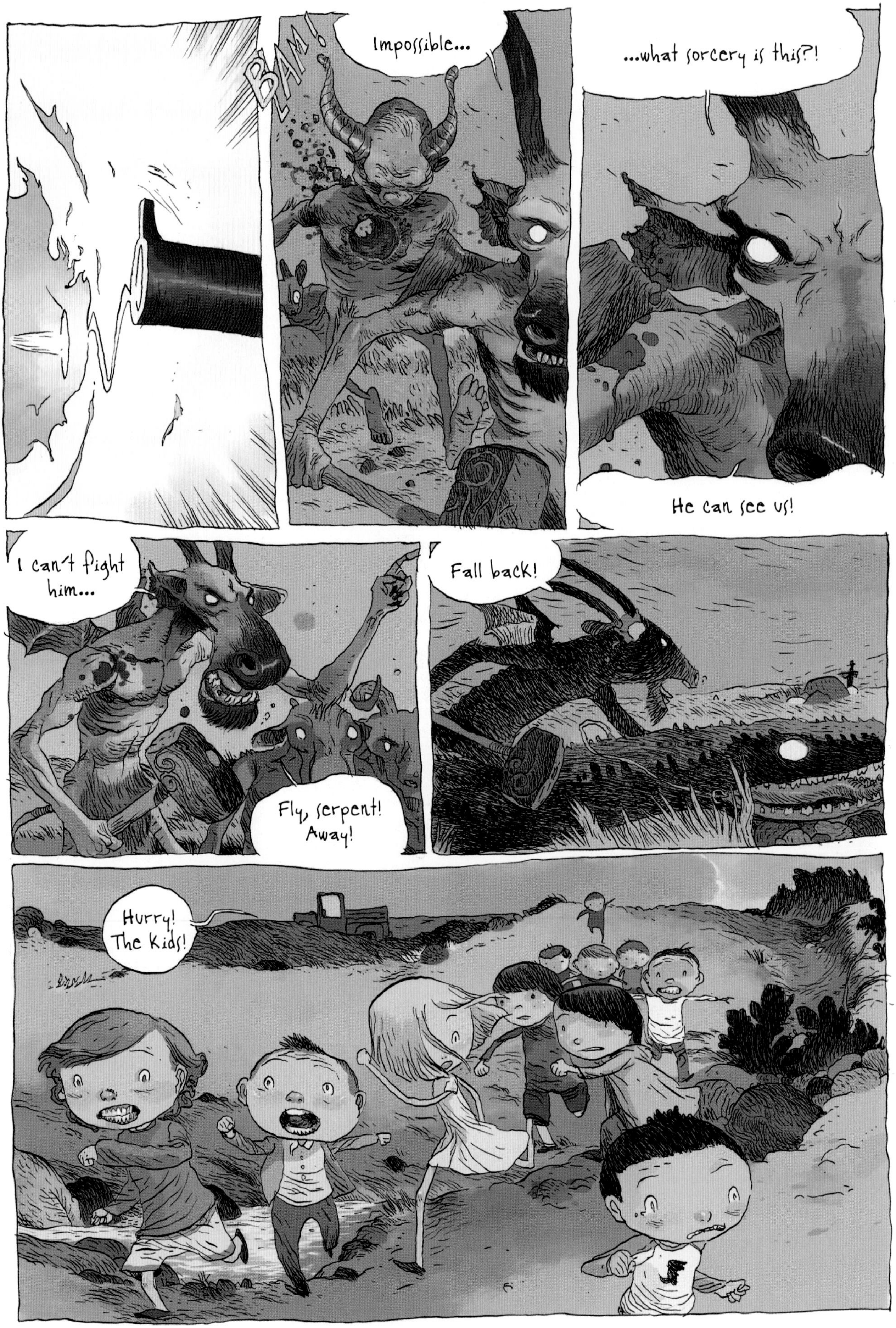
BLAM!
Impossible...
...what sorcery is this?!
He can see us!
I can't fight him...
Fly, serpent! Away!
Fall back!
Hurry! The kids!

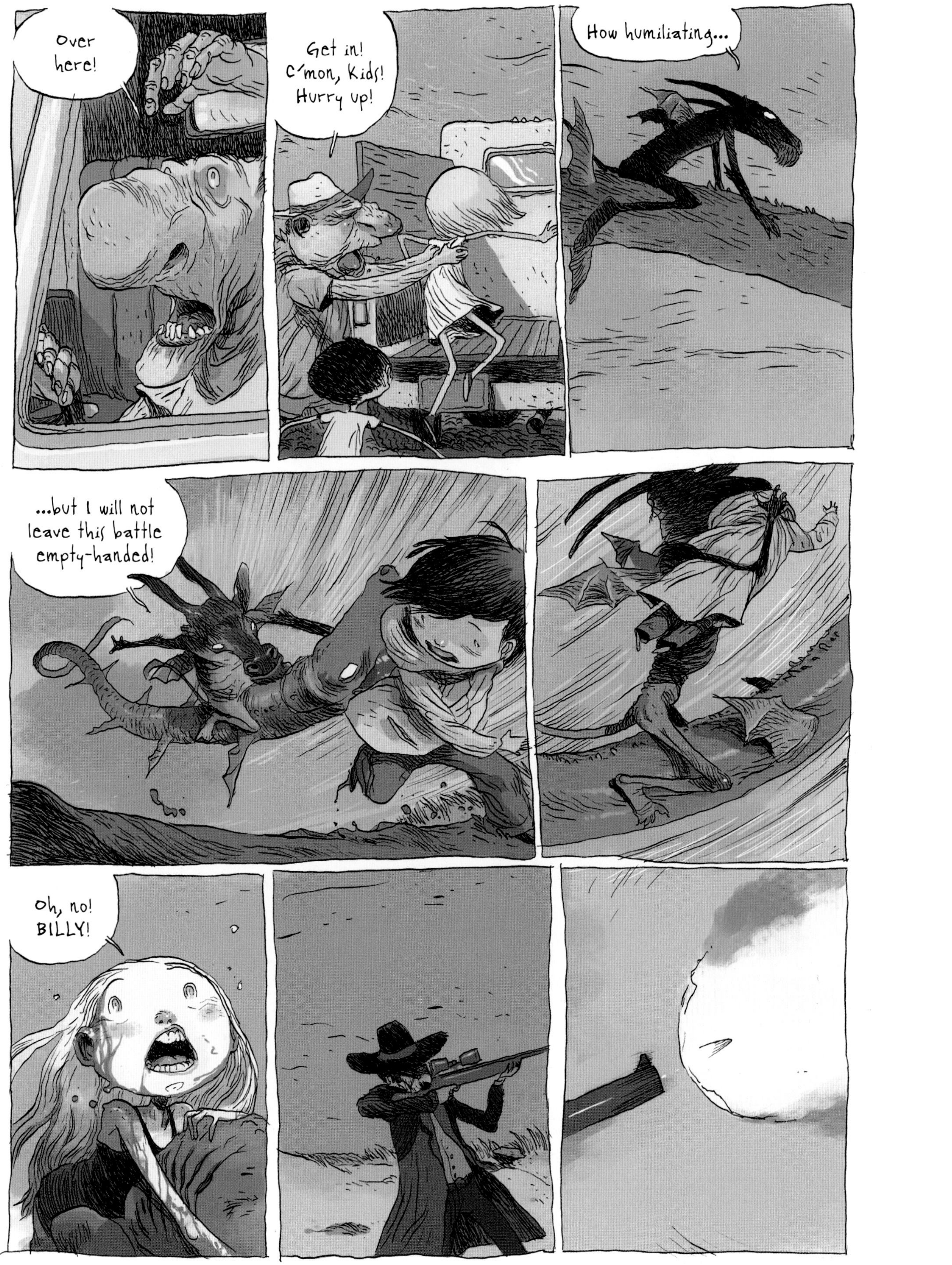
Over here!
Get in! C'mon, kids! Hurry up!
How humiliating...
...but I will not leave this battle empty-handed!
Oh, no! BILLY!

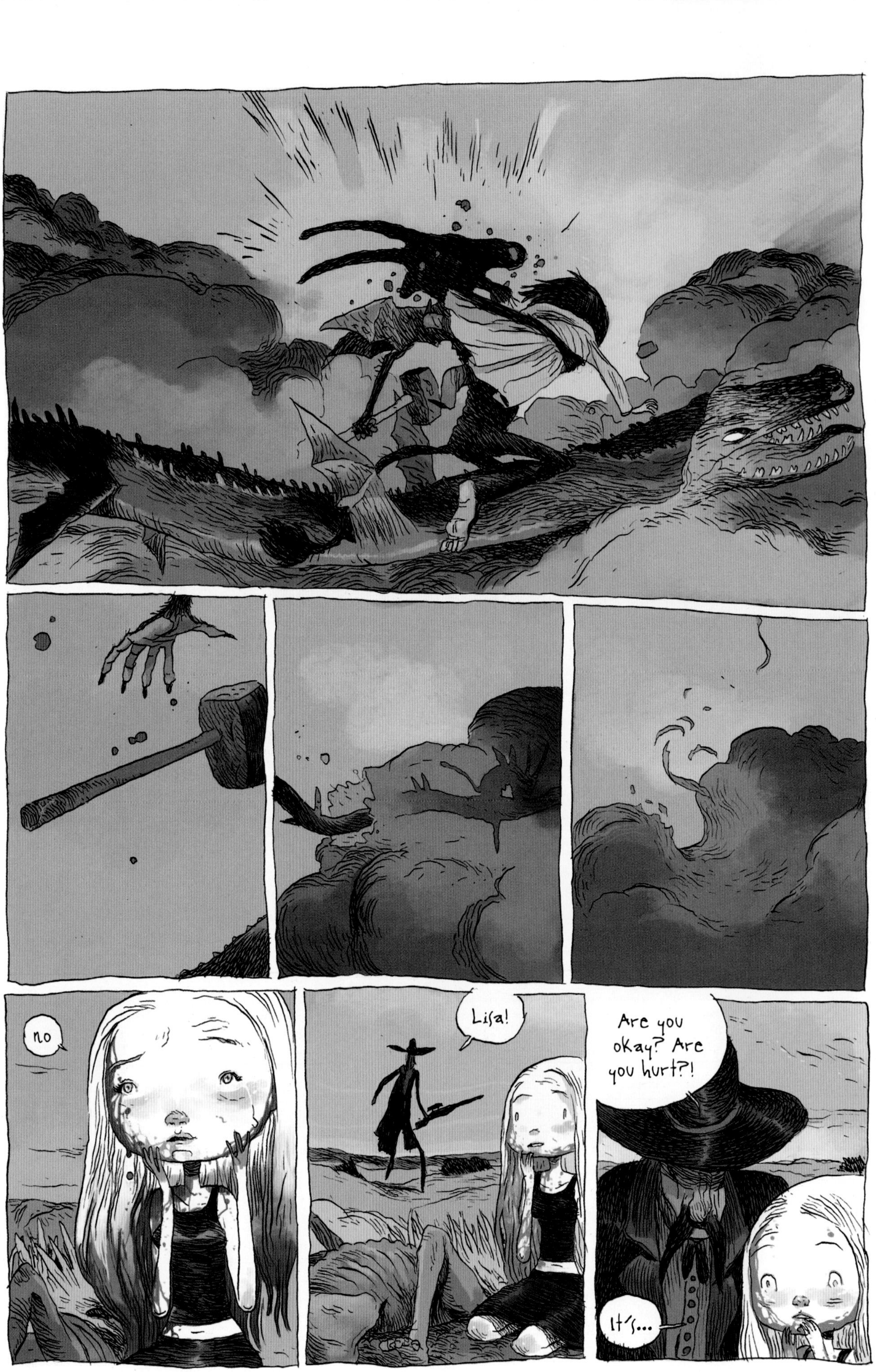
no
Lisa!
Are you okay? Are you hurt?!
It's...

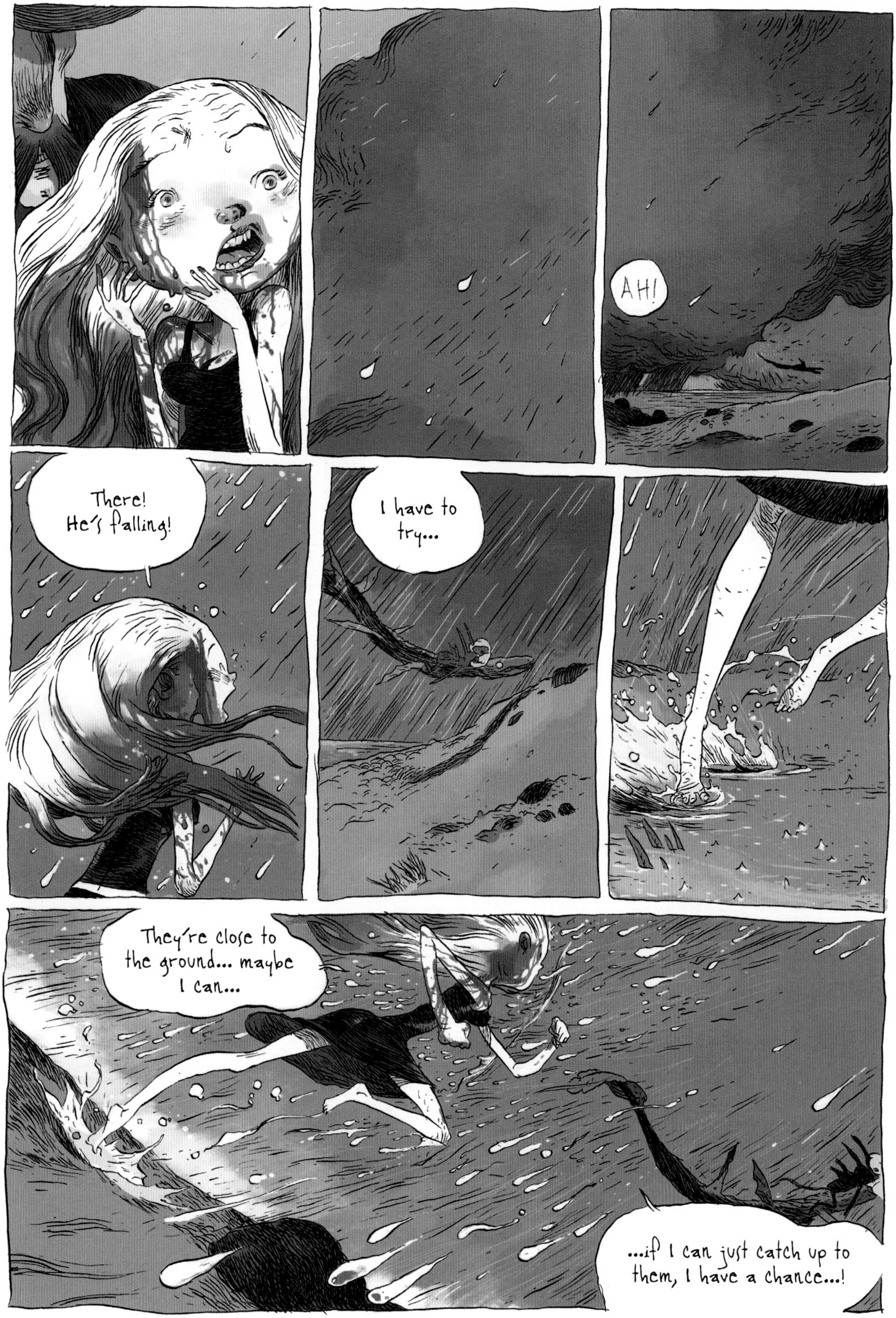
AH!
There! He's falling!
I have to try...
They're close to the ground... maybe I can...
...if I can just catch up to them, I have a chance...!

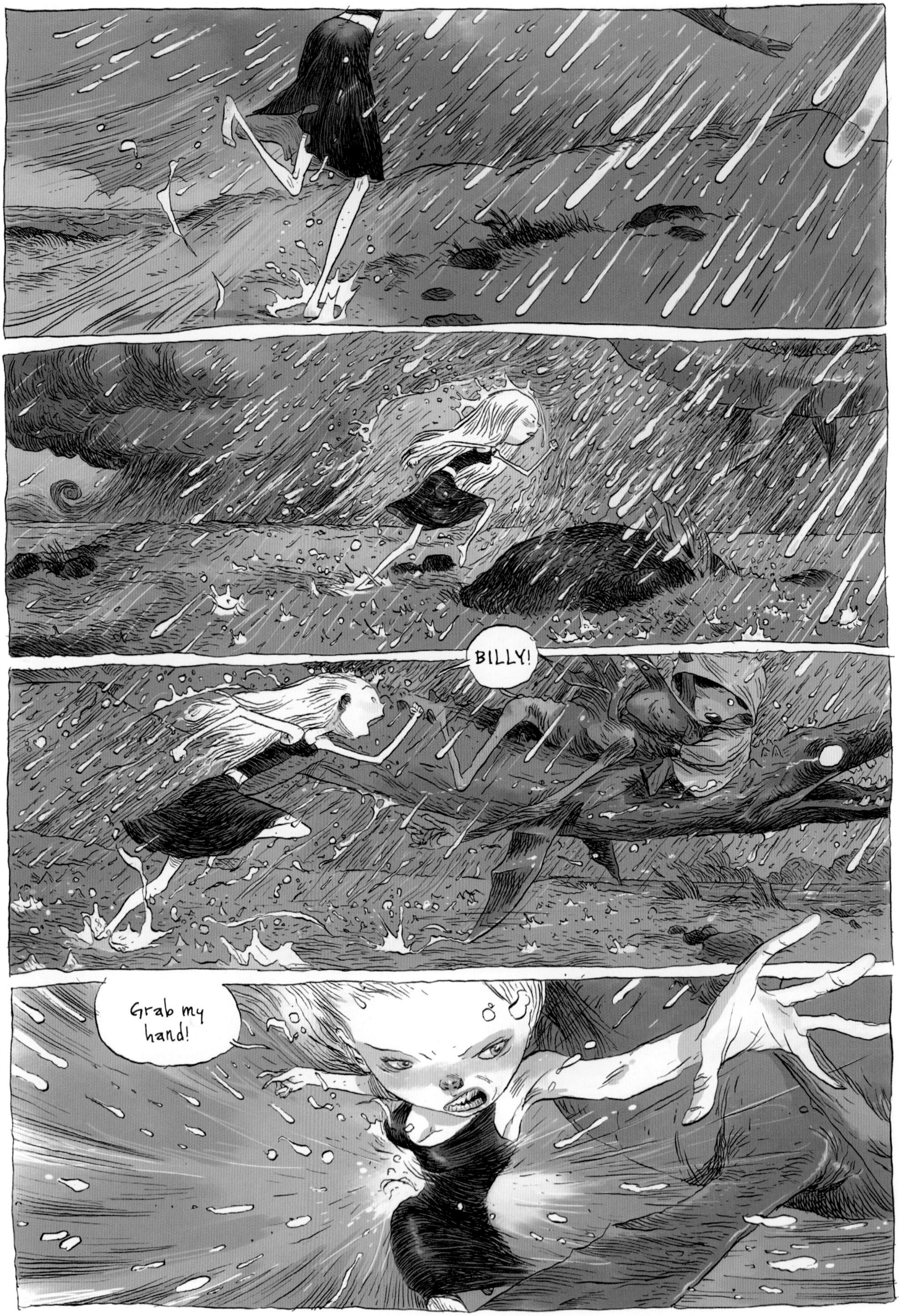
BILLY!
Grab my hand!

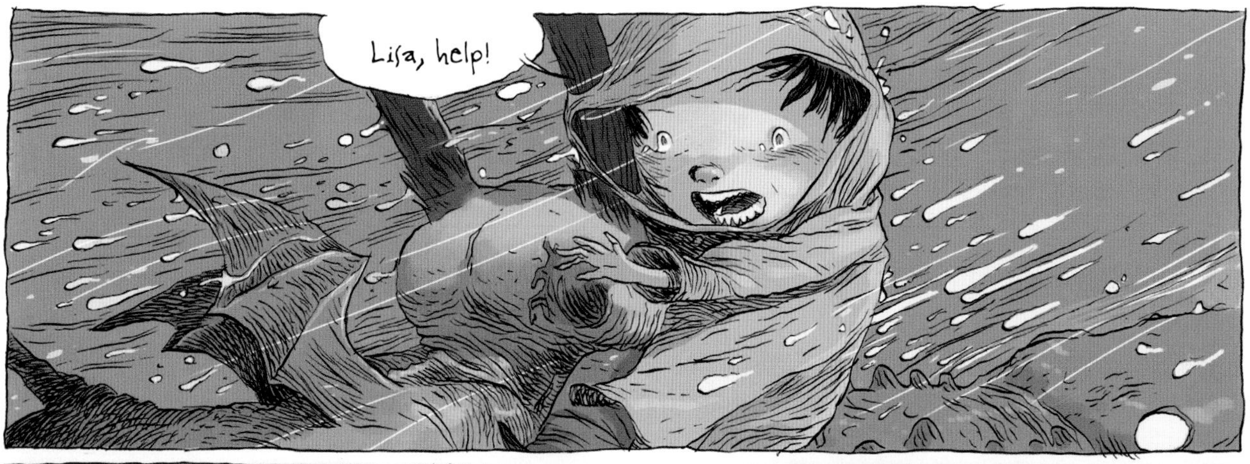
Lisa, help!
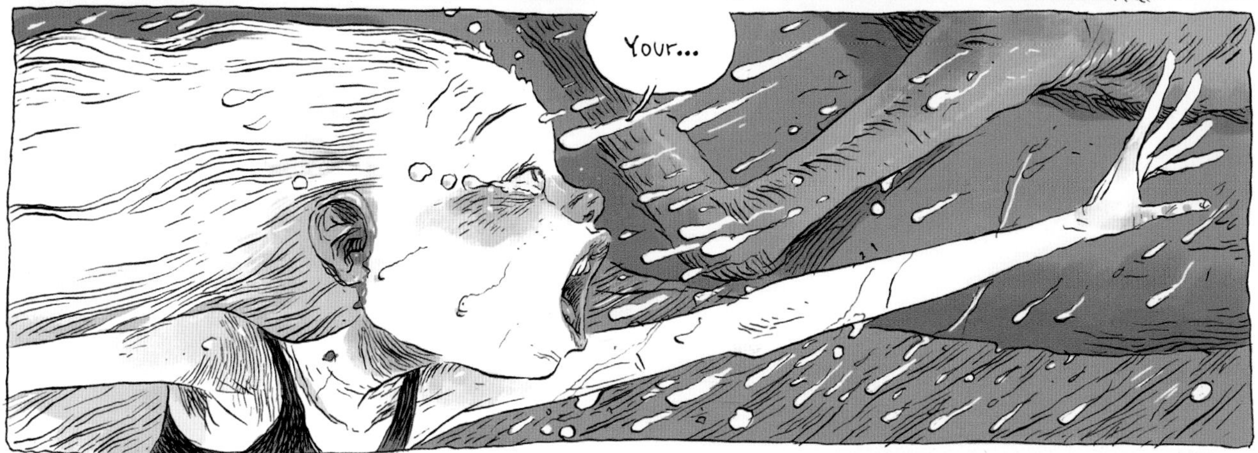
Your...
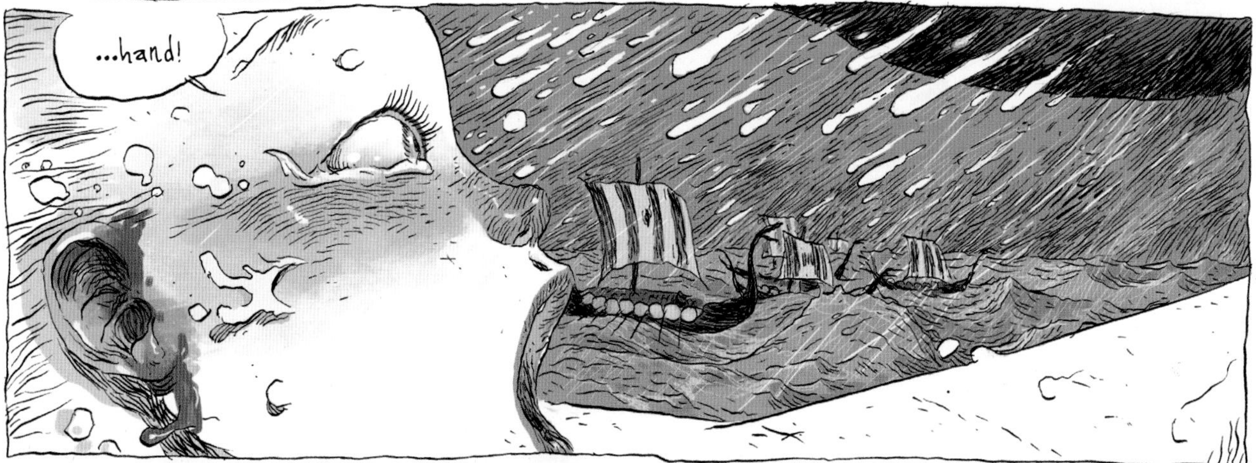
...hand!
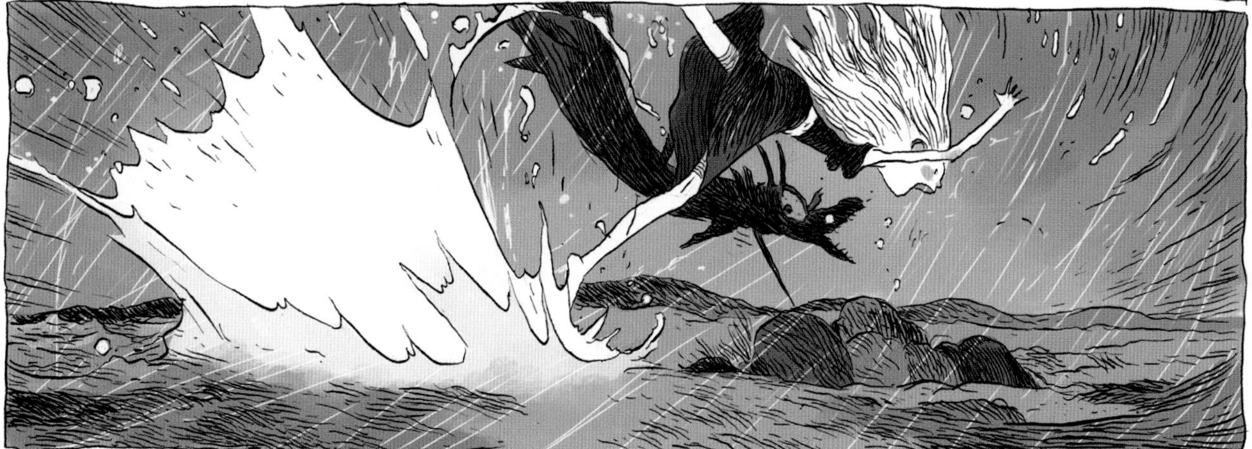

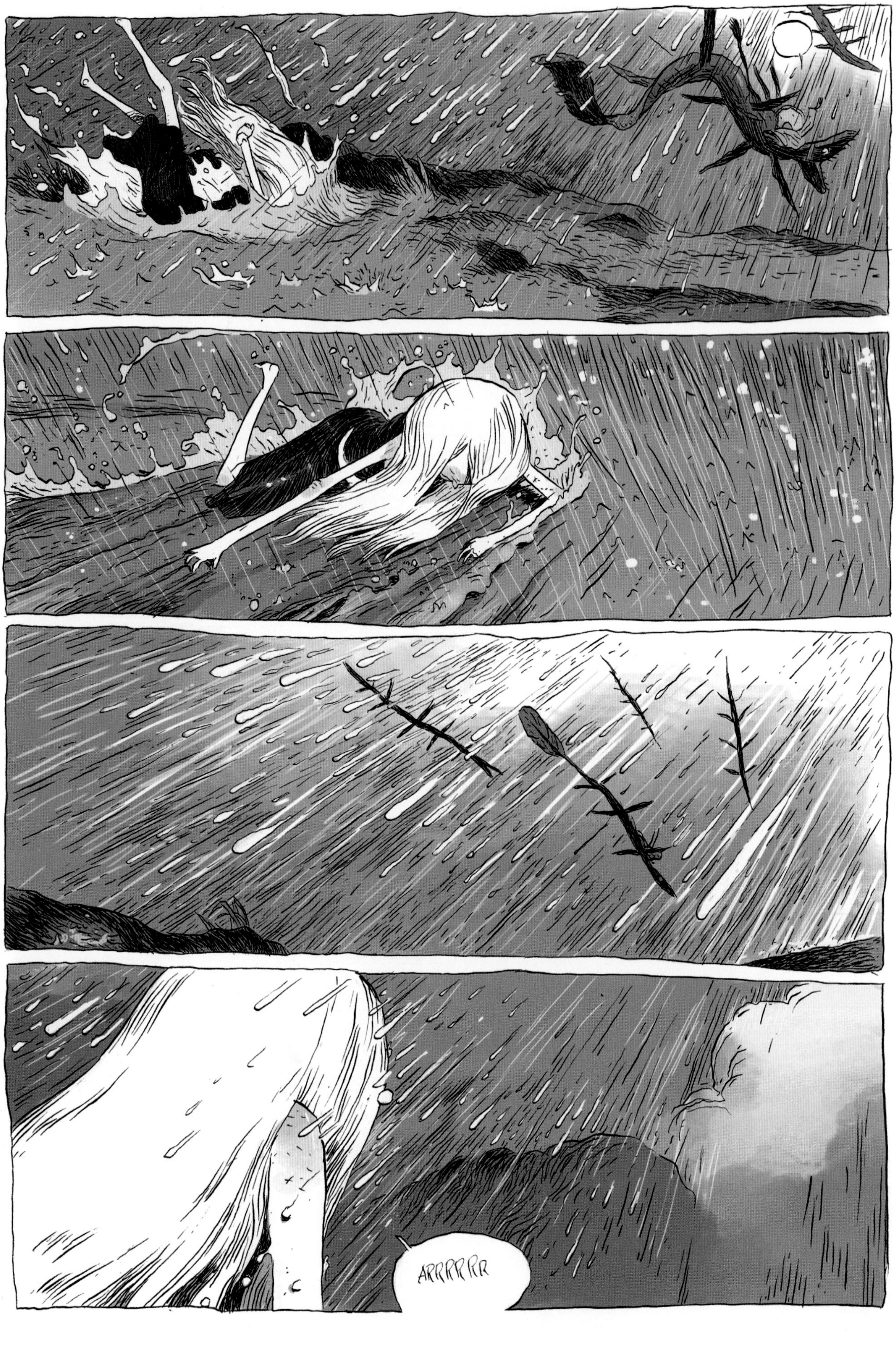
ARRRRRR

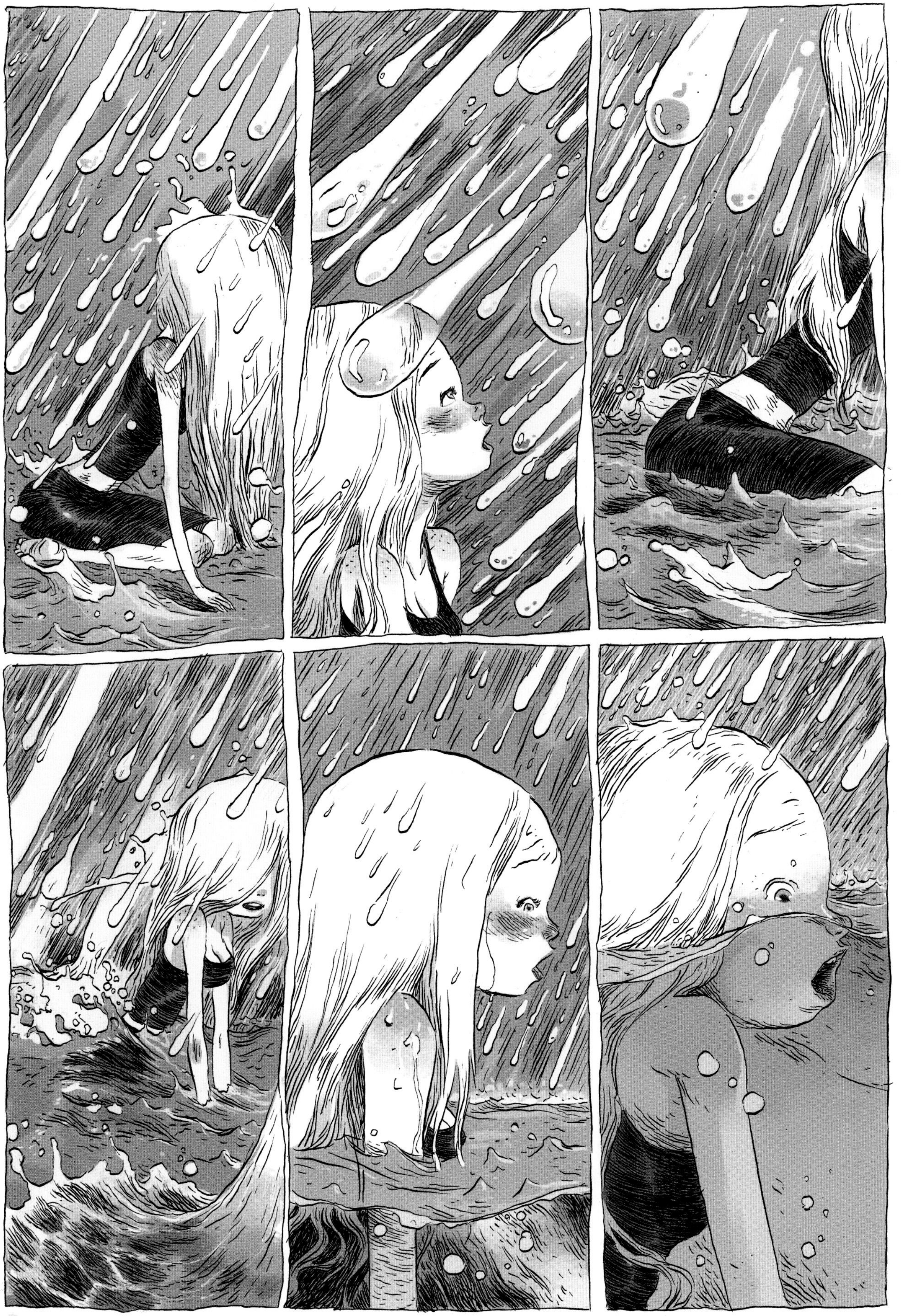

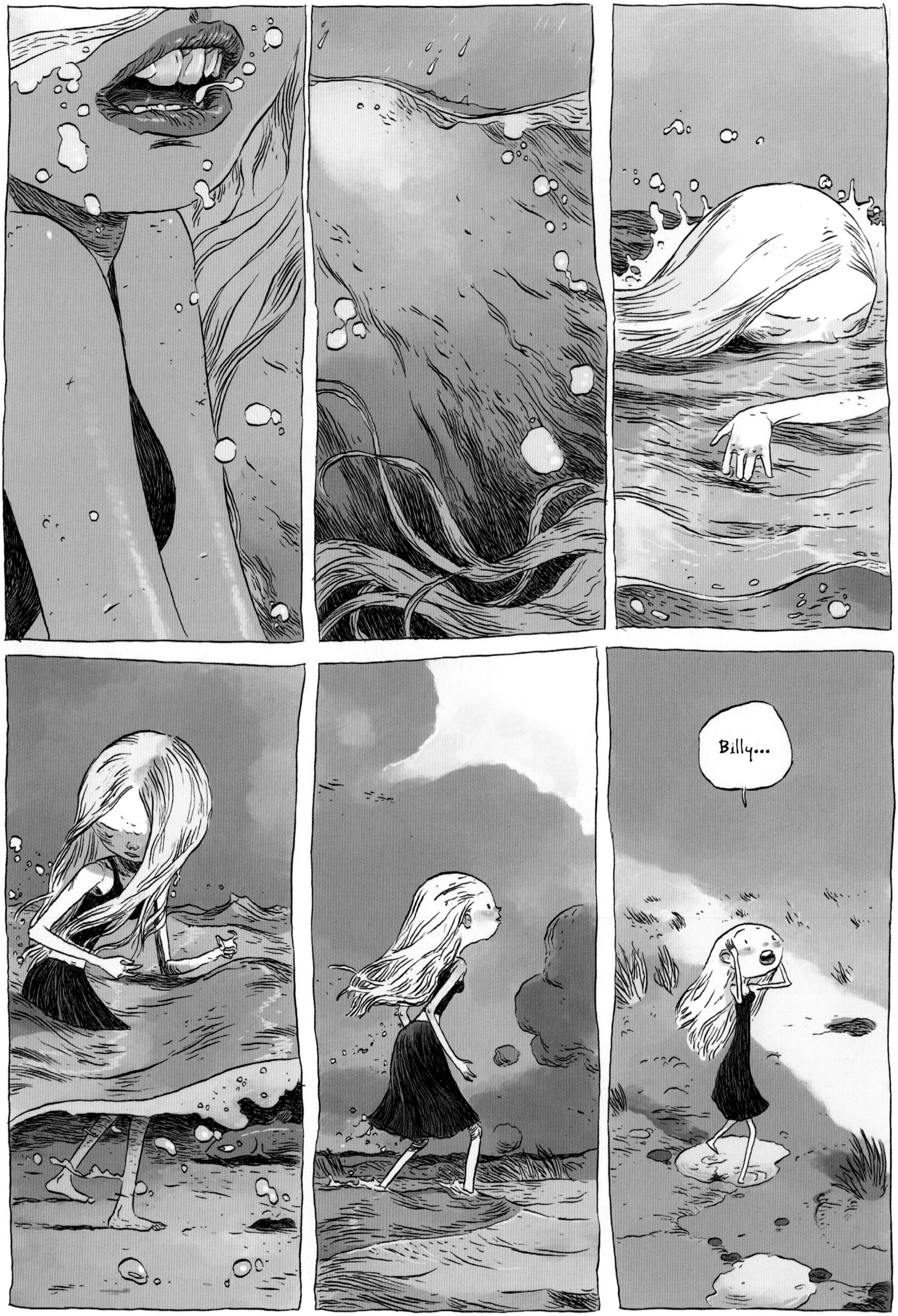
Billy...

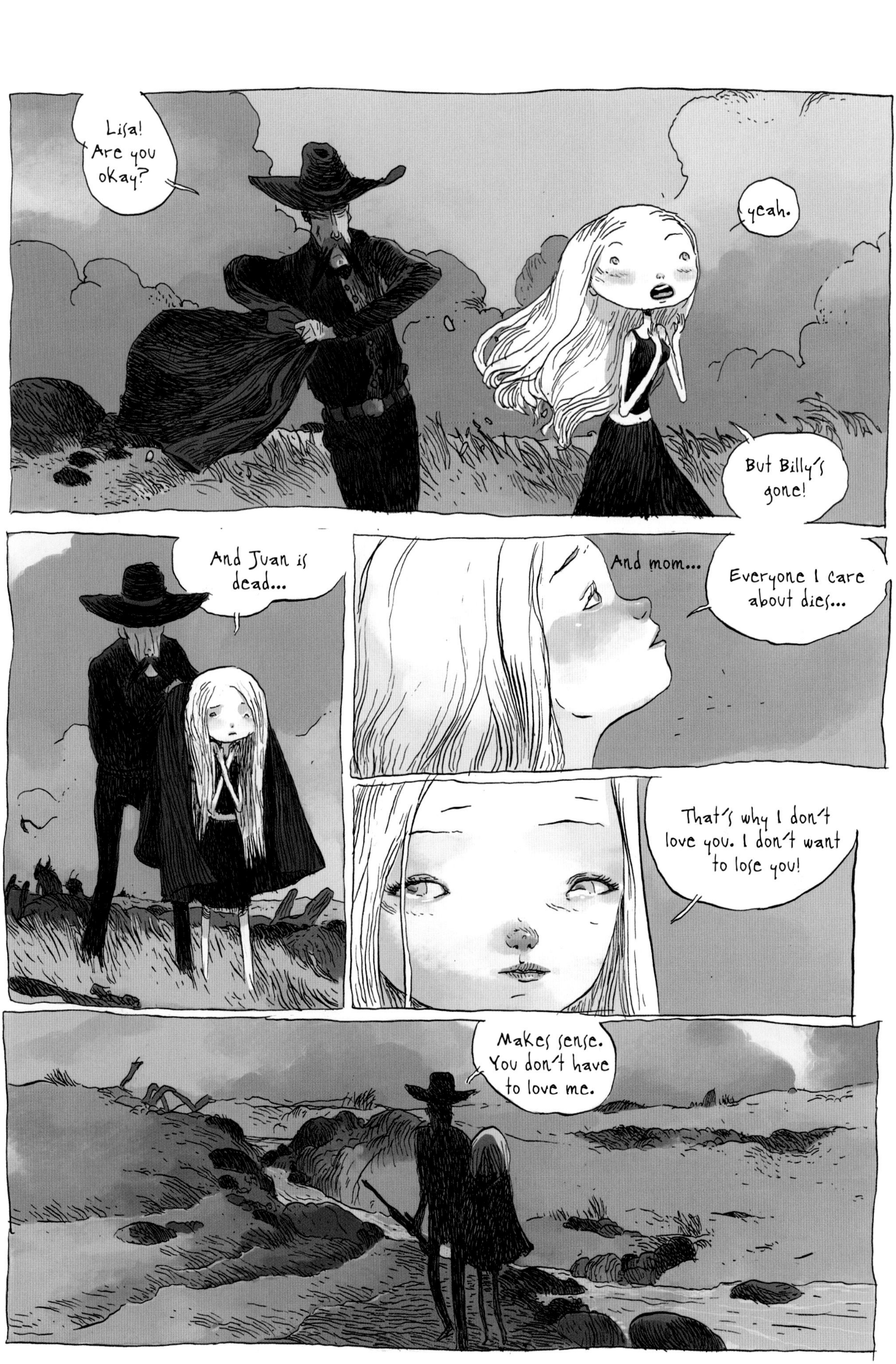
Lisa! Are you okay?
yeah.
But Billy's gone!
And Juan is dead...
And mom...
Everyone I care about dies...
That's why I don't love you. I don't want to lose you!
Makes sense. You don't have to love me.

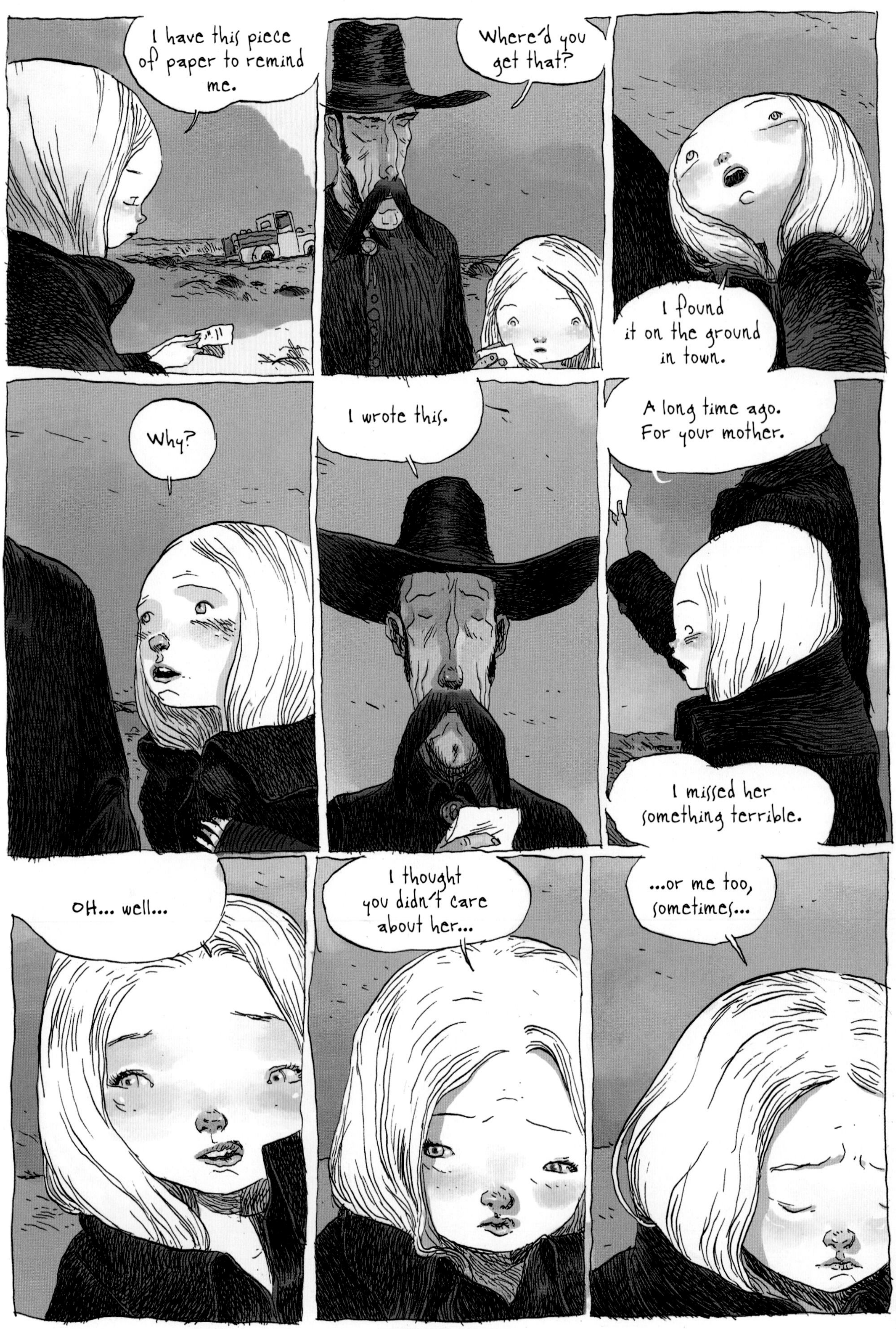
I have this piece of paper to remind me.
Where'd you get that?
I found it on the ground in town.
Why?
I wrote this.
A long time ago. For your mother.
I missed her something terrible.
OH... well...
I thought you didn't care about her...
...or me too, sometimes...

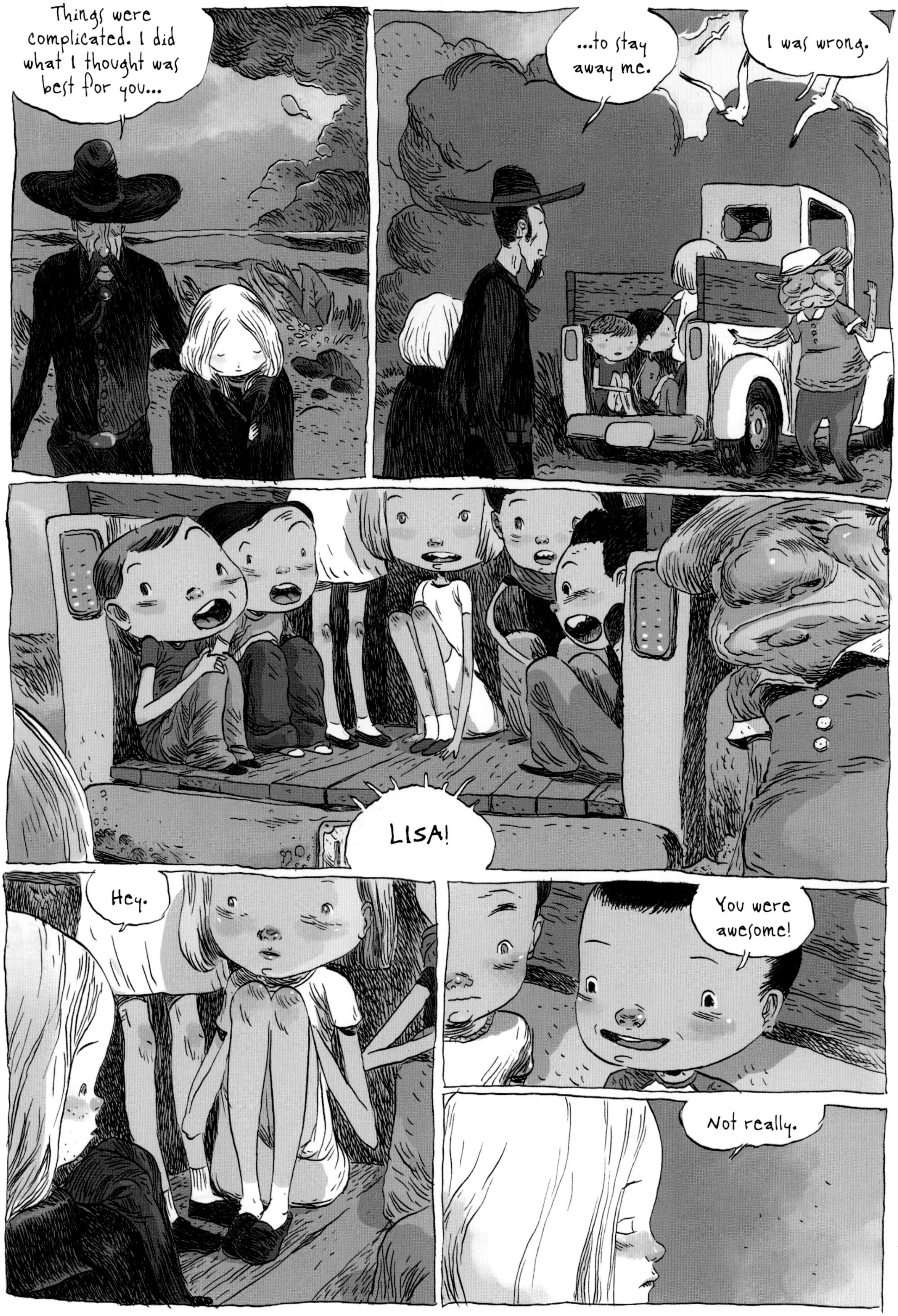
Things were complicated. I did what I thought was best for you...
...to stay away me.
I was wrong.
LISA!
Hey.
You were awesome!
Not really.

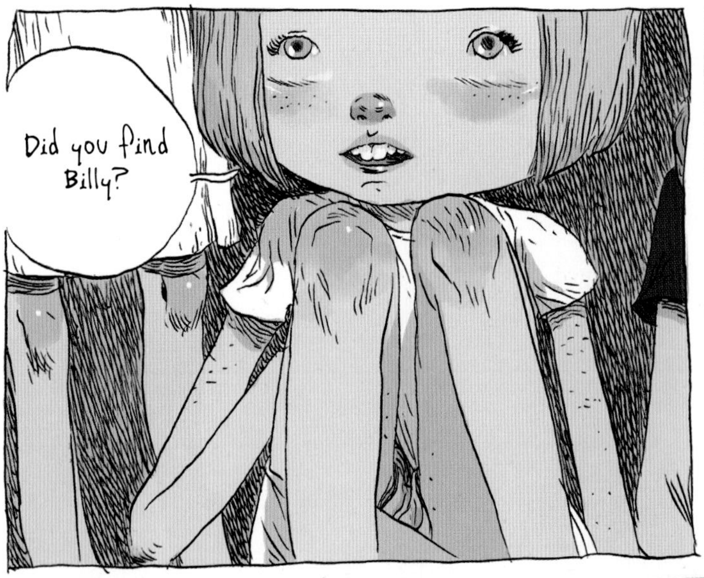
Did you find Billy?

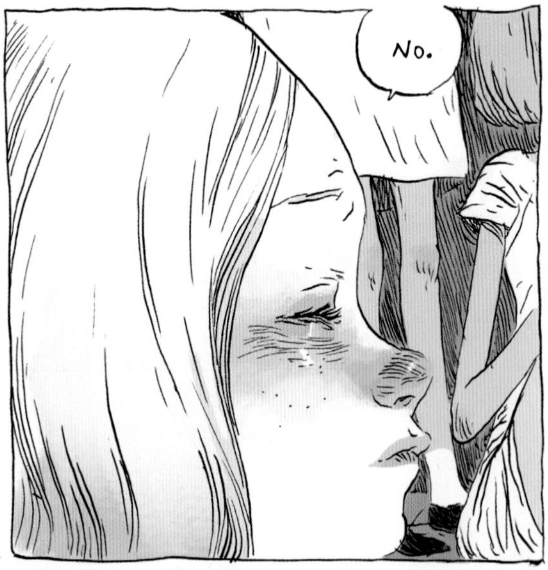
No.

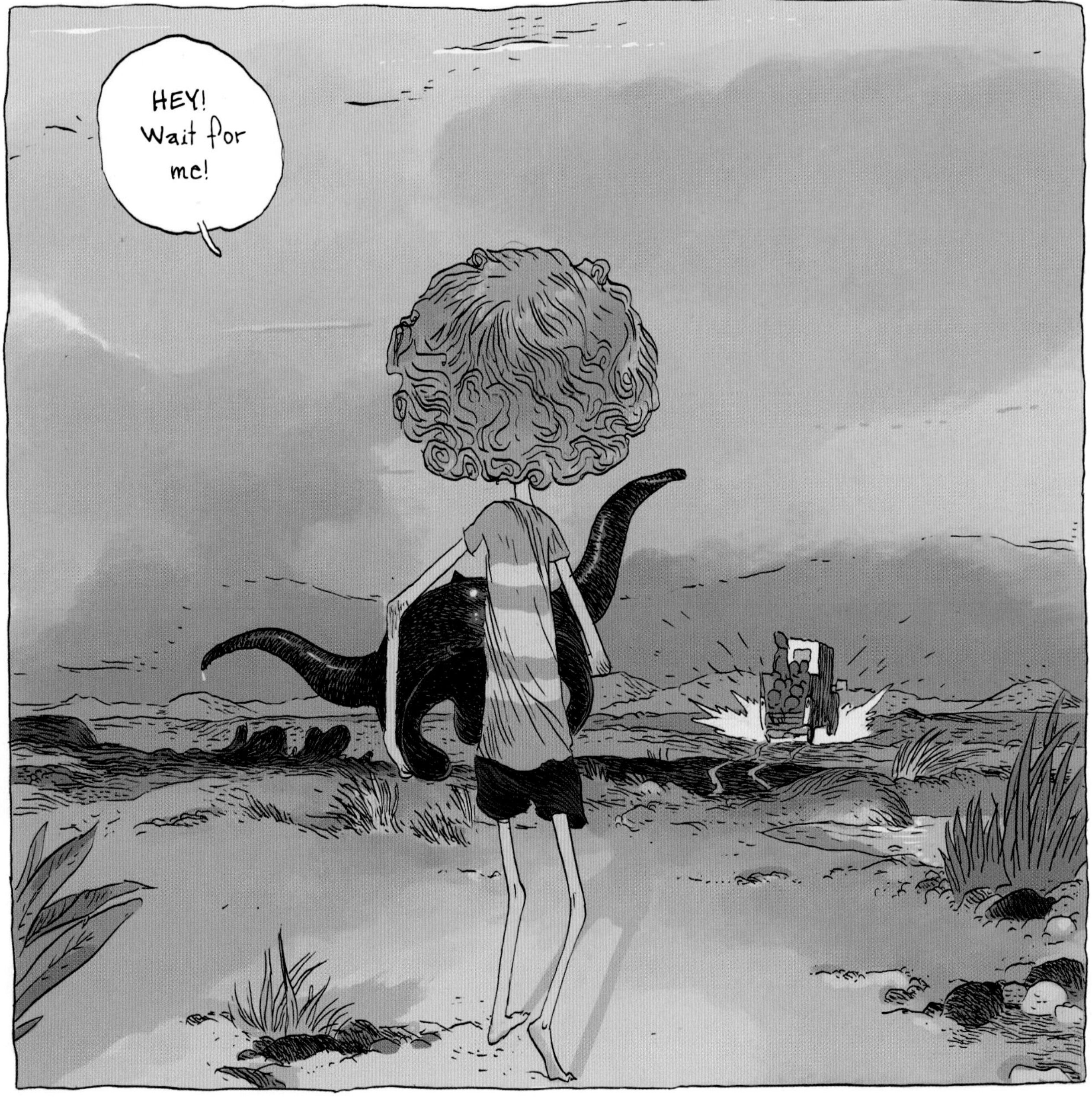
HEY! Wait for me!

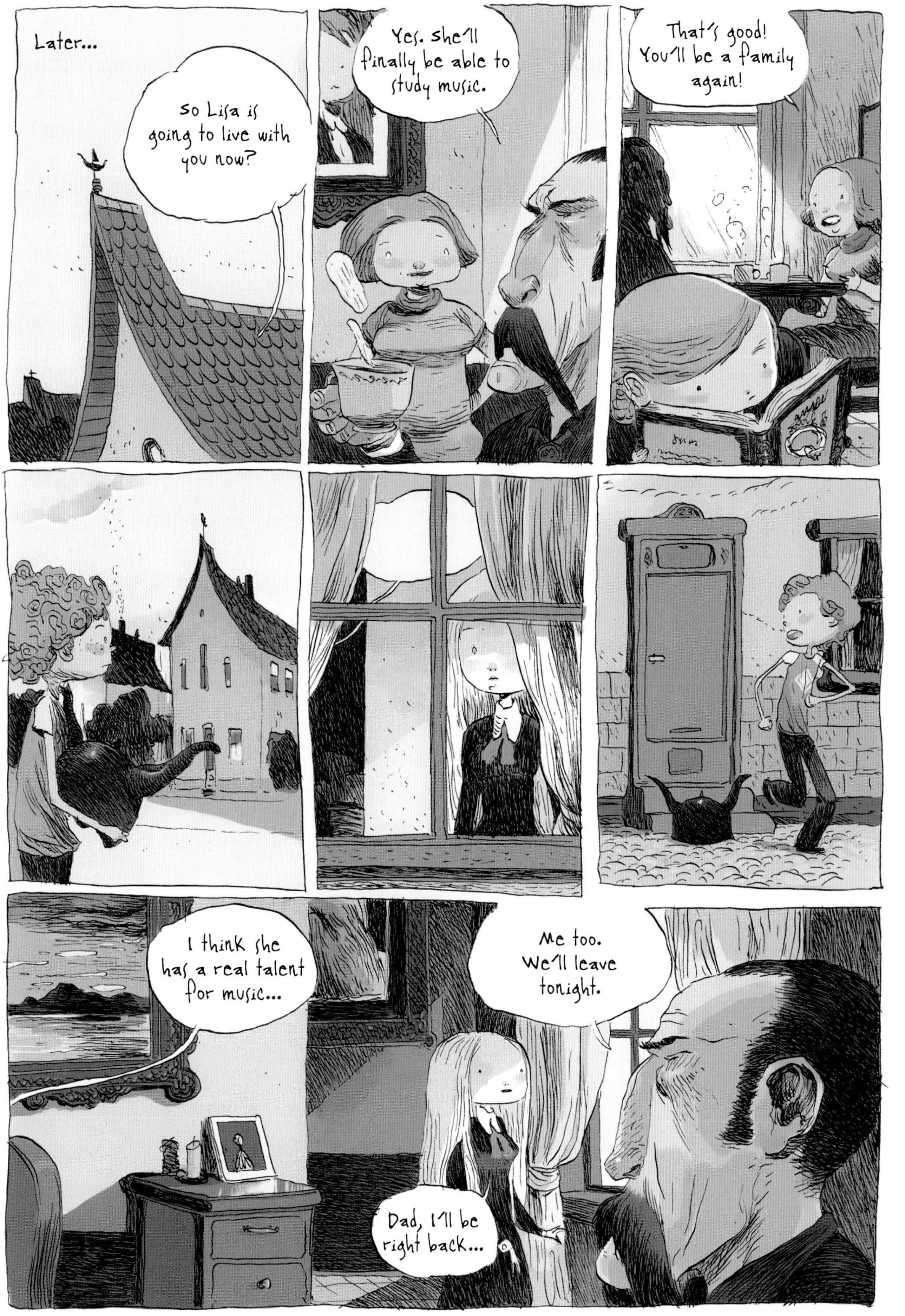
Later...
So Lisa is going to live with you now?
Yes. She'll finally be able to study music.
That's good! You'll be a family again!
I think she has a real talent for music...
Me too. We'll leave tonight.
Dad, I'll be right back...

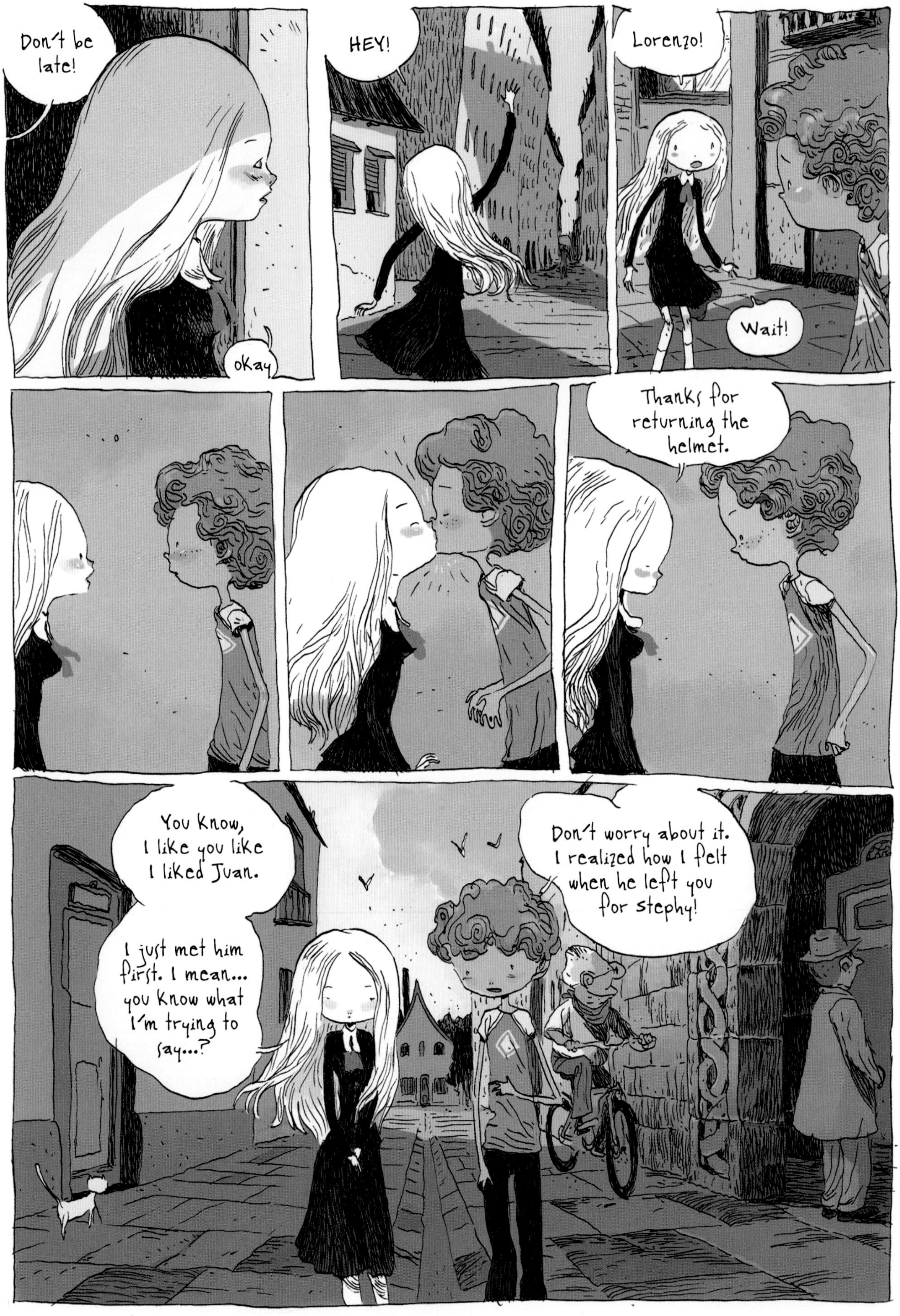
Don't be late!
oKay
HEY!
Lorenzo!
Wait!
. . .
Thanks for returning the helmet.
You know, I like you like I liked Juan.
I just met him first. I mean... you know what I'm trying to say...?
Don't worry about it. I realized how I felt when he left you for stephy!

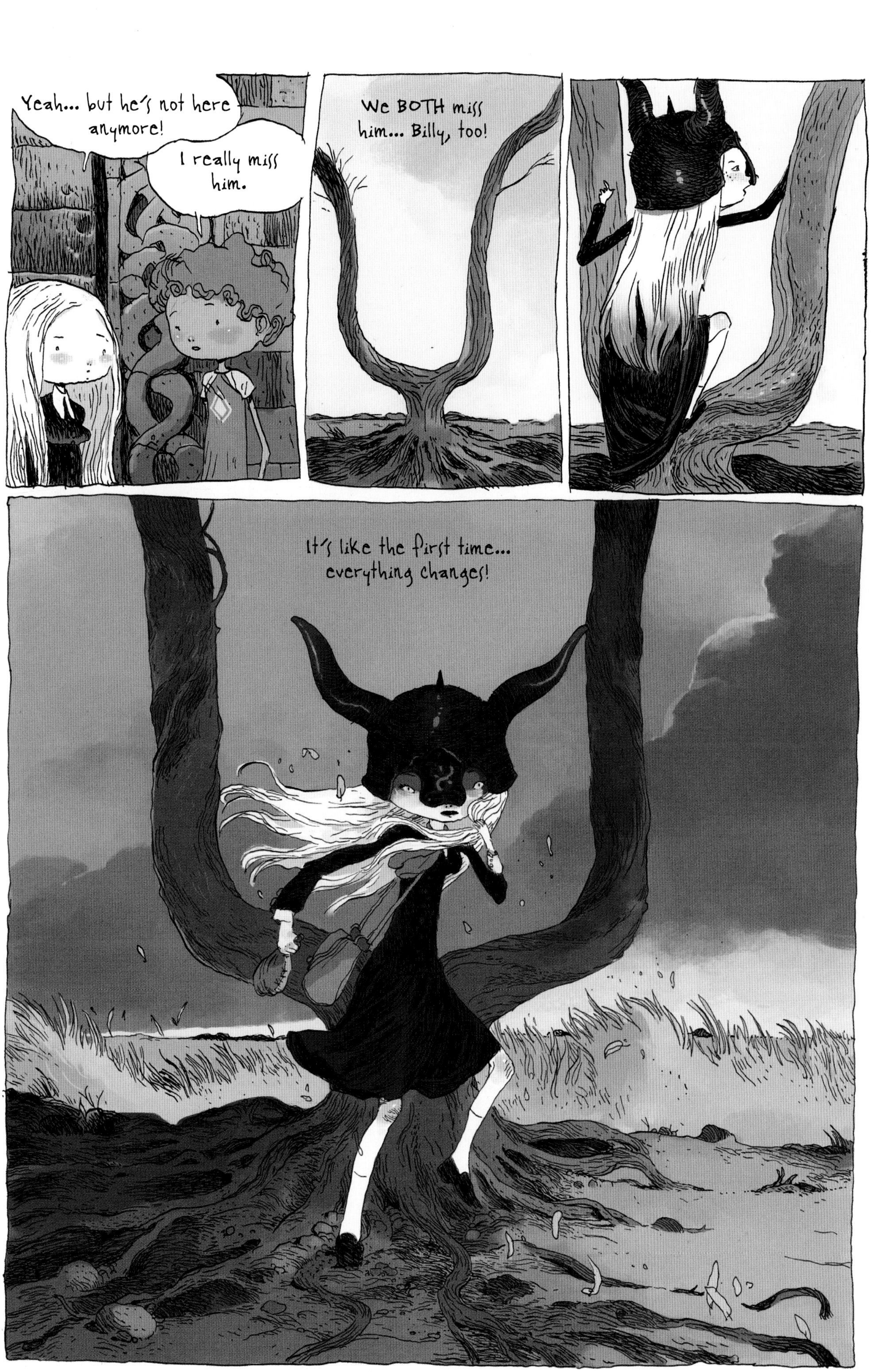
Yeah... but he's not here anymore!
I really miss him.
We BOTH miss him... Billy, too!
It's like the first time... everything changes!

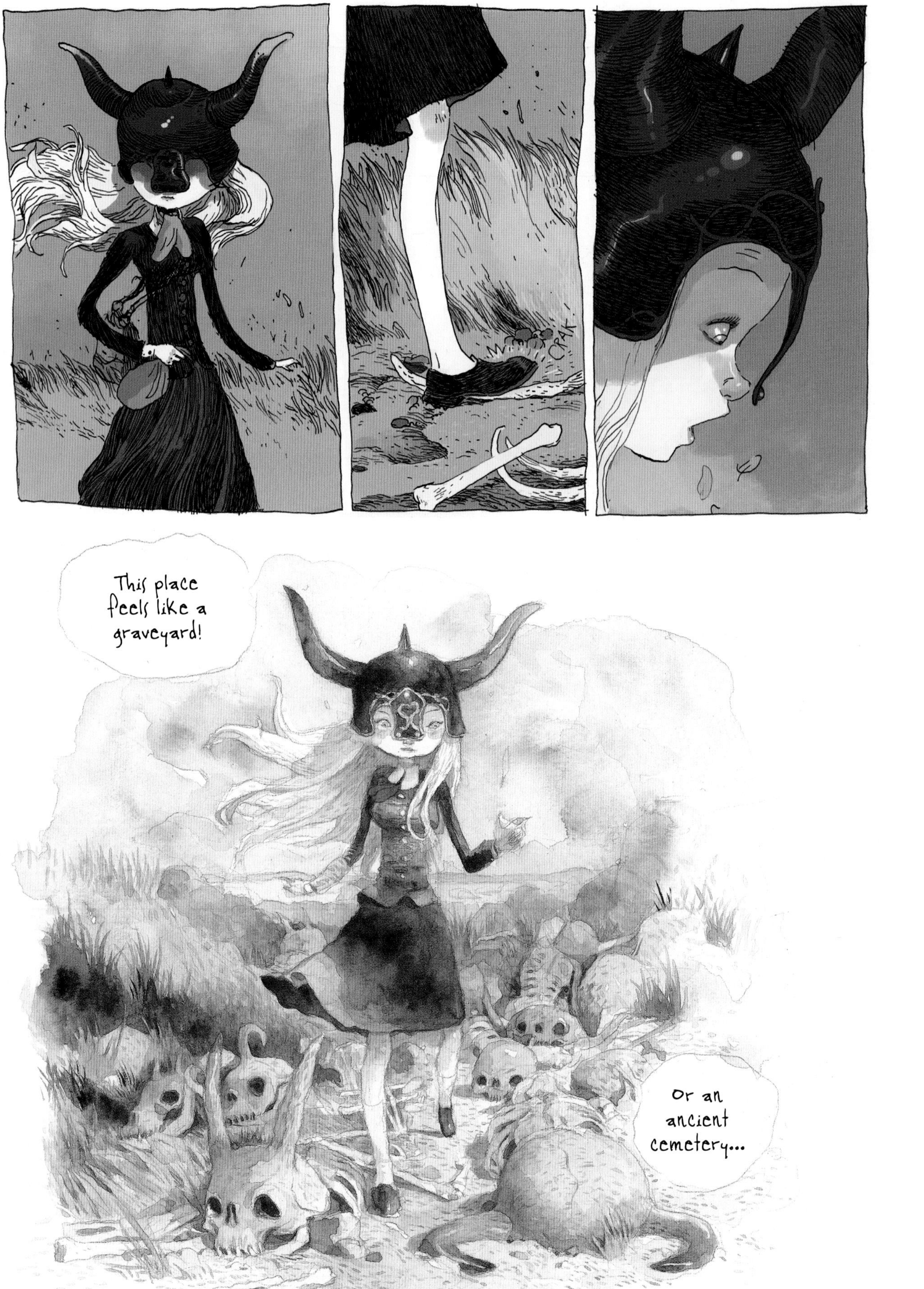
CRAK
This place feels like a graveyard!
Or an ancient cemetery...

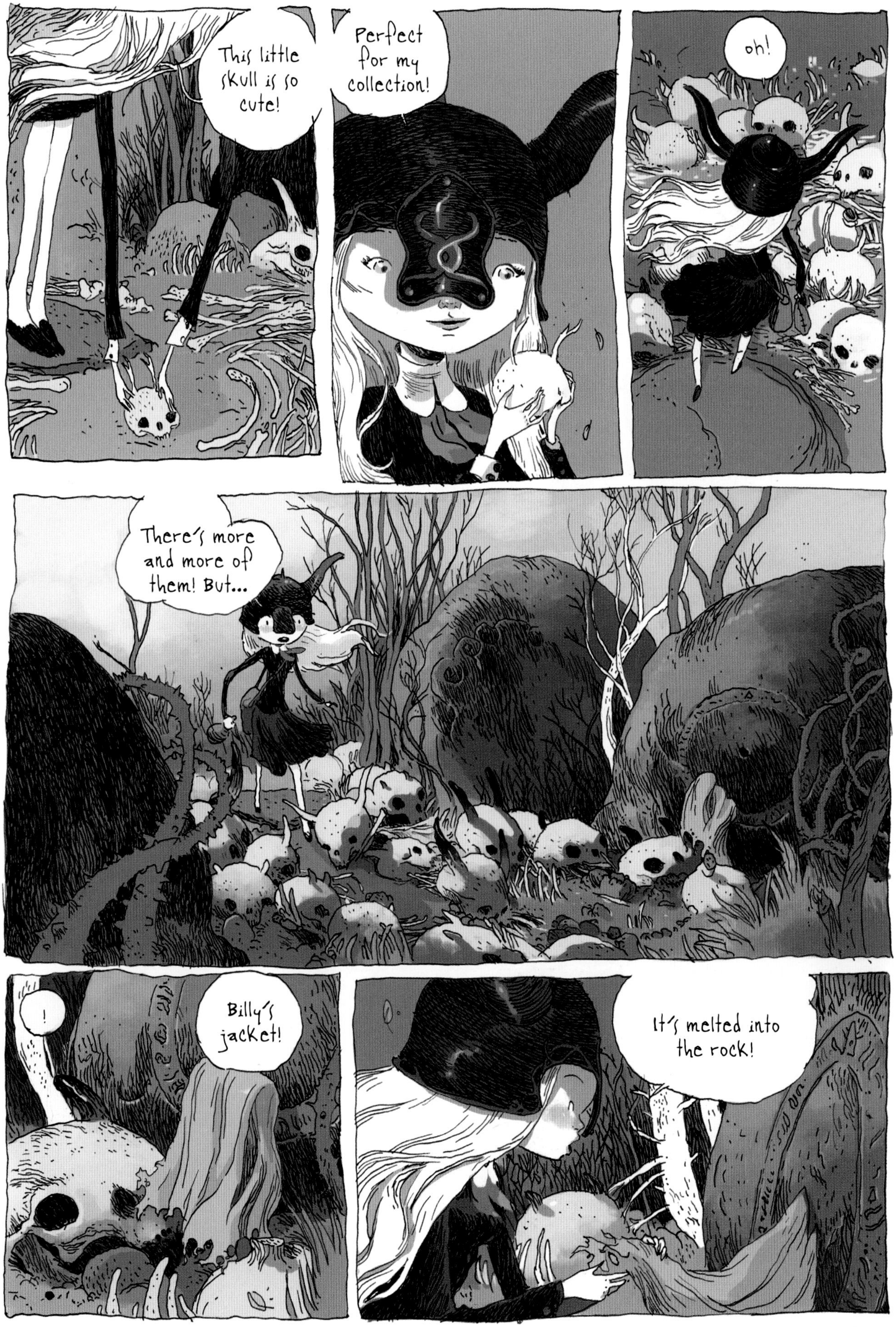
This little skull is so cute!
Perfect for my collection!
oh!
There's more and more of them! But...
!
Billy's jacket!
It's melted into the rock!

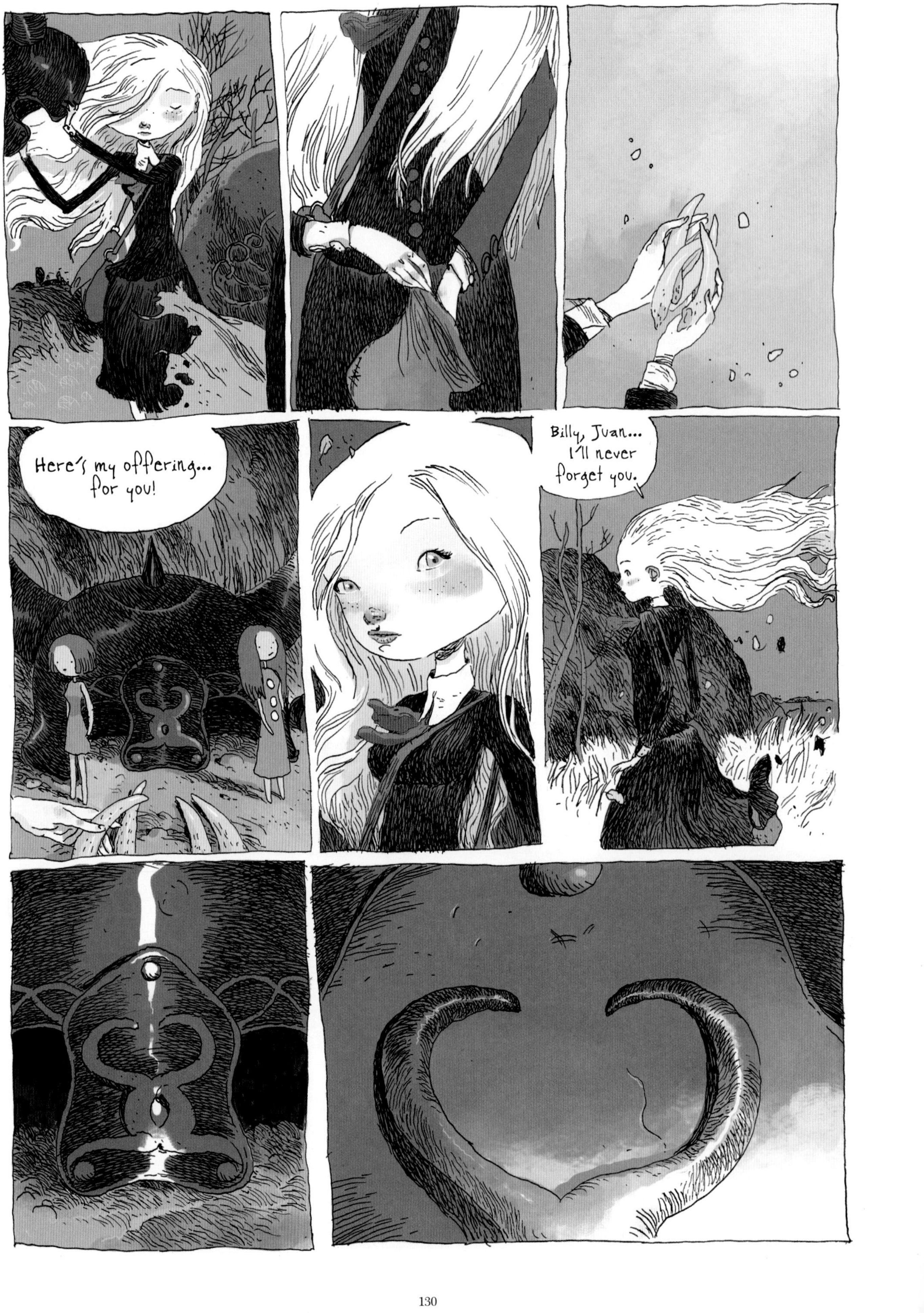
Here's my offering... for you!
Billy, Juan... I'll never forget you.

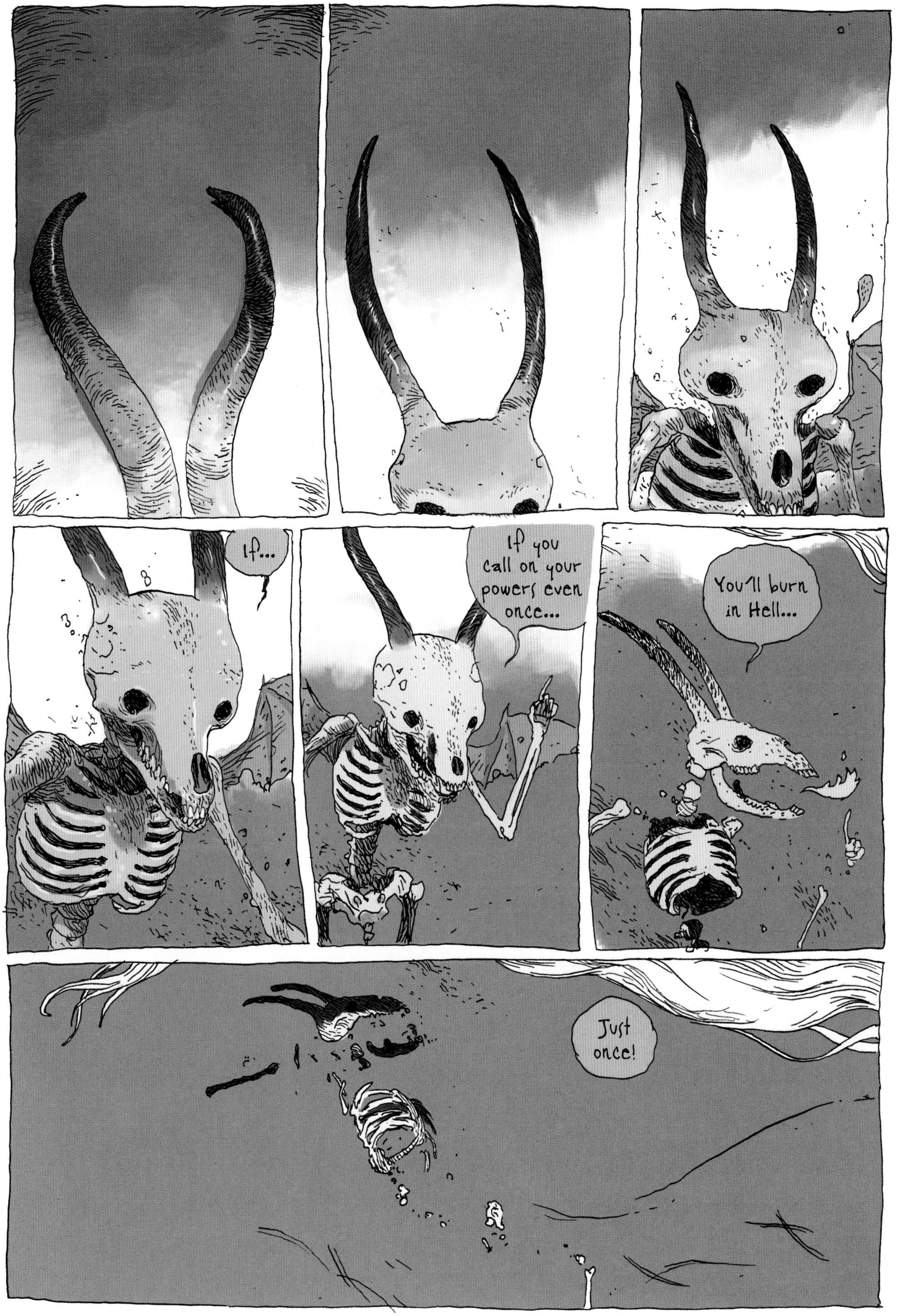
If...
If you call on your powers even once...
You'll burn in Hell...
Just once!

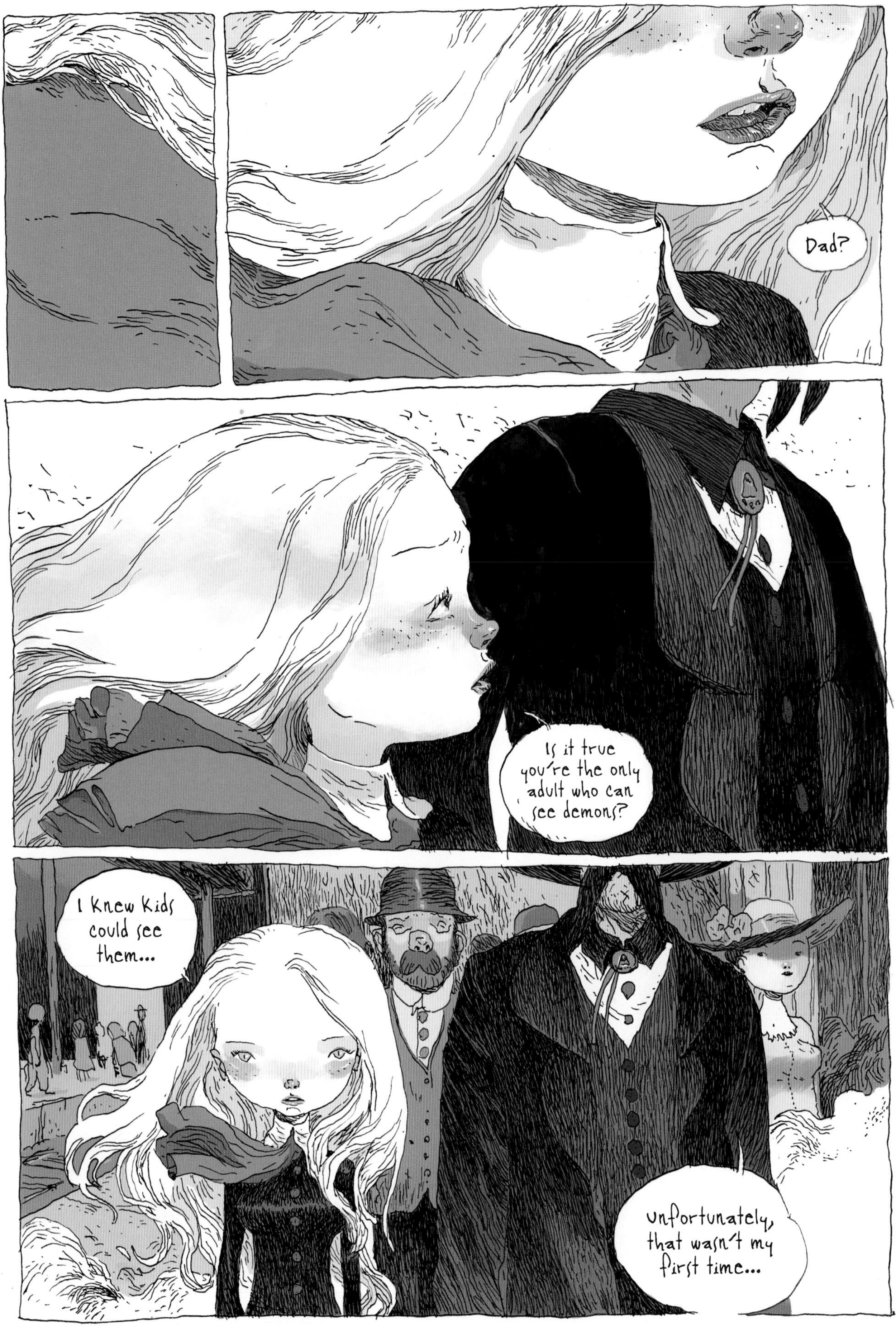
Dad?
Is it true you're the only adult who can see demons?
I knew kids could see them...
Unfortunately, that wasn't my first time...

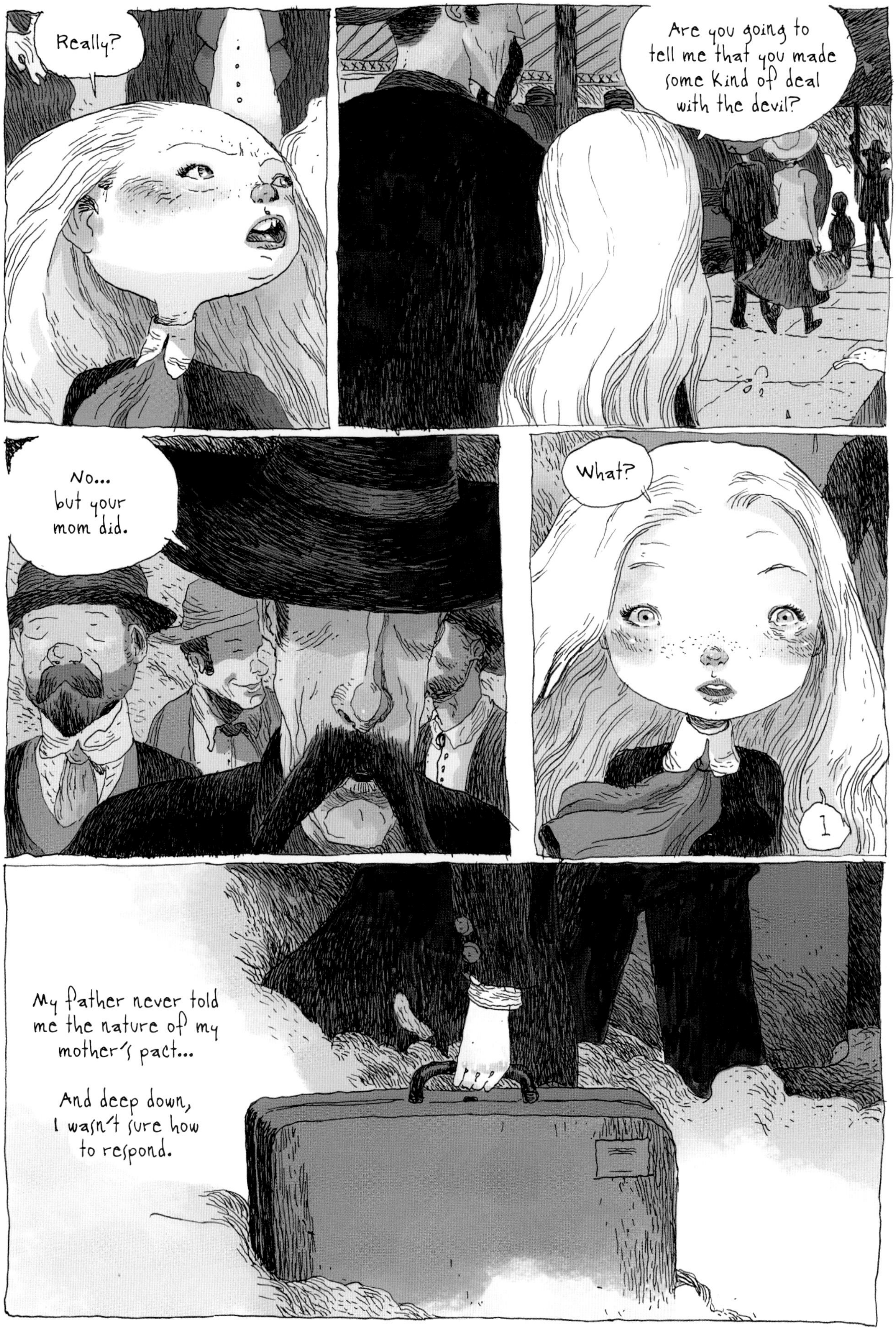
Really?
Are you going to tell me that you made some kind of deal with the devil?
No... but your mom did.
What?
!
My father never told me the nature of my mother's pact...
And deep down, I wasn't sure how to respond.

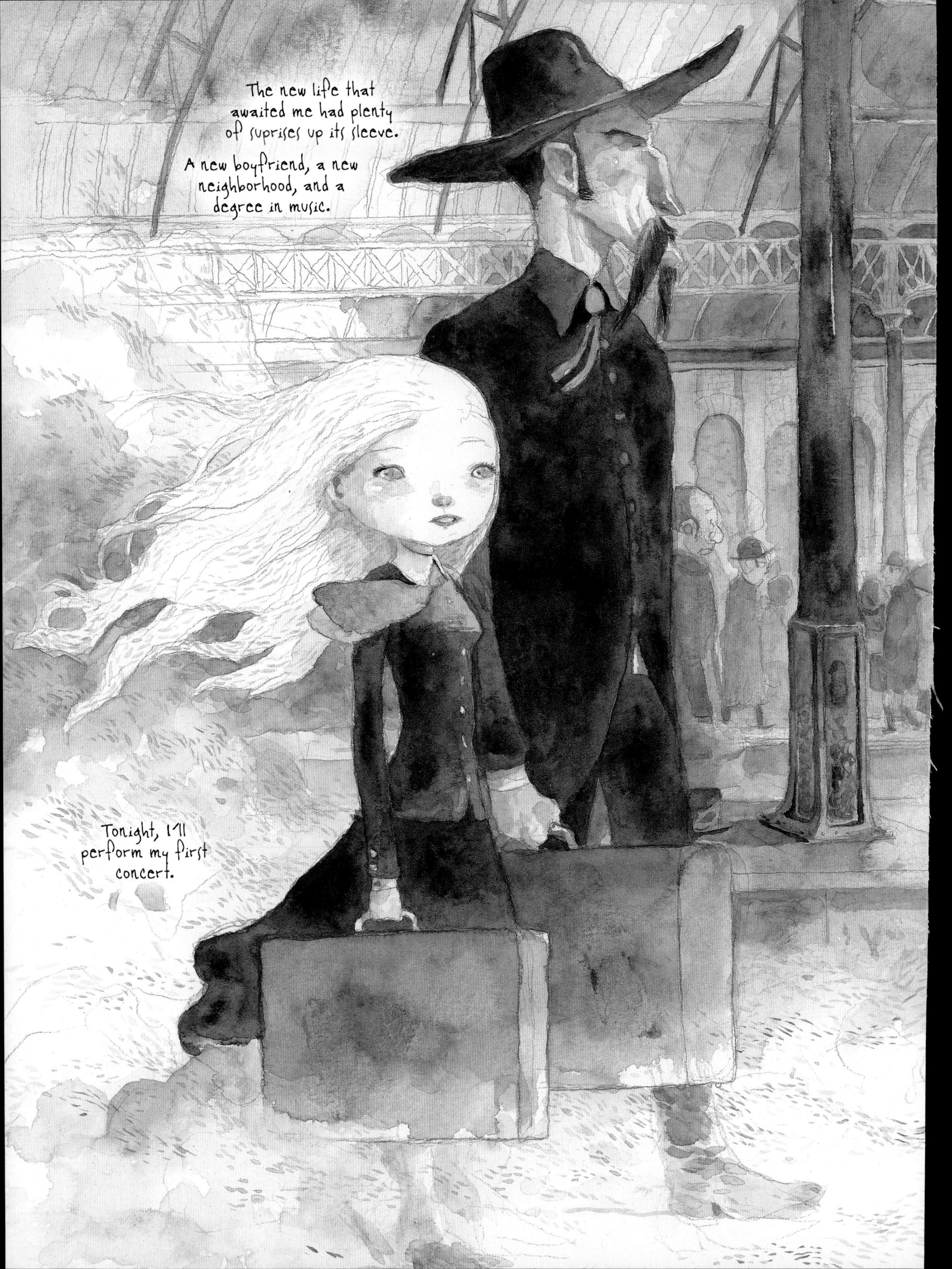
The new life that awaited me had plenty of suprises up its sleeve.
A new boyfriend, a new neighborhood, and a degree in music.
Tonight, I'll perform my first concert.

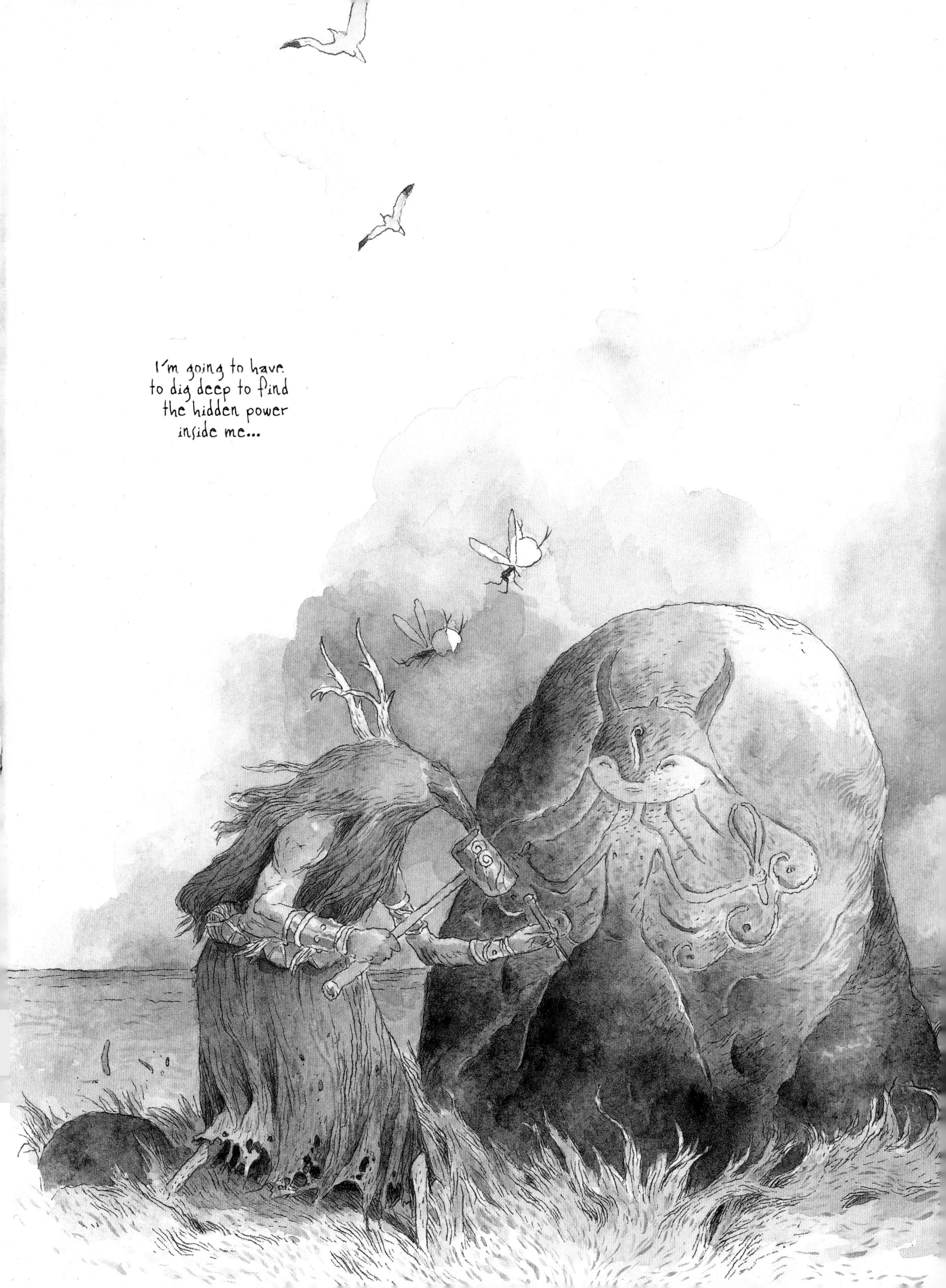
I'm going to have to dig deep to find the hidden power inside me...

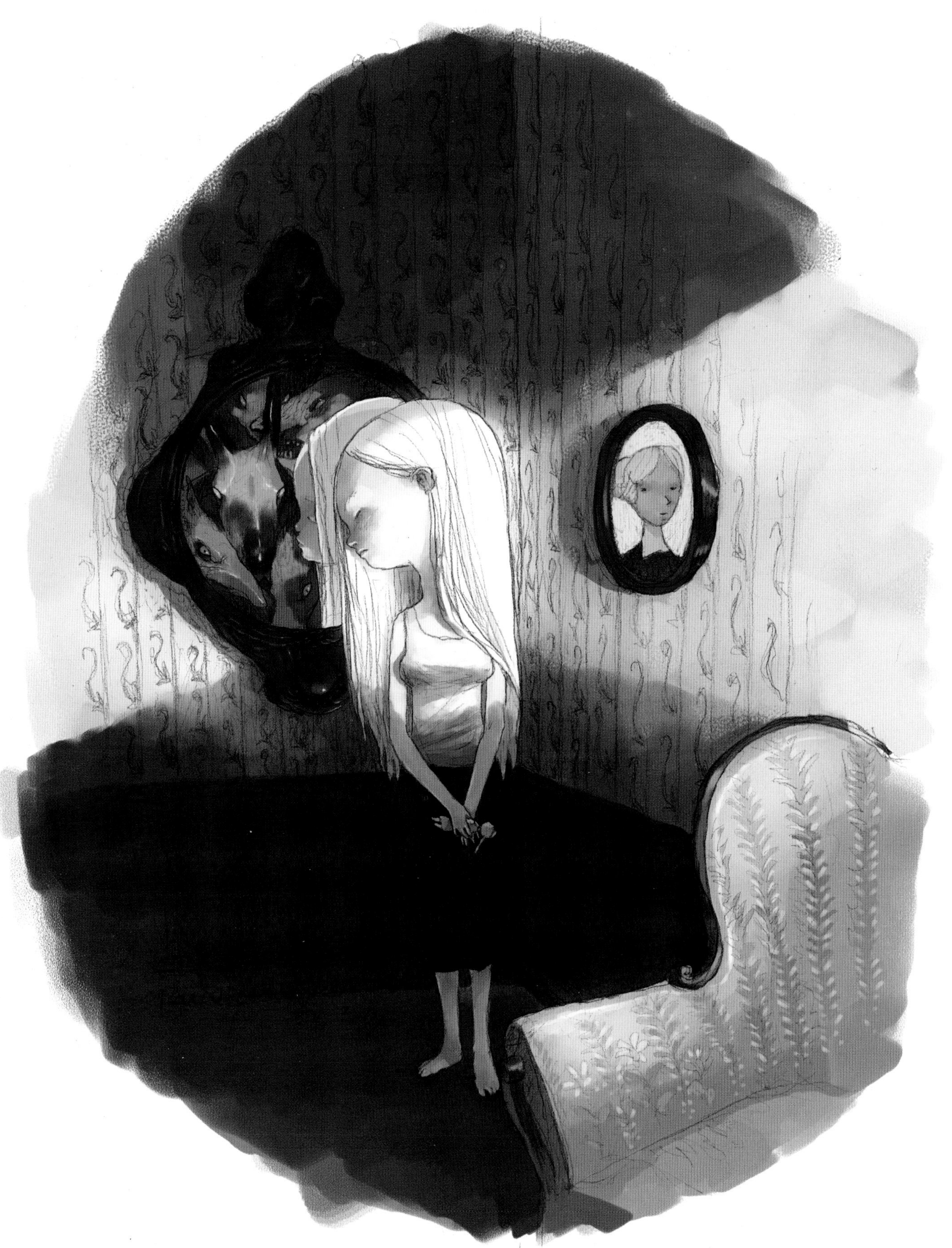

BONUS

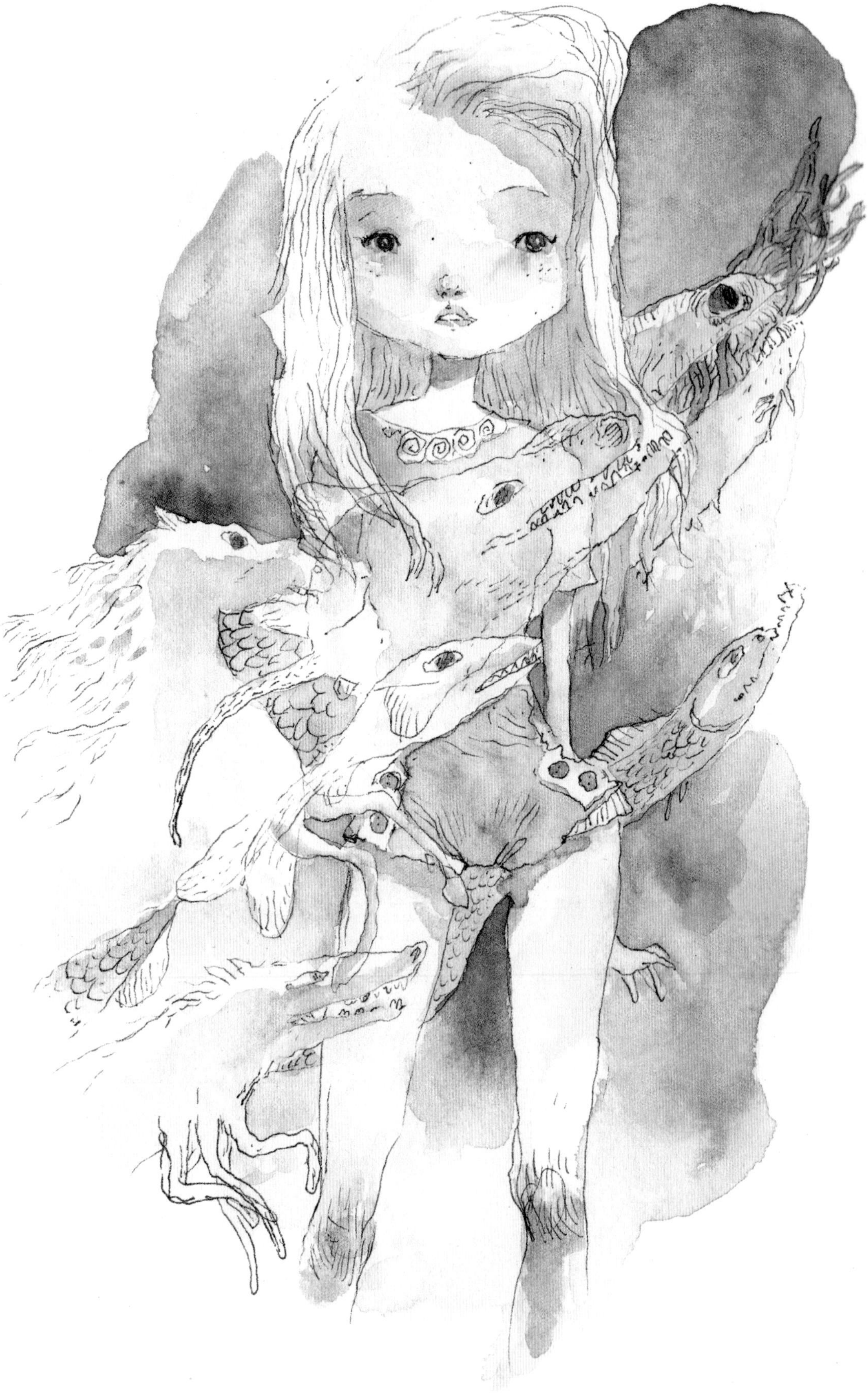

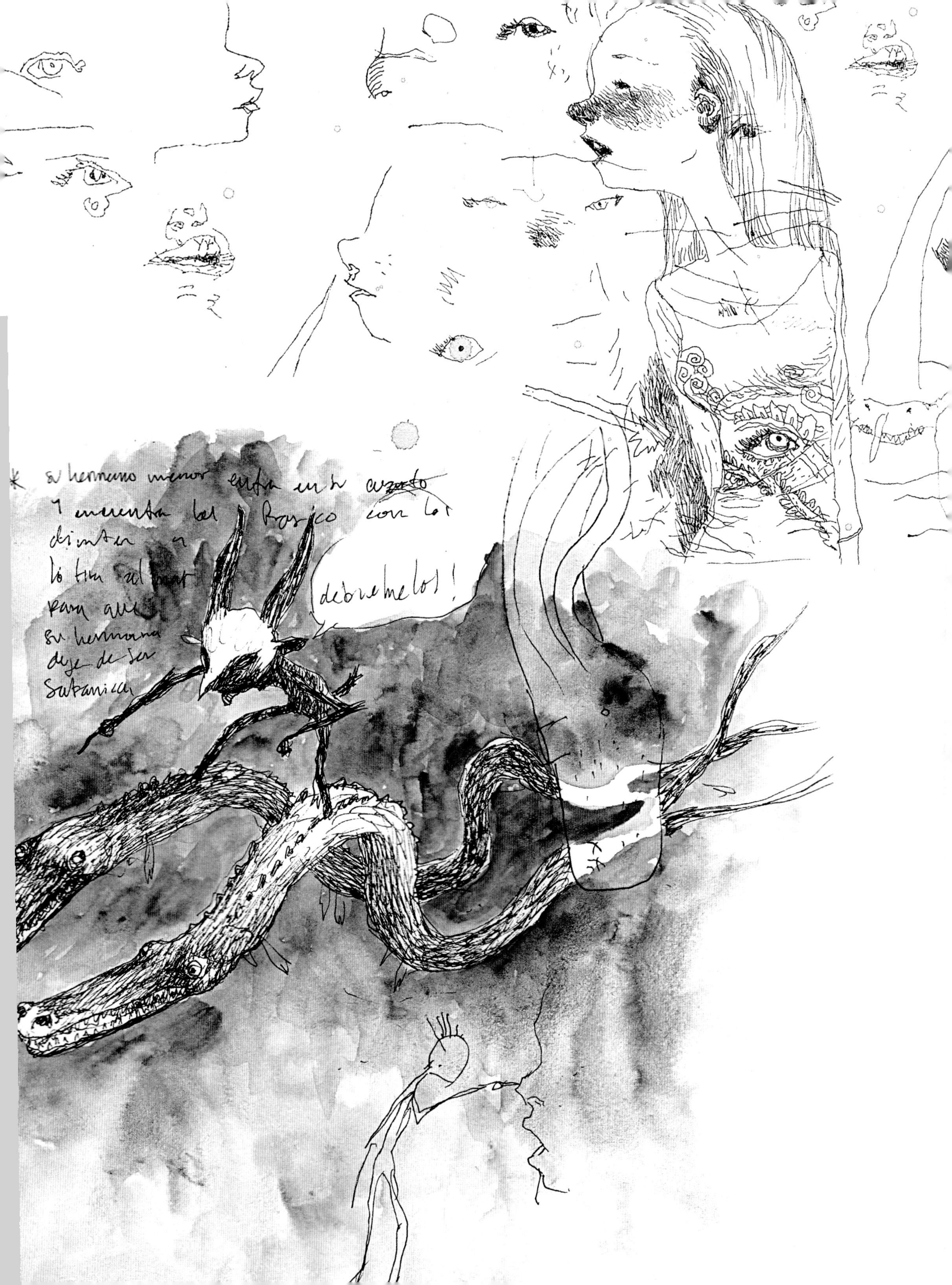
* su hermano menor entra en su cuarto
lo tira al mar
para que
su hermana
deje de ser
Satanica
debuemelos!

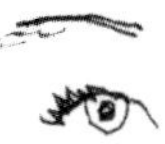

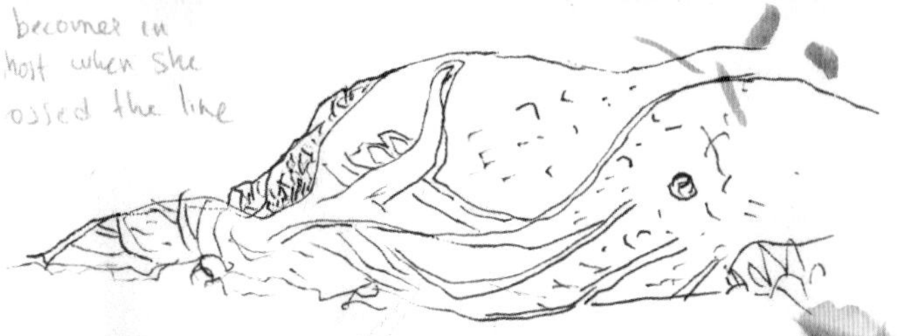
becomes in
host when she
ossed the line

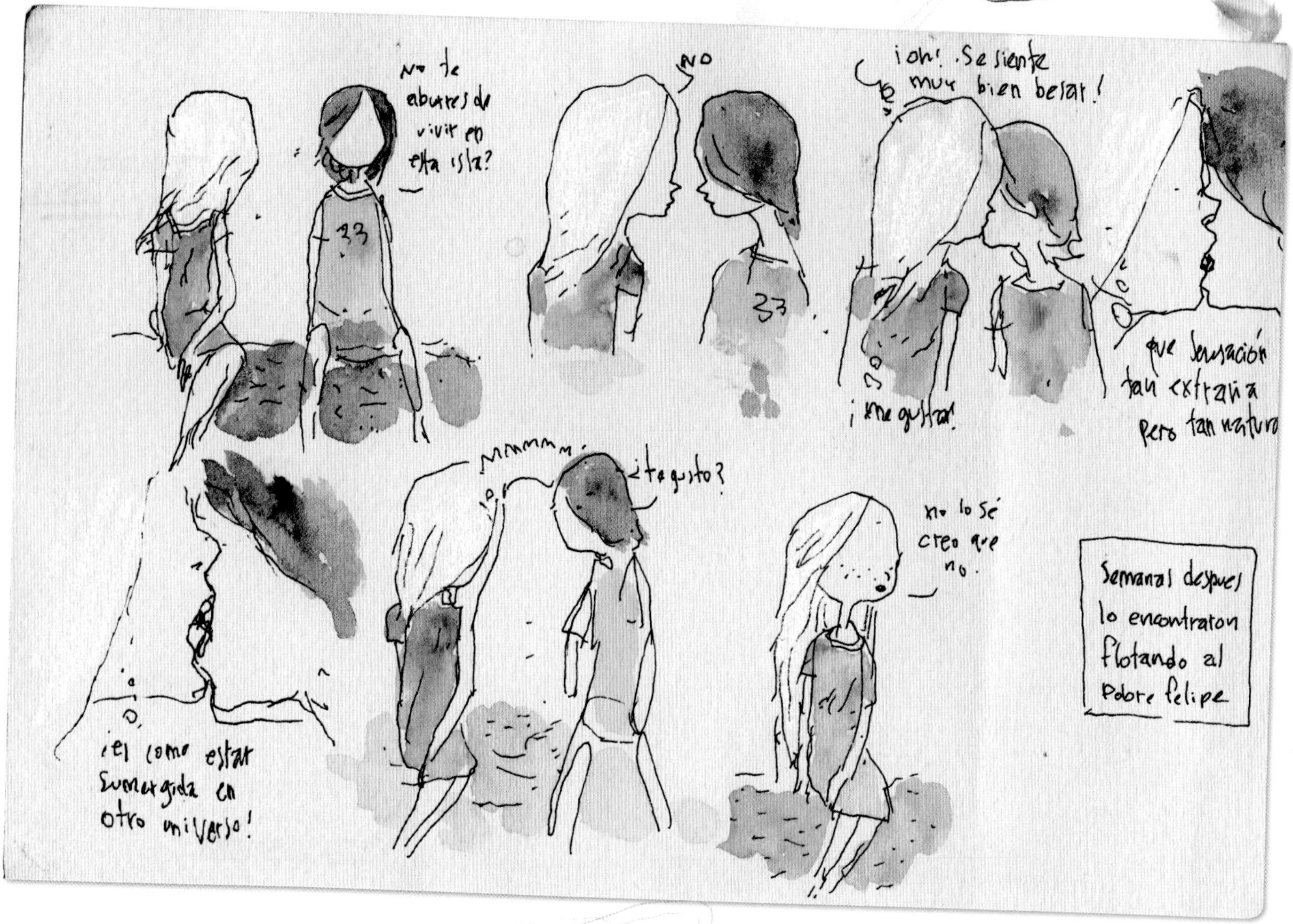
No te aburres de vivir en esta isla?
NO
¡oh! Se siente muy bien besar!
¡me gusta!
que sensación tan extraña pero tan natura
¡es como estar sumergida en otro universo!
Mmmmm
¿te gustó?
no lo sé creo que no.
Semanas después lo encontraron flotando al pobre felipe

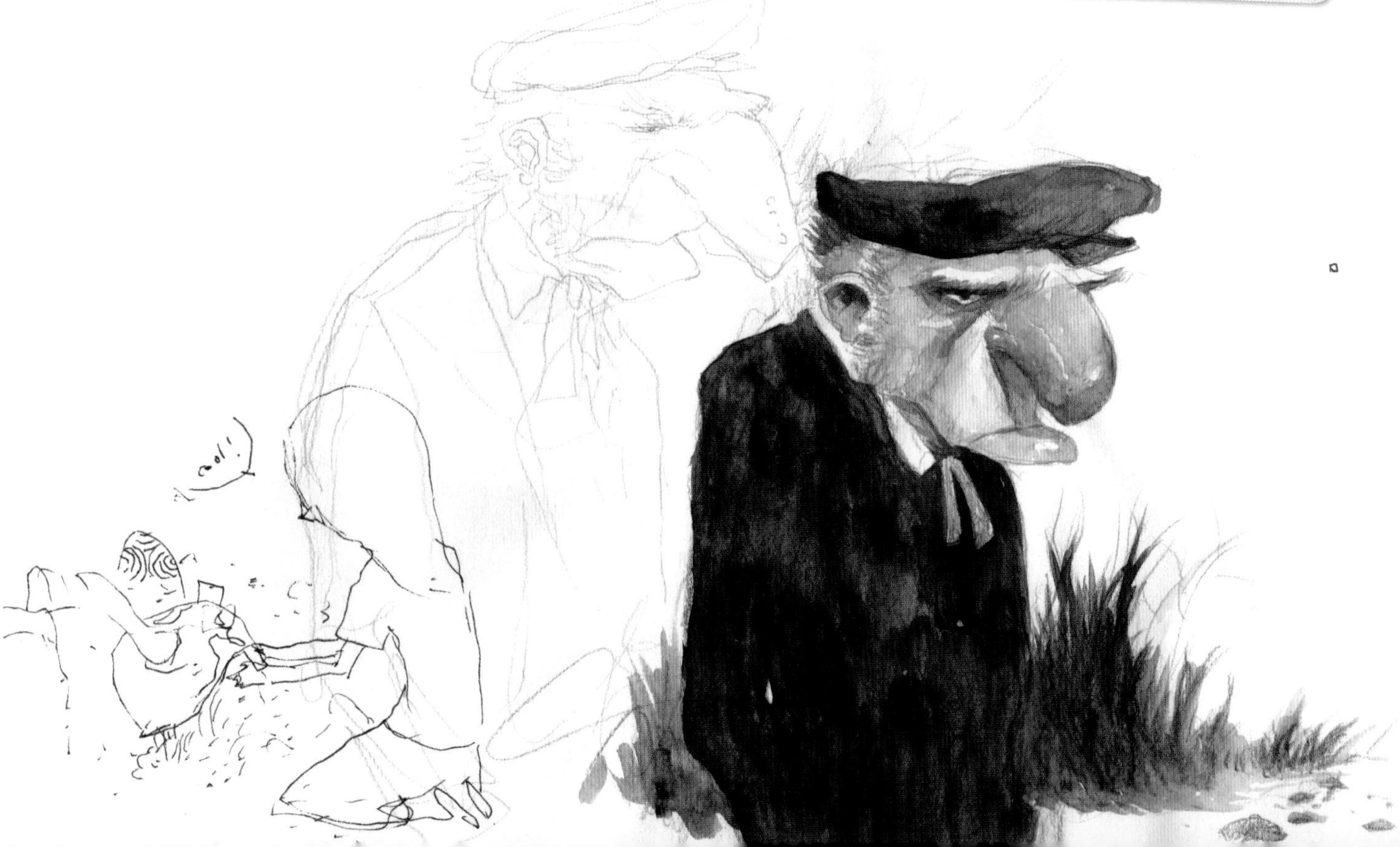

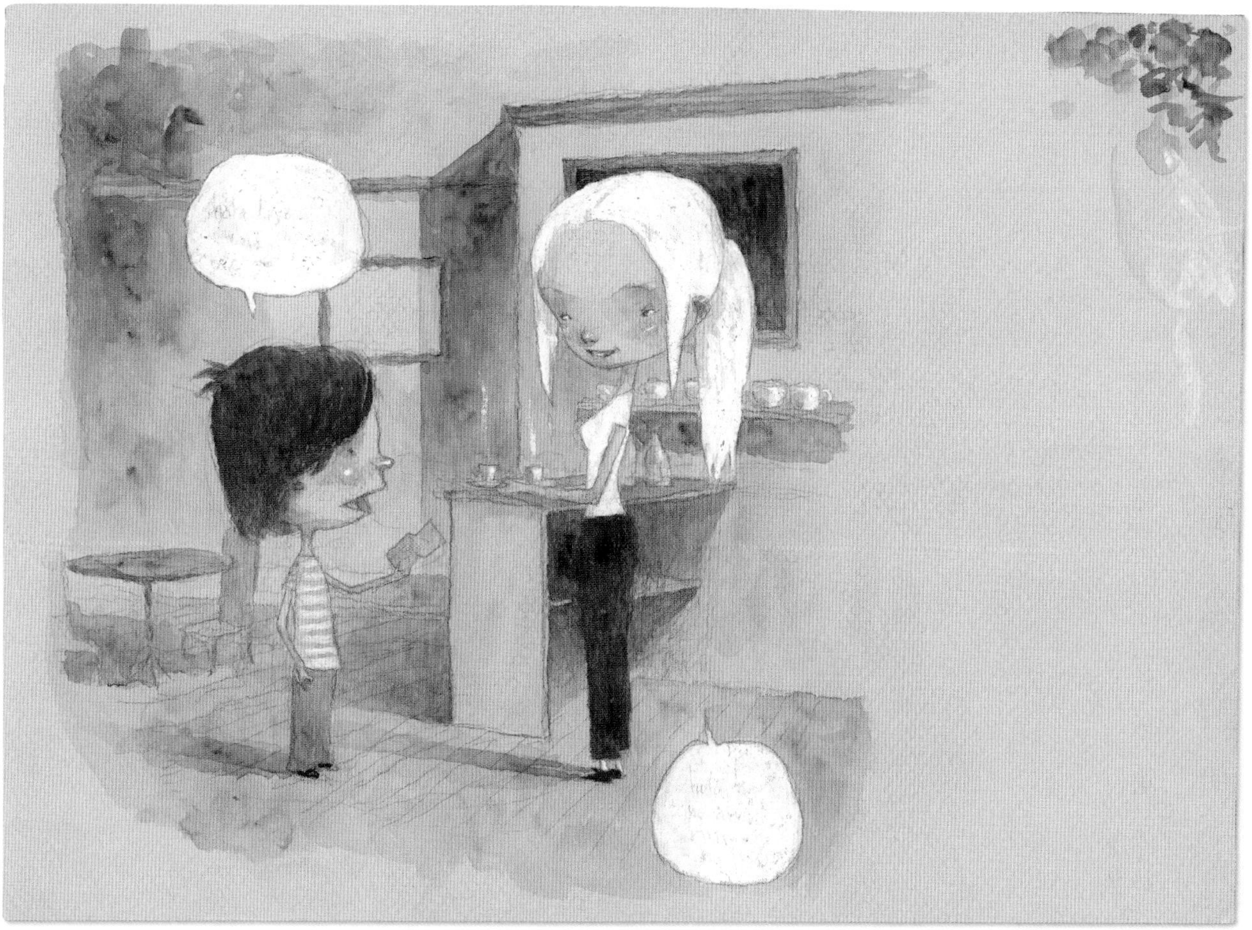

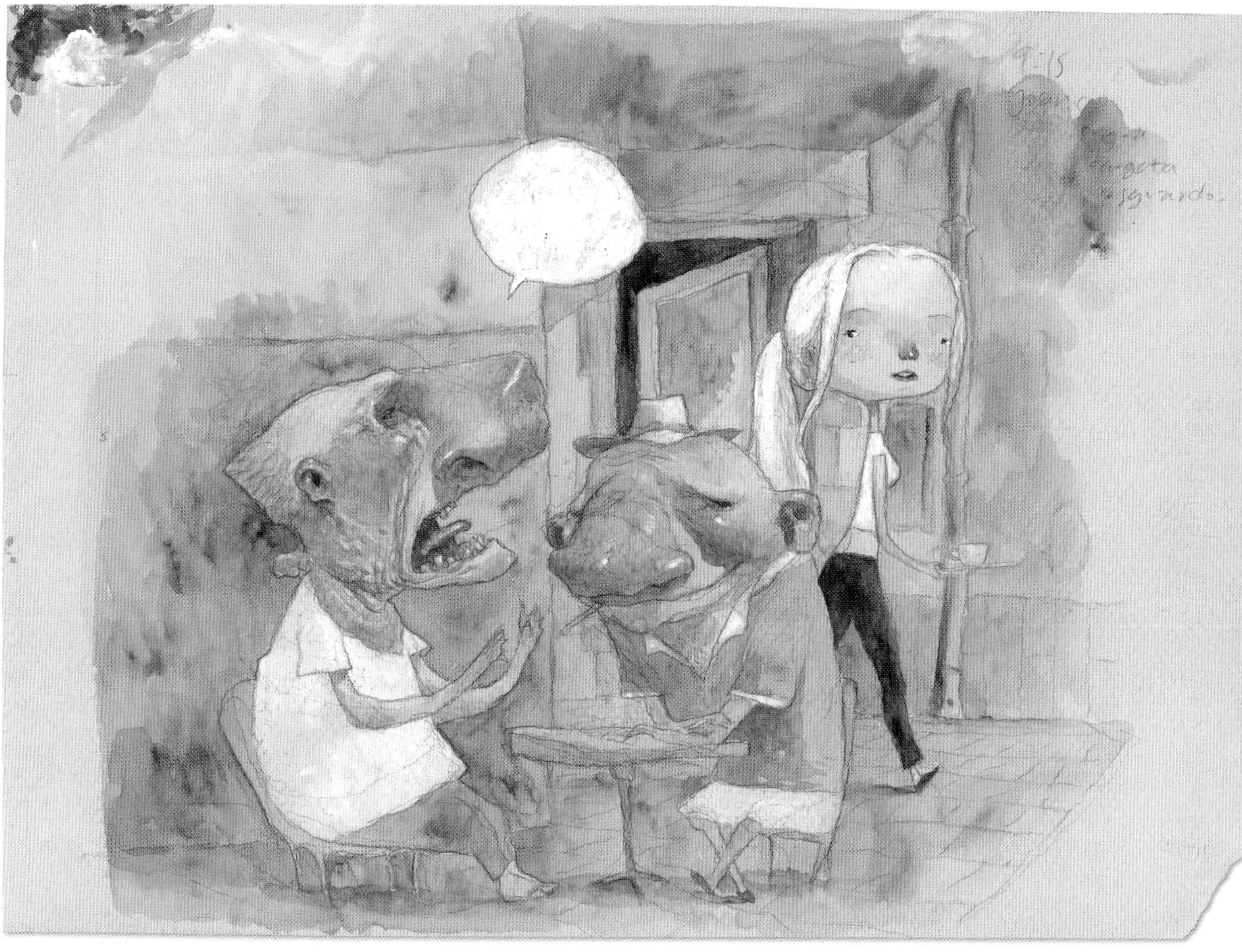

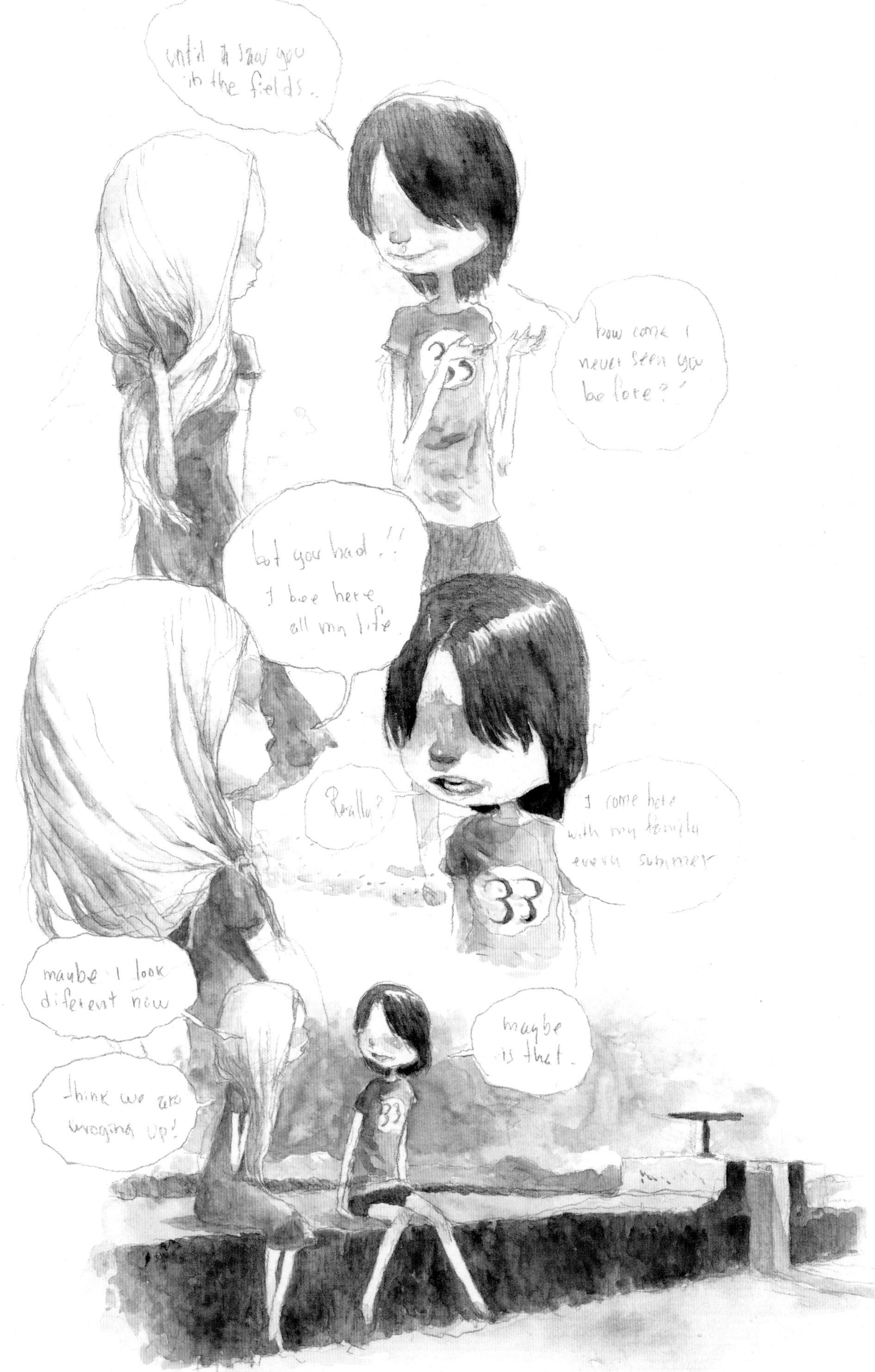
until I saw you in the fields..
how come I never seen you before?
but you had!! I bee here all my life.
Really?
I come here with my family every summer
maybe I look diferent now
maybe is that.
think we are growing up!

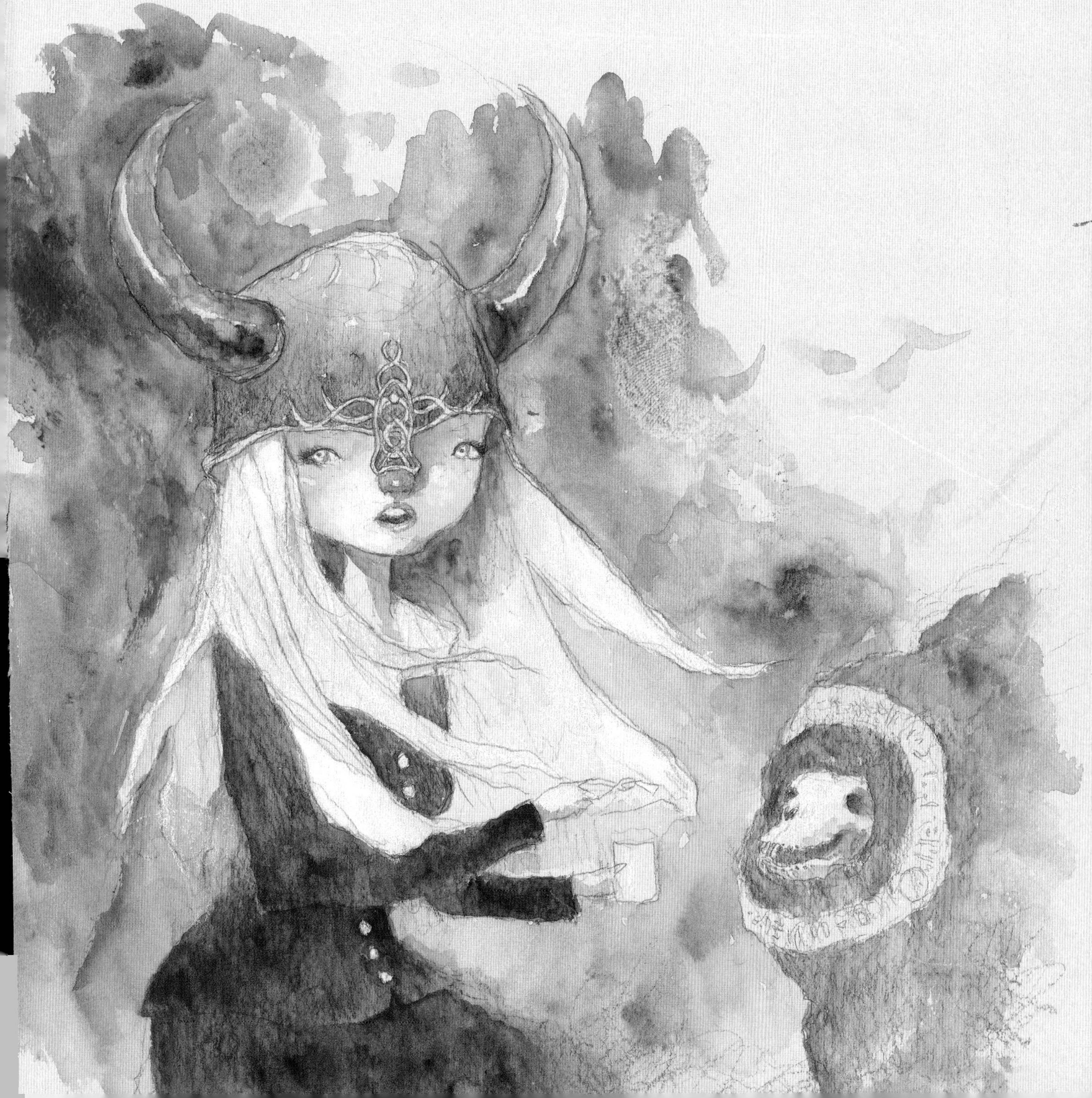

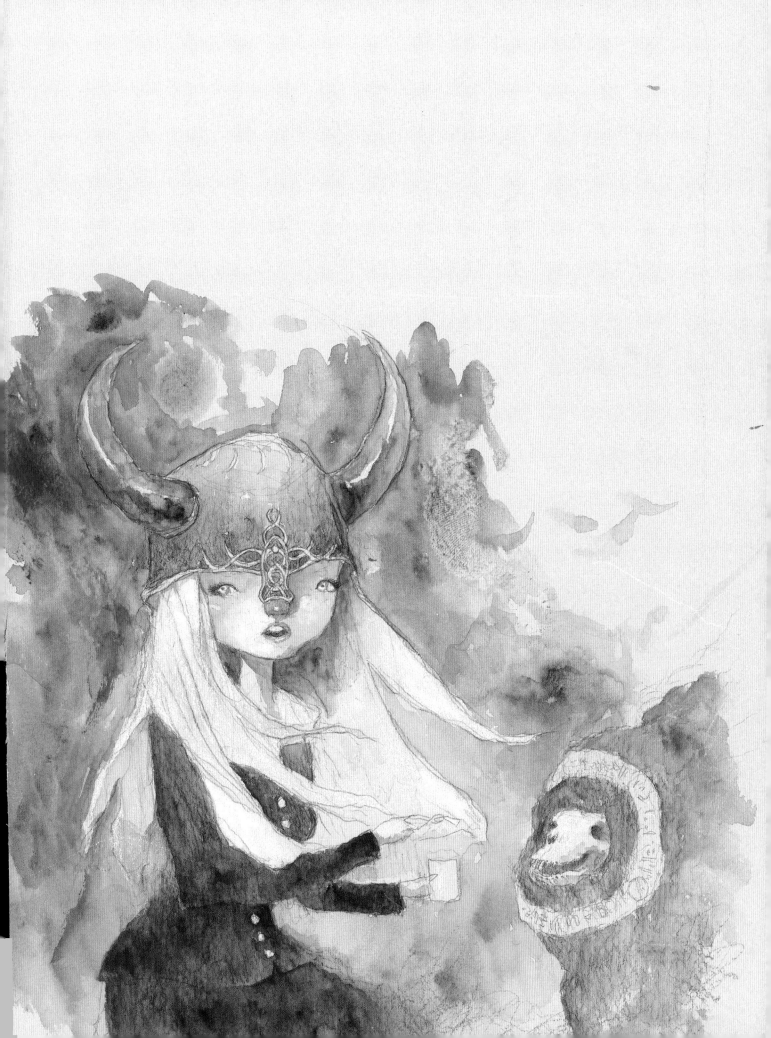

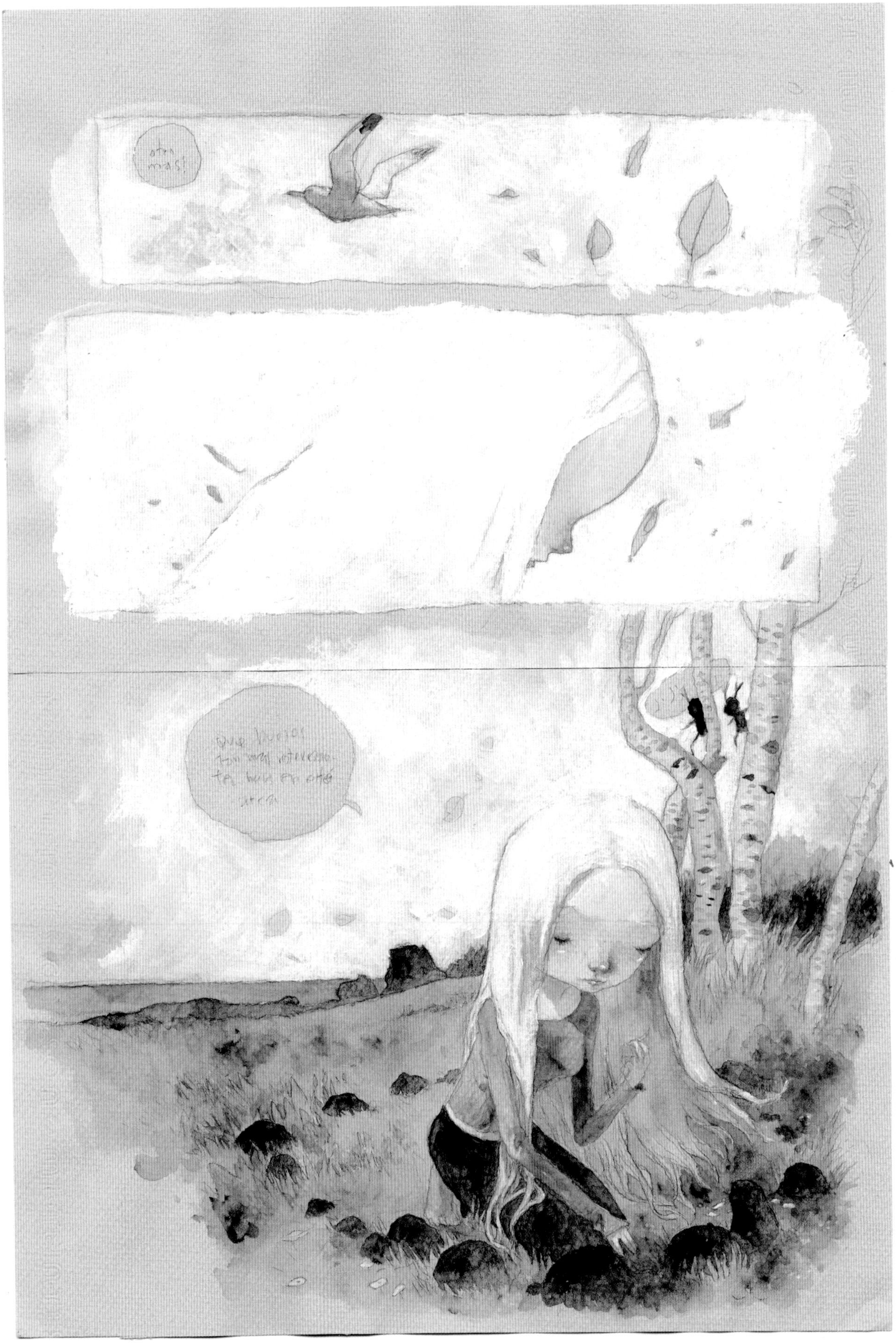
otra mas!

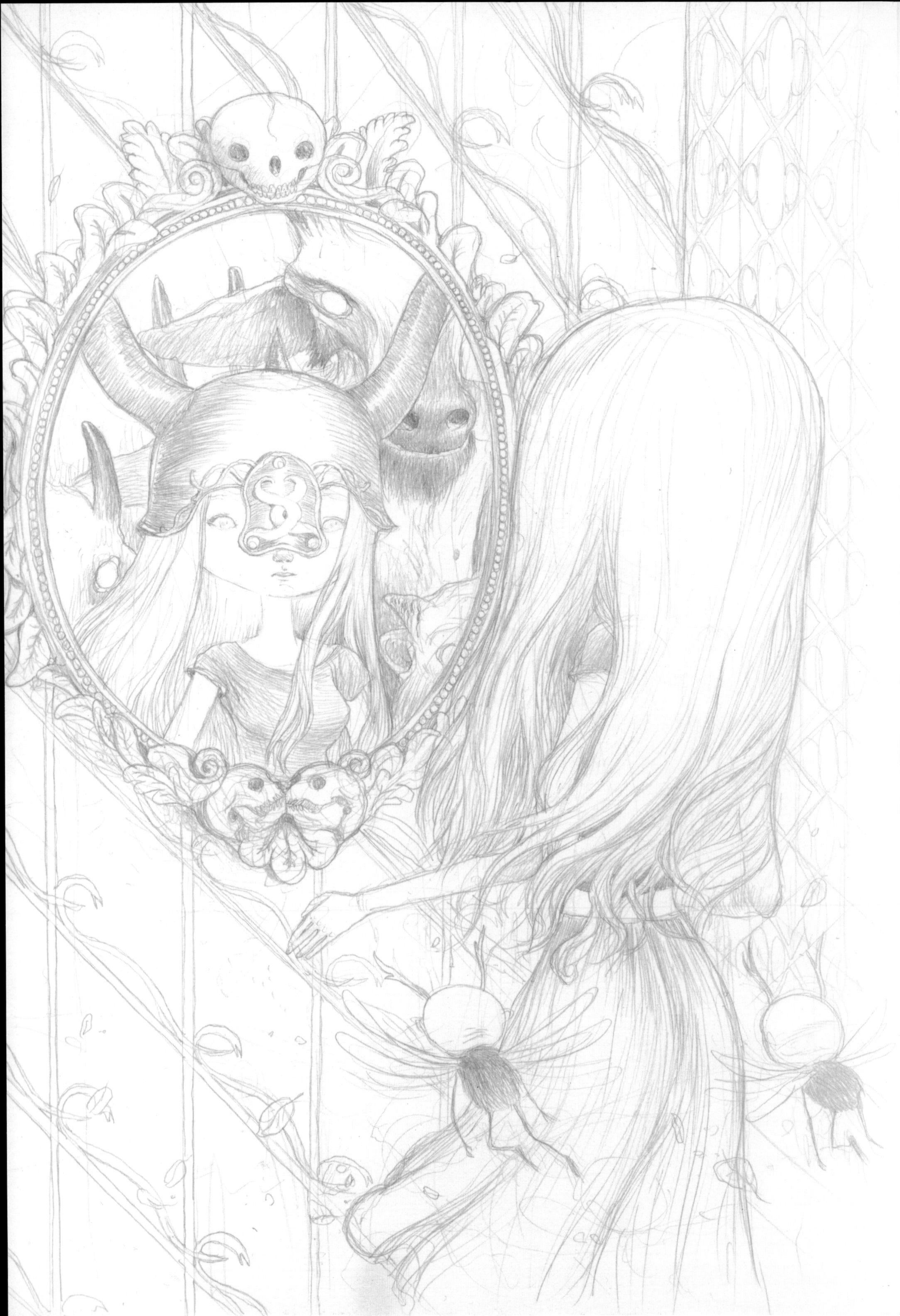